SHAKESPEARE'S THEMES
As Presented Throughout His Works

Paul Fletcher

Centaur Press
An imprint of Open Gate Press
London

First published in 2002 by Centaur Press,
an imprint of Open Gate Press
51 Achilles Road, London NW6 1DZ

Copyright © Paul Fletcher
All rights, by all media, reserved.

British Library Cataloguing-in-Publication Programme
A catalogue reference for this book is available from the
British Library.

ISBN: 0 900001 48 8

The Collins *Complete Works of William Shakespeare* (1994 edition)
has been used with permission for the giving of Act/scene/line references.

Produced by Bookchase (UK) Ltd.
Typeset by PDQ Typesetting, Newcastle-under-Lyme
Printed and bound in Great Britain by Biddles Ltd, *www.biddles.co.uk*

CONTENTS

Introduction	1
Shakespeare's View of Life	5
THE FIRST PART OF HENRY VI (c. 1590)	24
THE SECOND PART OF HENRY VI (c. 1590)	27
THE THIRD PART OF HENRY VI (c. 1591)	32
RICHARD III (c. 1591)	36
TITUS ANDRONICUS (c. 1591)	43
THE COMEDY OF ERRORS (c. 1592)	48
THE TAMING OF THE SHREW (c. 1592)	51
THE SONNETS (c. 1592–3)	57
VENUS AND ADONIS (1593)	61
THE TWO GENTLEMEN OF VERONA (c. 1593)	64
A LOVER'S COMPLAINT (c. 1593)	68
THE RAPE OF LUCRECE (1594)	70
LOVE'S LABOUR'S LOST (c. 1594)	73
KING JOHN (c. 1594)	77
ROMEO AND JULIET (c. 1595)	82
RICHARD II (c. 1595)	88
A MIDSUMMER NIGHT'S DREAM (c. 1596)	95
THE MERCHANT OF VENICE (c. 1596)	100
THE FIRST PART OF HENRY IV (c. 1596)	107
THE MERRY WIVES OF WINDSOR (c. 1597)	112
THE SECOND PART OF HENRY IV (c. 1598)	115
MUCH ADO ABOUT NOTHING (c. 1598)	120
HENRY V (1599)	125
JULIUS CAESAR (c. 1599)	131
AS YOU LIKE IT (c. 1600)	139

HAMLET (c. 1600)	145
THE PHOENIX AND TURTLE (1601)	154
TWELFTH NIGHT, OR WHAT YOU WILL (c. 1601)	155
TROILUS AND CRESSIDA (c. 1602)	162
ALL'S WELL THAT ENDS WELL (c. 1603)	167
OTHELLO (c. 1603)	172
MEASURE FOR MEASURE (c. 1604)	180
TIMON OF ATHENS (c. 1605)	185
KING LEAR (c. 1605)	190
MACBETH (c. 1606)	203
ANTONY AND CLEOPATRA (c. 1607)	211
CORIOLANUS (c. 1607)	221
PERICLES (c. 1608)	228
CYMBELINE (c. 1609)	233
THE WINTER'S TALE (c. 1610)	240
THE TEMPEST (c. 1611)	247
HENRY VIII (c. 1613)	255
A Note on THE TWO NOBLE KINSMEN	260
Brief Notes on the Chronology of Shakespeare's Works	263
General Notes	271
Index	290

Paul Fletcher read English at Cambridge and taught that subject throughout his working life, first at Tiffin Boys' School, Kingston-upon-Thames, and at The Judd School, Tonbridge, where he was head of the English department. Then, being great attracted to Scotland (his wife is half-Scottish), he became a lecturer in English at Langside College, Glasgow, where he remained until his retirement.

Introduction

Attempts have been made in recent times to see Shakespeare's plays in terms of modern attitudes to life. Influential in this respect was Jan Kott's book *Shakespeare Our Contemporary*[1] (in Polish 1964, English translation 1965), and I recall a remark made by the Shakespearean director Michael Bogdanov in connection with *The Taming of the Shrew* in a TV discussion programme (Channel 4, 15 January 1986): 'Look at it for what it means now and not what it meant 350 years ago.' Making the stage performance of a Shakespeare play meaningful to a modern audience certainly has its problems, but if one wishes to make a personal study of Shakespeare's plays I believe that such a study is best approached in the way that provides the main stimulus for studying literature in general – as an exploration of what an individual author thinks and feels about life, responding in his or her own way to the conditions and influences of his or her time.[2] And the interest in studying the literature of the past involves taking note of differences as well as similarities between the author's attitudes and those current in our own day.

Of course the value of literature depends not only on what is said but on the way it is said, and Shakespeare's plays are supremely valuable for the vigour and beauty of their language – the power of the language gives emotional reality to the plays even when the plots are improbable or unrealistic. But the essential meaning of a Shakespeare play, as of any work of imaginative literature of any depth, derives from its ideas, from the central theme and themes related to the central theme: we cannot respond fully to the feelings expressed in such a work without paying attention to the ideas to which those feelings are linked. The purpose of this book, therefore, is to bring out as clearly as possible Shakespeare's themes. The themes of individual plays are often discussed by their editors, but in this book an account is given of the themes that I take to be important for the understanding of all Shakespeare's works – poems as well as plays.

This book is intended not for the specialist but for any student of Shakespeare who, in possession of Shakespeare's complete works, wishes to make sense of these works as a whole. Although such a student will presumably know some of Shakespeare's works already, he/she will probably not know them all, and as regards the plays I shall try to make details of plot and characters clear to a reader who may not already know, or may have partly forgotten, the play under discussion. But in giving details of plot and characters my main concern will be to show how the main theme and related themes emerge as the play proceeds, and I shall give numerous Act, scene and line references, partly to facilitate consultation of the text, but more especially to help the reader keep track of just where points I discuss occur in the forward movement of the play. Since I am essentially concerned with interpretation I should stress that the interpretation of a Shakespeare play inevitably depends on one's judgment as to where, and through which characters, Shakespeare expresses his own ideas and attitudes: my interpretations, therefore, will at times differ, sometimes markedly, from other interpretations (just as other interpretations must differ from each other).[3] In this book I have thought it best to concentrate on what Shakespeare himself has to say and so have deliberately refrained from commenting on other interpretations: I leave it to the reader to make comparisons between my interpretations and other interpretations. I hope that at least my approach will help to promote a full response to Shakespeare's works.

For the purpose of giving Act, scene and line references I shall be using the 1994 edition (incorporating the 1951 edition) of the Collins *Complete Works of William Shakespeare*. In many references the line numbering as taken from the Collins edition will not vary much from the line numbering in other editions of the complete works: the greatest variations will occur when references are to scenes in the plays that are wholly or partly in prose (rather than in verse). From time to time the scene divisions in the Collins edition may be different from those in some other editions: there may then be a considerable difference in the line numbering. One slight disadvantage in using the Collins edition for line references is that the line numbers placed at intervals in the margin are taken from the 1863-6 Cambridge edition of Shakespeare's works, with the result that in the prose sections of the plays the Cambridge line numbers often do not correspond to the lines as printed in the Collins edition. Where I am unable to give a precise reference to a line or lines as printed in the Collins edition I shall cite the nearest number as given in the Collins margin and then add a plus or minus sign to indicate that the words I am quoting or wish to draw attention to will be found shortly after or shortly before the margin number I have cited. I may not always strictly adhere to the punctuation or textual reading as given in the Collins edition, and I shall follow the traditional practice of giving Act and scene numbers in the form of Roman numerals (whereas in the short commentaries in the 1994 Collins edition on Shakespeare's individual works Arabic numerals are used to indicate Act and scene numbers as well as line numbers).

In the Collins edition the arrangement of Shakespeare's plays is the traditional one, the arrangement that goes back to the First Folio of 1623 (published seven years after Shakespeare's death), where the plays were divided into Comedies, Histories and Tragedies. The 1986 Oxford *William Shakespeare: The Complete Works*, on the other hand, has tried to present the works in the order in which they were composed. (I decided against using this Oxford edition for line numbering since its departure from the traditional presentation of a number of Shakespeare texts might be a source of confusion for the student.) It is certainly desirable to be aware as far as possible of the order in which Shakespeare's works were written, so that we can see how far certain themes recur as he moves on from one work to another. Since, however, there is not sufficient evidence for scholars to be in complete agreement about the chronology of Shakespeare's works, I give at the end of this book brief notes to show how I have arrived at my own decisions about possible dates of composition (without any pretension of being a Shakespearean textual scholar myself) in order that I might deal with Shakespeare's works in something like chronological order. It should be noted that most of the dates of composition shown in this book are preceded by 'c.' (*circa*) to denote that the dates are only approximate and sometimes may scarcely be based on any firm evidence at all.

Shakespeare's works do indeed shed light on each other – as do the works of any major author – and I shall be making some comparisons as regards themes, usually by looking back from later works to earlier ones. But before proceeding to the examination of individual works I propose, as a general introduction to Shakespeare's themes, to give an account of his view of life – since the themes of a major author represent ideas that belong to a whole view of life. Shakespeare's view of life may be conveniently considered in connection with the three main areas of any comprehensive view of life: beliefs about the place of human life in the universe, social and political values, and personal values. In the account that follows the quotations from Shakespeare's works are quotations which I take as representing Shakespeare's own point of view. Some of the points made will be supported more fully in the examination of individual works.

Shakespeare's View of Life

Shakespeare's view of life may be broadly described as that of a Renaissance Christian – like a number of other prominent Renaissance authors,[4] Shakespeare (as, for instance, E. M. W. Tillyard has shown in his little book *The Elizabethan World Picture*, 1943) combined an interest in the literary culture of ancient Greece and Rome with a belief in traditional Christian doctrines. But as regards Christianity it should be remembered that in England in Shakespeare's time the theatre operated under censorship. Reference to current religious controversy was forbidden, as laid down by Queen Elizabeth in 1559, and in 1606 (some time after the midway point of Shakespeare's dramatic career) an Act was introduced (the Act to Restrain Abuses of Players) which banned the use on the stage of the word 'God' and the name Jesus Christ. In plays written after 1606 'God' came to be replaced by some such term as 'heaven' (or 'the heavens').

In Shakespeare's plays supernatural powers, both good and evil, are seen to be at work in human life on earth. In *Richard III* (V.iii.175) it is asserted that 'God and good angels fight on Richmond's side', and the Earl of Richmond, after defeating the evil tyrant Richard III in battle, becomes king (as Henry VII). And in *Macbeth* (IV.iii.238–9) those working for the removal of the tyrant Macbeth are the human instruments of 'the powers above'. In *1 Henry VI*, on the other hand, Joan, leader of the French against the English, is seen as 'a witch' (I.v.6) in communication with evil spirits (V.iii.8–23): she is a 'minister of hell' (V.iv.93). Similarly the Witches in *Macbeth* are 'The instruments of darkness' (i.e. instruments of evil, I.iii.124), endowed with supernatural powers (Macbeth is the object of their 'supernatural soliciting', I.iii.130). In that play the evil Lady Macbeth does not need to be tempted by the Witches, since of her own volition she appeals for inspiration from 'spirits /That tend on mortal [murderous] thoughts' (I.v.37–8). The fairies in *A Midsummer Night's Dream* clearly belong to the realm of fantasy in that here Shakespeare combines the fairies of folklore with creatures of his own invention, but they are probably to be taken as symbolic of supernatural activity impinging on human life, and in *The Tempest* supernatural activity takes the form of magic as practised by Prospero and the spirits who serve him. As for references in Shakespeare to the deities of ancient Greece and Rome, though St Augustine at the beginning of the medieval period took the view that they were evil spirits,[5] by Shakespeare's time stories about Greek and Roman gods and goddesses were regarded as myths that appealed to the imagination (as they were regarded by the Roman poet Ovid, whose *Metamorphoses*, completed in 8 AD and translated into English by Arthur Golding in 1565–7, was one of Shakespeare's favourite works). In Shakespeare, as in the works of other Renaissance poets and dramatists, these deities become personifications of various aspects of human nature – Venus in the poem *Venus and Adonis* represents physical 'desire' (lines 720 and 1074), Cupid (with his arrows) in *Romeo and Juliet* (I.i.206–7) and *A Midsummer Night's Dream* (III.ii.103) represents a force that causes a person to fall in love with someone of the opposite sex, Mars in *Henry V* (line 6 of the opening Chorus) represents a war-like spirit, and so on. But in *Cymbeline*, which is set in Roman times, the descent from the heavens of the Roman chief god Jupiter (V.iv.93–113) symbolises divine intervention, and in *The Winter's Tale* (III.ii.125–44) Apollo's oracle symbolises a form of divine communication. (Reference to the Christian God, it should be remembered, was not allowed on the stage after the 1606 Act.)

Human life is subject not only to supernatural powers but also to Fortune, regarded as 'fickle' – in *1 Henry VI* (V.iii.134) the French leader Reignier is resigned to 'fortune's fickleness', and in *Romeo and Juliet* (III.v.60) Juliet says 'O Fortune, Fortune, all men call thee fickle' – because good fortune or bad fortune is meted out indiscriminately. And with Fortune is associated Time, which brings endless alternation from good to bad and bad to good – in the poem *The Rape of Lucrece* we hear that Time contrives to 'turn the giddy round of Fortune's wheel' (line 952), and Time is addressed as 'O Time, thou tutor both to good and bad' (line 995). Shakespeare may well have believed that good or bad fortune was brought about by the planets and the stars: he certainly associates fortune with them – references are made to 'the planets of mishap' (*1 Henry VI* I.i.23), 'malignant and ill-boding stars' (*1 Henry VI* IV.v.6), 'star-crossed lovers' (*Romeo and Juliet* Prologue, line 6), and 'fortune's star' (*Hamlet* I.iv.32). But Fortune can be controlled by God – in the final speech of *Pericles* Pericles is described as having been 'assailed with fortune' but 'Led on by heaven and crowned with joy at last'. And human beings, though much affected by fortune, have it within them to stand up to adverse fortune. In *Hamlet* (III.ii.66–9) Hamlet says:

> blest are those
> Whose blood [passion] and judgment are so well commingled
> That they are not a pipe for Fortune's finger
> To sound what stop she please.

In *Troilus and Cressida* (I.iii, in the speech beginning line 31) we hear that 'In the reproof of chance/Lies the true proof of men': courage shows itself when it 'Retorts to chiding fortune'. And in *Antony and Cleopatra* (III.xiii.31–4) Enobarbus deplores Antony's weak submission to fortune:

> I see men's judgments are
> A parcel of their fortunes, and things outward
> Do draw the inward quality after them...

In the *Henry VI* plays and in *Macbeth* it is indicated that future events may be predicted by both good and bad supernatural powers. In *3 Henry VI* (IV.vi.68–74) it is supernaturally revealed that the Earl of Richmond will subsequently bring 'bliss' to England by becoming king (as actually happens at the end of *Richard III*). In *1 Henry VI* (V.iii.18–23) the evil spirits with whom Joan is in communication make it clear to her that France is doomed to defeat, and in *Macbeth* the Witches are able to predict various future events. But, though certain future events, including human actions, may be predictable, human beings are still regarded as morally responsible for their actions. Shakespeare offers no explanation as to how a predictable future can be reconciled with a human being's responsibility for making moral choices, but there was the traditional explanation that God has foreknowledge of how human beings will choose to act.[6] It would appear that this kind of foreknowledge is imparted by the powers of evil to the Witches in *Macbeth*: their foreknowledge in I.iii of future events consequent upon the murder of King Duncan must surely include their knowing beforehand that Macbeth will decide to murder Duncan, even though in I.vii he at first decides against the murder.

The assumed explanation for suffering in human life derives from the Christian doctrine of Original Sin, according to which all human beings have inherited the tendency to sin from Adam (expelled for his disobedience from the Garden of Eden), though release from punishment is afforded by faith in Christ. (See *Genesis* 3 and Paul's *Epistle to the Romans* 5.) Christ by his death has atoned for human sinfulness: in *Richard III* (I.iv.185–6) Clarence speaks of 'redemption/By Christ's dear blood, shed for our grievous sins'; in *Richard II* (II.i.56) John of Gaunt describes Christ as 'the world's ransom, blessèd Mary's Son'; in the opening speech of *1 Henry IV* (I.i.26–7) King Henry speaks of Christ as having been 'nailed/For our advantage on the bitter cross'; and in *Measure for Measure* (II.ii.73–5) Isabella says that God (through Christ) has exercised His power to rescue human souls that were previously 'forfeit':

> Why, all the souls that were were forfeit once,
> And He that might the vantage best have took
> Found out the remedy.

A similar reference to the inborn sinfulness in human nature is made by Portia in *The Merchant of Venice* (IV.i.194–5) when she tells Shylock that were it not for God's mercy no human being could expect to be saved:

> in the course of justice none of us
> Should see salvation: we do pray for mercy...

There are good human beings who overcome the effects of original sin, but salvation comes in the next world, so that even truly good human beings may suffer in their lives on earth, where they are to be commended for showing 'patience' (the virtue praised by Paul in *Romans* 5:3) – such patience is shown by Marina in *Pericles* (V.i.136–8), Hermione in *The Winter's Tale* (II.i.106), and the Duke of Buckingham in *Henry VIII* (II.i.36).

We may note that Shakespeare's Christianity, though partly sectarian, is capable of taking a broader view. In *Twelfth Night* the word 'Puritan' is introduced in a spirit of light comedy (II.iii.129 + ff.): the foolish Sir Andrew Aguecheek, on hearing that Malvolio, the pompous steward, is 'a kind of Puritan', exclaims 'O, if I thought that, I'd beat him like a dog', but when challenged to give a reason he cannot give one. More damningly, the sanctimonious but corrupt Angelo in *Measure for Measure* is described as 'precise' (I.iii.50), which in Shakespeare's time denoted a Puritan. In *Pericles*, on the other hand, 'puritan' is used favourably to mean a pure person: Marina, forced to work in a brothel, is so effective in making the clients there feel morally ashamed that 'she could make a puritan of the Devil if he would cheapen [bargain for] a kiss of her' (IV.vi.10–). As regards Roman Catholicism, Shakespeare does indeed show a Protestant contempt for the Papacy. According to *1 Henry VI* (V.i.28–9, 51–4) the Pope has made Beaufort, Bishop of Winchester, a cardinal in return for a promised sum of money. In *King John* the Papal legate plays at power politics, and in *Henry VIII* the Papacy is closely associated with the worldly Cardinal Wolsey, whose arrogance has been promoted by the Pope ('him that made him [Wolsey] proud – the Pope', II.ii.53).[7] But Shakespeare has a great respect for friars, as represented by Friar Lawrence in *Romeo and Juliet* and Friar Francis in *Much Ado about Nothing*, and in *Measure for Measure* the Duke as a conscientious ruler seeks assistance from Friar Thomas, whom he addresses as 'holy father' (I.iii.l).

As regards social and political values, Shakespeare's firm belief is in the ideal of concord or harmony. This comes out clearly in the series of historical plays – *Henry VI* in three Parts and *Richard III* – that appeared early in Shakespeare's career.

For his historical material in these four plays Shakespeare drew on the chronicles of Edward Hall and Raphael Holinshed, but, as Tillyard has shown in a valuable chapter (Ch. 2, 'The Historical Background') in his *Shakespeare's History Plays* (1944), Shakespeare also derived from Hall a political philosophy. Hall in his chronicle *The Union of the Two Noble and Illustre Families of Lancaster and York* (1542, earliest surviving edition 1548) deplored the 'dissension' that occurred in England during the Wars of the Roses (1455–85), which were brought to an end with the crowning of Henry VII. Tillyard quotes Hall as saying: 'as by discord great things decay and fall to ruin, so the same by concord be revived and erected.' In *1 Henry VI* (IV.i.188–94) the public-spirited Duke of Exeter deplores discord amongst leading nobles: 'This jarring discord of nobility... There comes the ruin, there begins confusion.' And in *2 Henry VI* (II.i.57) King Henry himself says: 'When such strings jar, what hope of harmony?' One may add that for Shakespeare an important aspect of social harmony is 'love' in what may be taken as the Christian sense of love of one's fellow human beings. In *1 Henry VI* (III.i.68) King Henry pleads for 'love and amity', and in a later play Coriolanus asks the Roman gods to 'Plant love among us' (*Coriolanus* III.iii.35).

Harmony in human society is linked with 'order' and 'degree' (acceptance of one's place in a social hierarchy) – the 'order' and 'degree' that were insisted on in one of the Church of England 'Homilies' which were required to be read out regularly to church congregations. In *Shakespeare's History Plays* (Ch. 1, sec. 4) Tillyard quotes (in the original spelling) a passage from the 1547 Homily entitled 'An Exhortation concerning Good Order and Obedience to Rulers and Magistrates'. This passage asserts the following: 'Euery degree of people, in their vocacion, callyng, and office, hath appointed to them their duetie and ordre... Take awaie Kynges, Princes, Rulers, Magistrates, Judges, and suche states of God's ordre... and there muste nedes folowe all mischief and utter destruccion.' In Shakespeare's *Henry V* (I.ii.180–3) the Duke of Exeter (an earlier Duke of Exeter than the one in *1 Henry VI*) talks of good government as depending on people of different social rank performing harmoniously together like singers of a part-song:

> For government, though high, and low, and lower,
> Put into parts, doth keep in one consent,
> Congreeing in a full and natural close,
> Like music.

(Exeter's speech is then followed up by the Archbishop of Canterbury who speaks at length about how a beehive can provide a model for 'order' in human society.) Similarly a well-known speech in *Troilus and Cressida* (I.iii. 109–10) stresses the importance of 'degree' in the promotion of social harmony:

> Take but degree away, untune that string,
> And hark what discord follows.

But rulers and magistrates are under the obligation to administer justice.[8] In *Macbeth* (IV.iii.91–4) 'justice' comes first in a list of a dozen 'king-becoming graces'. Richard II, as a king, is shown to be utterly corrupt in the administration of justice. When in the first scene of *Richard II* Bolingbroke asks for 'justice' (I.i.106) against Mowbray, Duke of Norfolk, for the killing of the Duke of Gloucester, the only 'justice' (I.i.203) offered by Richard is that the matter should be settled by combat between Bolingbroke and Mowbray. Then, in the second scene, John of Gaunt (brother of the Duke of Gloucester) reveals that he knows it was Richard himself who was responsible for the death of Gloucester. John of Gaunt condemns Richard for being false to his divinely appointed office (I.ii.37–40):

> God's is the quarrel – for God's substitute,
> His deputy anointed in His sight,
> Hath caused his [Gloucester's] death, the which if wrongfully,
> Let heaven revenge.

Shakespeare also, of course, gave expression to Elizabethan patriotism, the most notable example being John of Gaunt's description of England as 'This royal throne of kings...This other Eden, demi-paradise...Dear for her reputation through the world' (*Richard II* II.i.40–58). This patriotism, it must be confessed, is of the jingoistic kind. The concluding speech of *King John* boasts that

> This England never did, nor never shall,
> Lie at the proud foot of a conqueror,

and in *Henry V* the Chorus at the beginning of Act II extols England's greatness as preparations are made for the invasion of France:

> O England, model to thy inward greatness,
> Like little body with a mighty heart.

And in France, in the fighting before Harfleur, King Henry urges his soldiers on with the cry 'God for Harry, England and Saint George!' (III.i.34). It should be noted, however, that in a later play Shakespeare presents a very different view of patriotism – at the end of *Cymbeline*, written in the reign of King James, not of Queen Elizabeth, a war fought by Britain in defiance of the Roman emperor is condemned as Cymbeline, the British king, gladly submits to the superior authority of Rome (V.v.458–61), and this submission receives the blessing of 'the powers above' (V.v.464–5). (Could Shakespeare's change of attitude, I wonder, be connected with the fact that, whereas Queen Elizabeth encouraged a patriotic resistance to Spain, King James made peace with Spain?)

In *Henry V* patriotism is seen as a justification for military violence (III.i.5–6):

> when the blast of war blows in our ears
> Then imitate the action of the tiger.

Earlier in that play (I.ii.102–11) the Archbishop of Canterbury, recalling the time when Henry V's ancestor Edward III was at war with France, describes with patriotic enthusiasm how King

Edward was able to watch his son the Black Prince and his men 'Forage in blood of French nobility [noblemen]. O noble English...' And in *Macbeth* violence is praised in a war against a group of rebels – at the beginning of that play Macbeth, before he later succumbs to evil, is hailed as 'brave Macbeth', 'worthy gentleman' (I.ii.16,24) for having ripped open on the battlefield the body of the treacherous rebel leader: Macbeth 'unseamed him from the nave [navel] to the chaps [jaws]' (I.ii.22). But Shakespeare is in no doubt about peace being preferable to war. At the end of *Richard III* the Earl of Richmond, due to be crowned Henry VII, hopes that his heirs, in an England now at last rid of civil war, will 'Enrich the time to come with smooth-faced peace' (V.v.33). And in the last scene of *Henry V* peace is welcomed as 'Dear nurse of arts, plenties, and joyful births' (V.ii.35). As for military violence, in a later play, *Coriolanus*, Coriolanus's mother is heavily satirised for glorifying military violence for its own sake – she thinks of the Trojan warrior Hector wounded in battle as being a more beautiful sight than his mother when performing her maternal function (I.iii.40–2):

> The breasts of Hecuba
> When she did suckle Hector looked not lovelier
> Than Hector's forehead when it spit forth blood...

As regards personal values (also of importance socially in that it is especially desirable that they should be manifested by those in authority), integrity is rated highly by Shakespeare. 'Integrity' is a word actually used by Shakespeare – in the opening scene of *Titus Andronicus* (I.i.48) Bassianus speaks of 'uprightness and integrity', and in *Henry VIII* Wolsey hypocritically lays claim to 'integrity' (III.i.51; later, after a moral conversion, he talks about 'integrity' more sincerely, III.ii.453), whereas Archbishop Cranmer's 'integrity' is genuine (V.i.114). The words 'honour' and 'truth' are also used to convey the same kind of human quality. In *2 Henry VI* (III.i.203) the Duke of Gloucester is praised for his 'honour, truth and loyalty'; in *Richard II* (II.i.138) the last words we hear from the dying John of Gaunt are 'Love they to live that love and honour have'; and in *Macbeth* (IV.iii.114–17) Malcolm describes Macduff's detestation of evil qualities in a ruler as 'this noble passion,/Child of integrity' and praises his 'good truth and honour'. A stout upholder of integrity ('truth') is the Bastard (Philip Faulconbridge, illegitimate son of Richard I) who in *King John* (IV.iii.144–5) sees John's appalling lack of integrity as desecrating England as a whole:

> The life, the right, and truth of all this realm
> Is fled to heaven.

Also regarded as being of supreme value by Shakespeare is the place of love in various personal relationships. There is love between members of a family, as shown in *King Lear* by Cordelia as a devoted daughter and Edgar as a devoted son, and as shown in *As You Like It* by Rosalind and Celia as cousins 'whose loves/Are dearer than the natural bond of sisters' (I.ii.254–5). There is love between friends of the same sex: between Hermia and Helena (*A Midsummer Night's Dream* III.ii.201–15) there is an 'ancient love' going back to their childhood days, and in the Sonnets the Poet (who may or may not resemble Shakespeare himself) expresses an intense love for a young man (Sonnet 20 makes it clear that this love excludes a physical relationship). Intense love felt by one man for another also occurs in *Henry V* (IV.vi.11–27) where the Duke of York, before dying on the battlefield, passionately kisses the Earl of Suffolk who is already dead ('And so, espoused to death, with blood he sealed/A testament of noble-ending love'), and in *Twelfth Night* (II.i.42–3) a sea captain who has rescued Sebastian from the sea after shipwreck is prepared to risk encountering enemies because he cannot bear to be parted from Sebastian ('I do adore thee so/That danger shall seem sport'). There is also love in other situations – in *As You Like It* a banished duke is attended in exile by 'loving lords' (I.i.89+) and the young Orlando, driven out of the family household by his elder brother, is attended by an elderly servant, Adam, 'Who after me hath many a weary step/Limped in pure love' (II.vii.130–1).

The form of love with which Shakespeare is most concerned is, of course, love between man and woman. In two early comedies this love is acclaimed as divine inspiration. In *The Comedy of Errors* (III.ii.33–40) Antipholus of Syracuse, falling in love at first sight, says to Luciana:

Teach me, dear creature, how to think and speak...
Are you a god? Would you create me new?
Transform me, then, and to your power I'll yield.

And according to Berowne in *Love's Labour's Lost* (IV.iii .340–1):

when Love speaks the voice of all the gods
Makes heaven drowsy with the harmony.

This love is an emotion that transcends sexual desire, such desire being lust which needs to be controlled by 'reason' ('The expense of spirit [vital energy] in a waste of shame/Is lust in action...Past reason hunted...Past reason hated' – Sonnet 129; 'careless [reckless] lust stirs up a desperate courage...beating reason back' – *Venus and Adonis* lines 556–7; 'My will [lust] is strong, past reason's weak removing' – Tarquin's words before committing rape, *The Rape of Lucrece* line 243). Shakespeare shows, however, that a characteristic even of true love in its initial stages is a certain kind of madness or blindness ('Love is blind' and is afflicted by 'folly' – *The Two Gentlemen of Verona* II.i.60+); 'Madman! Passion! Lover!' Mercutio says of Romeo – *Romeo and Juliet* II.i.7; 'Love looks not with the eyes but with the mind...Nor hath Love's mind of any judgment taste' – *A Midsummer Night's Dream* I.i.234–6).[9]

Heterosexual love is firmly related to marriage, and chastity is required before marriage. When the lovers in *A Midsummer Night's Dream* are in the wood during the night Demetrius warns Helena of the need to protect 'the rich worth of your virginity' (II.i.219), and Hermia asks Lysander to 'Lie further off', that a becoming distance may be kept between 'a virtuous bachelor and a maid' (II.ii.44, 57–60). And in *The Tempest*

Prospero, just before the betrothal of his daughter Miranda to Ferdinand, insists that chastity must be observed until a full marriage ceremony is performed (IV.i.15–21):

> If thou dost break her virgin knot before
> All sanctimonious ceremonies may
> With full and holy rite be ministered
> ... disdain and discord shall bestrew
> The union of your bed...[10]

(In a poem ascribed to Shakespeare and known by the title *The Phoenix and Turtle* chastity even within marriage – 'married chastity', line 61 – is applauded, presumably as an exceptional dedication to a love entirely spiritual. This certainly contrasts with the full approval given to Juliet's yearning, after her secret marriage to Romeo, for the coming together of 'a pair of stainless maidenheads' in the 'amorous rites' of marriage – *Romeo and Juliet* III.ii.8–13.) In marriage a wife should obey her husband, just as a ruler's subjects should obey their ruler – as Katherina says in the final scene of *The Taming of the Shrew* (V.ii.155–6):

> Such duty as the subject owes the prince,
> Even such a woman oweth to her husband.

Katherina refers to a woman's husband as her 'lord' (V.ii.138,146), and a husband is referred to in this way by Juliet (*Romeo and Juliet* III.ii.98), Portia (*The Merchant of Venice* III.iv.17–18), Helena (*All's Well That Ends Well* II.v.83, 86; III.ii.101,110), Desdemona (*Othello* I.iii.189, 251; III.iv.30, 32), and Hermione (*The Winter's Tale* I.ii.61). But Katherina's husband, Petruchio, though high-handed in his taming of Katherina, is good-humoured and he does love her: the husband to whom a wife owes obedience is referred to by Katherina not only as 'lord' but as a 'loving lord' (V.ii.160). Shakespeare's view of marriage is in fact in line with the Church of England marriage ceremony, which, as established in 1549, calls upon the woman to 'obey' her husband and the man to 'love' and 'cherish' his wife as she is to 'love' and 'cherish' him. (These requirements are themselves in line with Paul's teaching in *Ephesians* 5:22,25: 'Wives, submit yourselves unto your own husbands... Husbands, love your wives...') And, though Shakespeare upholds male authority in marriage, he condemns fathers who try to oppose their daughters' wishes in the choice of a husband – fathers such as Sylvia's father (the Duke of Milan) in *The Two Gentlemen of Verona*, Hermia's father (Egeus) in *A Midsummer Night's Dream*, Anne Page's father in *The Merry Wives of Windsor*, and Desdemona's father (Brabantio) in *Othello*.

Apart from love, another human emotion highly valued by Shakespeare is 'compassion' or 'pity'. In *Richard III* (IV.iii.6–7) the two murderers of the princes (Richard's two nephews), though these murderers were 'fleshed villains, bloody dogs', are afterwards filled with remorse – they 'Melted with tenderness and mild [gentle] compassion'. And in *King John* Hubert, persuaded to undertake the murder of John's nephew, cannot but respond to Arthur's appeal for 'compassion' (IV.i.89) and becomes his protector. In *King Lear* Edgar, though unjustly proclaimed a criminal by his father, Gloucester, is nevertheless moved by 'good pity' (IV.vi.225) to give immediate help after Gloucester's eyes have been put out by the husband of Regan, Lear's cruel daughter. And even Macbeth, before murdering Duncan, is briefly deterred by pity – 'pity, like a naked new-born babe' (*Macbeth* I.vii.21).

On several occasions in his plays Shakespeare touches on the Christian doctrine that one should forgive those by whom one has been wronged instead of seeking personal revenge. In *As You Like It* Orlando, though he has been grossly maltreated by his elder brother Oliver, rescues him from being attacked by a lioness – as Oliver reports with gratitude (IV.iii.127–9):

> But kindness, nobler ever than revenge...
> Made him give battle to the lioness...

And in *The Tempest* Prospero, when he has his enemies at his mercy, says (V.i.26–8):

> Yet with my nobler reason 'gainst my fury
> Do I take part. The rarer action is
> In virtue than in vengeance.

(Similar in spirit is Portia's appeal to Shylock, in *The Merchant of Venice* IV.i.177–82, to show mercy to Antonio, who cannot repay the money Shylock lent him. Shylock, however, deaf to such an appeal, is not to be deterred from exacting 'revenge' against Antonio for having scorned him as a Jewish usurer – see III.i.44 + ff.) And in two of his early plays, *3 Henry VI* and *Titus Andronicus*, Shakespeare shows the futility of acts of revenge and counter-revenge. But it should be noted that, while deploring 'revenge' in the sense of personal malice, Shakespeare also uses this word in an approving sense to mean rightful punishment, punishment meted out in the interests of justice. In the poem *The Rape of Lucrece* Lucrece, having been raped by Tarquin, son of the Roman king, begs to be 'revenged' (line 1683) for the sake of 'justice' (line 1687), whereupon she herself commits suicide: in due course Tarquin is accordingly banished. In *Richard II* the dying John of Gaunt (in words I quoted earlier) leaves it to heaven to punish Richard for the death of Gaunt's brother: 'Let heaven revenge' (I.ii.40). And when in *Macbeth* Malcolm calls upon Macduff to work for 'revenge' against Macbeth (IV.iii.214), following the murder at Macbeth's orders of Macduff's wife and children, it is suggested here that Malcolm and Macduff are to be the instruments of divine punishment: 'the powers above/Put on their instruments' (IV.iii.238–9).

We should also notice, as regards personal values, Shakespeare's concern with a moral balance between certain opposites.[11] An early example of this is a balance between pity and punishment. In *2 Henry VI* Humphrey, Duke of Gloucester, who during Henry VI's minority has ruled England as 'Protector', is a professed man of 'pity' but has not let pity interfere with the punishment of murderers and heartless thieves (III.i.124–32), and he orders a beggar to be beaten for fraudulently claiming to have been miraculously cured of blindness by St Alban and also for pretending to be a cripple

(II.i.97–149). Humphrey thus contrasts with the naive young Henry, described by his queen as being 'Too full of foolish pity' (III.i.225): though this remark reveals the Queen's lack of respect for pity, Henry is indeed too quick to show pity where it is not deserved, as in his pity for the evil Cardinal Beaufort when the Cardinal is on his deathbed (III.iii). (In *3 Henry VI*, however, the King rightly expresses pity for those killed in civil war – 'O, pity, pity, gentle heaven, pity!', II.v.96 – in contrast with his pitiless supporter Lord Clifford who, in revenge for the killing of his father in battle by the Duke of York, kills young Rutland, York's son, an 'innocent child' – I.iii.8 – in the company of his tutor.)

A kind of balance with which Shakespeare is especially concerned is the balance between reason and passion.[12] This is an extension of the need for a balance between reason and desire[13] which I have already mentioned in connection with love – Sonnet 147 may be quoted here as describing the state of misery that results when desire (the Poet's desire for his mistress) has outstripped the power of reason to control it:

> My love is as a fever...
> Past cure I am, now reason is past care,
> And frantic mad with evermore unrest.

As for reason and passion, *Titus Andronicus*, an early Shakespeare play, shows Titus as a man completely at the mercy of his 'passions' (III.i.218), following the mutilation of his daughter: unable to respond to the plea of his brother Marcus – 'But yet let reason govern thy lament' (III.i.219) – Titus lapses into madness. I have already quoted Hamlet's recognition of the need for 'blood and judgment' (i.e. passion and reason) to be 'commingled' if one is to stand up to 'Fortune' (*Hamlet* III.ii.66–9): here Hamlet goes on to say 'Give me that man/That is not passion's slave' (III.ii.69–70). And in *Othello* Othello becomes a tragic example of 'passion's slave'. His awareness, earlier in the play (II.iii.196–9), of the danger of his giving way to passion is prophetic of the state of mind in which, in the last scene, he murders his devoted wife whom he falsely believes to be adulterous:

> Now, by heaven,
> My blood begins my safer guides to rule,
> And passion, having my best judgment collied [darkened],
> Assays [attempts] to lead the way.

(This imbalance between 'passion' and 'judgment' should be distinguished from a similar imbalance which, as we have seen, was regarded by Shakespeare as normal in the early stages of true love.) And similar to the need for a balance between reason and passion is the need for a balance between reason and 'imagination' – whereas Duke Theseus in *A Midsummer Night's Dream* (V.i.4–22) shows narrowness in regarding the 'imagination' of lovers and poets as being offensive to 'cool reason', Hotspur in *1 Henry IV* (I.iii.199–200) shows a lack of political and military judgement in being too easily carried away by 'imagination', as also is noted, after his death, in *2 Henry IV* (I.iii.30–2).

A further example of a desirable balance between opposites is that between mirth and seriousness, although Shakespeare also praises mirth as having a therapeutic value of its own.[14] We are meant to give a sympathetic hearing to Gratiano when he says to the downcast Antonio in *The Merchant of Venice* (I.i.78–79):

> Let me play the fool.
> With mirth and laughter let old wrinkles come.

And Hamlet realises how his whole attitude to life has been soured by the loss of mirth ('I have of late... lost all my mirth... and indeed it goes so heavily with my disposition that this goodly frame, the earth, seems to me a sterile promontory...', II.ii.290 + ff.): later he recalls with appreciation the King's jester, now dead, as being 'a fellow of infinite jest', with 'flashes of merriment that were wont to set the table on a roar' (V.i.176 + ff.). The need for balance comes out in *1 Henry IV*. It is a healthy sign that the Prince can enjoy making merry with

Falstaff and his cronies (when he takes part in a prank on Falstaff he says it will afford 'laughter for a month and a good jest for ever', II.ii.91–2), but as the play proceeds we see that as future king he is able to take his responsibilities seriously. In *Antony and Cleopatra* this kind of balance is shown to be lacking in the two chief Roman leaders, Mark Antony and Octavius Caesar. Caesar, the puritanical power-politician, dislikes Antony for giving himself up to 'mirth' and 'pleasure' (I.iv.19, 33 – 'our graver business/Frowns at this levity' Caesar says when attending a feast in Egypt, II.vii.118–19), but on the other hand Antony clearly shirks his political responsibilities.

So much for some of Shakespeare's positive ideals. Not surprisingly, the evil qualities portrayed by Shakespeare are often the opposites of his positive ideals. Hence the opposite of integrity or honour is 'policy', in the sense of crooked dealing. It is said of the Duke of Suffolk in *2 Henry VI* (IV.i.83) 'By devilish policy art thou grown great', and in *Titus Andronicus* (II.i.104–5) Aaron's advice, in suggesting that Demetrius and Chiron should rape Titus's daughter, is ' 'Tis policy and stratagem must do/That you affect [What you desire]'. Hate is strongly condemned as the opposite of love. In *Romeo and Juliet* (I.i.93) the Prince of Verona rightly condemns the 'cankered hate' that exists between the Montague and Capulet families (it is this hate that leads to the deaths of Romeo and Juliet), and in *Coriolanus* hate poisons relations between the upper and lower classes. And as for the virtue of pity, Richard, Duke of Gloucester, who obtains the throne by means of a series of murders, prides himself on being pitiless: 'I that have neither pity, love, nor fear' (*3 Henry VI* V.vi.68), 'Tear-falling pity dwells not in this eye' (*Richard III* IV.ii.64). The evil qualities of cunning ('policy'), malice ('hate') and pitilessness are combined in the 'Machiavel', a type of character who delights in performing acts of trickery and villainy in general.[15] Aaron, for instance, as he contemplates a treacherous double murder, says enthusiastically (*Titus Andronicus* III.i.203–4): 'O, how this villainy/Doth fat me [fill me with pleasure] with the very thoughts of it!' Other Shakespearean Machiavels are Richard

III, Don John in *Much Ado about Nothing*, Iago in *Othello*, Edmund in *King Lear*, and Iachimo in *Cymbeline*.

In Shakespeare's earlier plays the conflict between good and evil is presented mainly as a conflict between good characters and evil characters, but in the later plays both good and evil are shown to be at work in a single person. In *Julius Caesar* the 'noble Brutus' (I.ii.62) becomes an assassin. Hamlet, recognised by Ophelia as having 'a noble mind' (III.i.150), is tainted by evil in the cruel remarks he makes to her (III.i.), and the erstwhile 'noble' Othello (acclaimed as 'noble' in II.ii) succumbs completely to the evil influence of Iago. And Macbeth has a sufficiently strong conscience to reject the idea of murdering Duncan (I.vii.12–25), before being persuaded by Lady Macbeth to go ahead with the murder. (Macbeth succumbs to evil much more quickly than Othello.) The power of both good and evil to sway human beings is shown by Shakespeare to be sometimes unpredictable. Cassius in *Julius Caesar*, seen as evil in the early part of the play in his persuasion of Brutus to lead the conspiracy to murder Caesar, becomes in IV.iii the genuinely devoted friend of Brutus. More sudden is the moral conversion of the villains Edmund and Iachimo in the final scenes of *King Lear* and *Cymbeline* respectively – the same kind of conversion occurred in Borachio in V.i of *Much Ado about Nothing*. In *The Winter's Tale*, on the other hand, there is a sudden eruption of evil in Leontes (in I.ii), which takes the form of an almost insane conviction that his queen, Hermione, is unfaithful. Shakespeare's plays suggest that in human life there is a never-ending battle between good and evil, just as there is a continual alternation between good and bad Fortune, but at least most of his plays (not all of them) end with the triumph of the good: this is especially true of Shakespeare's last plays.

Finally, we must face the fact that Shakespeare reflects certain biases of his time. While paying a token tribute to the medieval ideal of a united Christendom – according to *1 Henry VI* (V.i.1–14) there should be peace between England and France as the 'professors of one faith', and according to *Henry V* there should be 'Christian-like accord' (V.ii.344) between these two nations – Shakespeare follows the chronicles of Hall and

Holinshed[16] in showing a strong nationalist bias. At the end of both *1 Henry VI* and *Henry V* peace is to be established entirely on English terms, and early in *Henry V* (in I.ii) what today would be regarded as a highly dubious claim to the French throne receives the Archbishop of Canterbury's blessing. (I have already noted, however, that in one of his last plays, *Cymbeline*, Shakespeare reaches the point of almost condemning nationalism.) Shakespeare's praise of violence in war (in *Henry V* and at the beginning of *Macbeth*) and his unquestioning acceptance of male authority in marriage are other examples of what would not meet with general acceptance today. Where Shakespeare especially reflects the prejudices of his contemporaries is in his attitude to non-Christians. His presentation of Shylock in *The Merchant of Venice* shows the same anti-Semitism as Marlowe's presentation of Barabas in *The Jew of Malta* (see Note 15 on Barabas as a Machiavel type of character). There are also incidental remarks which assume Jews to be villainous: 'I am a Jew else, an Ebrew Jew' says Falstaff in *1 Henry IV* (II.iv.172), and 'If I do not love her, I am a Jew' says Benedick in *Much Ado about Nothing* (end of II.iii). And Muslims, usually under the name of Turks, come in for contemptuous dismissal by various Shakespearean characters – 'What, think you we are Turks or infidels?' says Gloucester, posing hypocritically as a true Christian in *Richard III* (III.v.41); the Bishop of Carlisle in *Richard II* (IV.i.92–5) speaks of the Duke of Norfolk as fighting 'in glorious Christian field' against 'Turks and Saracens' (i.e. both Turkish and Arab Muslims); the Duke in *The Merchant of Venice* (IV.i.32) refers to 'stubborn Turks and Tartars' (Mongols); and Othello, confronted by fighting between two Venetians in Cyprus, condemns such behaviour as belonging rather to barbarous Turks (*Othello* II.iii.162–4): 'Are we turned Turks...?/For Christian shame, put by this barbarous brawl.' And in *Macbeth* (IV.i.26–9) prejudice is shown against Jew, Turk and Tartar together by referring to all three of them as providing ingredients ('Liver of blaspheming Jew... Nose of Turk, and Tartar's lips') for the evil brew in the Witches' cauldron.

We see, therefore, that when we look at his view of life as a whole Shakespeare in various respects is *not* our contemporary. But with Shakespeare, as with other major authors, we should find that, even though some elements may be unacceptable to us, there will remain much to which we can respond sympathetically. Surely, for instance, we can respond to Shakespeare's conception of human life as a perpetual battle between good and evil, and his insistence on the need for integrity in those in authority and his belief in the supreme value of love are surely to be applauded. We should in fact be able to draw inspiration from Shakespeare as a great proclaimer of positive values. But to respond effectively to Shakespeare we must make the effort to project our minds back into the world to which he belonged.

THE FIRST PART OF HENRY VI (c.1590)

I assume that Tillyard was right in arguing in *Shakespeare's History Plays* that *1 Henry VI* was planned by Shakespeare as part of a tetralogy consisting of *Henry VI* in three Parts and *Richard III*. The overall theme of the whole tetralogy is England in a state of disorder, which comes to an end with the ascent to the throne of Henry VII, England's first Tudor king. In *1 Henry VI* the theme is disorder as caused by discord amongst the leading noblemen, discord which by the end of the play appears on the surface to be resolved, though beneath the surface the forces of disorder are still at work.

The play opens with the funeral of Henry V, praised by the Duke of Bedford as an exemplary king ('England ne'er lost a king of so much worth', I.i.7). Hostility immediately breaks out between the Duke of Gloucester, 'Protector' of England (since Henry VI is not of age), and a leading churchman, Beaufort, Bishop of Winchester. The two men denounce each other and Bedford appeals for an end to such discord (I.i.44):

Cease, cease these jars and rest your minds in peace.

Then a Messenger arrives to report the loss of English territory in France,[17] which, says the Messenger, is due to 'want of men and money', caused by the existence of 'factions' amongst the 'English nobility' (I.i.69–78). We hear from another Messenger that Lord Talbot, the commander of the English troops in France, is a man of 'undaunted spirit' (I.i.127), but in a later scene (I.v) the English troops are seen to be unable to stand up to the French 'witch' (I.v.6, 21), Joan of Arc,[18] referred to in this play as Joan la Pucelle (Joan the Maid).

In I.iii the enmity between Gloucester and Winchester (now a cardinal) gives rise to fighting between their serving-men. In II.iv and v a source of further discord is revealed – a challenge to the legality of Henry VI's position as king. In II.iv in a garden of the Temple (one of the London Inns of Court concerned with legal education) a discussion is going on, in the presence of a lawyer, about a claim to the throne put forward by Richard Plantagenet. Those who support Plantagenet's claim pluck white roses from the garden, and those who support Henry VI pluck red roses: the lawyer is impressed by Plantagenet's claim and so plucks a white rose. (Shakespeare thus prepares the way for the outbreak of the Wars of the Roses which dominate the action in *3 Henry VI*.) The grounds of Plantagenet's claim become apparent in the next scene (II.v), where his dying uncle gives him full details about his descent through his mother from Edward III's third son, as against King Henry's descent from Edward III's fourth son.

King Henry, who appears in the play for the first time in III.i., does his best to overcome discord but meets with only superficial success. He appeals to Gloucester and Winchester to 'join your hearts in love and amity' (III.i.68), and the two enemies publicly exchange 'love' for one another (III.i.135) – but Winchester's insincerity is shown in his 'aside' (III.i.141): 'So help me God, as I intend it not!' In the same scene the question of Plantagenet's claim to the throne appears to be settled when the King confers on Plantagenet the title of Duke of York and Plantagenet vows life-long 'obedience' to Henry (III.i.164–73). The Duke of Exeter, however, in a soliloquy at the end of the scene, shows he is in no doubt about the falsity of these reconciliations (III.i 189–91):

This late dissension grown betwixt the peers
Burns under feignèd ashes of forged love,
And will at last break out into a flame.

The question of York's (Plantagenet's) claim to the throne does in fact remain a burning one, as we find out in IV.i, where a quarrel breaks out between York and the Earl of Somerset (plucker of a red rose in the Temple garden scene), following an exchange of insults between one of Somerset's men and one of York's men who have been displaying a red rose and a white rose respectively (IV.i.78–110). The King tries to resolve this quarrel by requiring Somerset and York to work together in leading a joint military force against the French as their common enemy (IV.i.164–8), but once again Exeter is apprehensive about the consequences of 'This jarring discord of nobility' (IV.i.188). And in a later scene we find that Winchester's enmity towards Gloucester has not abated – in his 'aside' in V.i.56–62 Winchester expresses his determination to humiliate Gloucester.

As regards the war in France, Joan has managed to persuade the Duke of Burgundy, previously England's ally, to join the French (III.iii), and, at a time when Talbot badly needs support from York and Somerset, Somerset fails to send his horsemen to work with York's footsoldiers (IV.iii.9–14): Talbot is wounded and dies on the battlefield (IV.vii). Despite these setbacks England in the last Act of the play appears to be in command of the situation in so far as Joan is taken prisoner (V.iii) and Charles the Dauphin[19] agrees to a truce whereby, instead of being King of France in his own right, he will submit to the authority of the King of England (V.iv.169–75). In actual fact Charles's acceptance is of little value, since it follows an 'aside' from the French Duke of Alençon (V.iv.163–4) in which he advises Charles to

> take this compact of a truce,
> Although you break it when your pleasure serves.

Alençon is clearly identified as an unscrupulous 'Machiavel' character – his advice to Charles justifies York's description of him as 'that notorious Machiavel' (V.iv.74). But England is shown to have her own Machiavel. The Earl of Suffolk is smitten by the charms of Margaret, daughter of Reignier, a French Duke who is also King of Naples, and Suffolk, since he is already married, wishes to make Margaret his 'paramour' (V.iii.81–2). In the last scene of the play (V.v) Suffolk persuades King Henry to marry Margaret who, he assures Henry, will be a perfect wife to him, and the play ends with Suffolk's self-congratulation on having found a way to acquire Margaret as his mistress and through her to wield supreme political power (V.v.107–8):

> Margaret shall now be Queen and rule the King,
> But I will rule both her, the King, and realm.

THE SECOND PART OF HENRY VI (c. 1590)

The theme of *2 Henry VI* is England in a state of disorder as caused by the pursuit of power by various individuals, a pursuit of power which culminates in the outbreak of civil war.

In contrast to the evil characters, but unable to withstand them, are the young King Henry and the Protector, the Duke of Gloucester. Henry is naively trusting – in the opening scene, even though Suffolk, in arranging a marriage between Henry and Margaret Regnier of France, has handed over two important parts of English territory in France, Henry expresses gratitude to Suffolk and promotes him from Marquis to Duke – it appears that he has already been promoted to Marquis from Earl, his title at the end of *1 Henry VI*. Henry in fact is a saintly person, whose new queen says of him (in contempt) that 'all his mind is bent to holiness' (I.iii.53). As for Gloucester, it is stressed in this play that he is a man of integrity – praised by the common people as 'Humphrey, the good Duke of Gloucester' (I.i.154), and praised too by the Earl of Salisbury (I.i.178–9), who himself, along with the Earl of Warwick, wishes to promote 'the public good' (I.i.194,198–201). Integrity is Gloucester's great virtue despite his inability to restrain himself from quarrelling with Cardinal Beaufort (Beaufort, Bishop of Winchester, who became a cardinal in *1 Henry VI*, is often referred to in *2 Henry VI* as 'the Cardinal'): Gloucester quarrelled with Beaufort in *1 Henry VI* and does so again in *2 Henry VI* (II.i.16–54), this discord now being deplored by Henry ('When such strings jar, what hope of harmony?', II.i.57), just as it was by the Duke of Bedford in *1 Henry VI* (I.i.44). Contrasting with Henry's naivety is Gloucester's shrewdness, as is brought out in the incident where he is not taken in by Saunder Simpcox, a beggar who claims to have been blind and had sight miraculously bestowed upon him at St Alban's shrine – Gloucester proves Simpcox to have been lying and then performs the 'miracle' of making Simpcox, who appears to be crippled, leap over a stool after being beaten (II.i.97–149). But as the play proceeds we see that such shrewdness cannot prevent Gloucester from being the victim of those who are determined to remove him from power.

Various contenders for power are revealed in the first Act. The Duke of Buckingham proposes that he and the Duke of Somerset, along with Suffolk, should work for Gloucester's overthrow (I.i.162–4). Though Cardinal Beaufort is also a party to the plot, Buckingham and Somerset privately agree that one or other of them should become Protector to the exclusion of the Cardinal (I.i.167–74). In a soliloquy at the end of the first scene the Duke of York who, despite a justifiable claim to the throne, appeared in *1 Henry VI* (III.i.167–8) to have abandoned his claim by vowing life-long 'obedience' to Henry, decides that he will side with Gloucester and with Salisbury and Warwick (whom he refers to as 'the Nevilles' since Salisbury was the son of Ralph Neville and Warwick is Salisbury's son) until the time seems ripe for him to bid for power (I.i.235–7):

> And therefore I will take the Nevilles' parts
> And make a show of love to proud Duke Humphrey,
> And, when I spy advantage, claim the crown.

In the second scene of the play another contender for power turns out to be Gloucester's own wife, who wants to be Queen rather than Duchess – she urges Gloucester to make himself King (I.ii.11):

> Put forth thy hand, reach at the glorious gold.

Gloucester immediately rejects such a suggestion, but the Duchess seeks to engage a witch and a 'conjurer' (one who raises spirits) in order to obtain aid from evil spirits (I.ii.74–7): unbeknown to the Duchess, her contact man in these dealings is being paid by the Cardinal and Suffolk to bring shame on the Duchess and so on Gloucester as her husband (I.ii.93–106). In the next scene we hear of Suffolk's own tactics. He tells Queen Margaret (his mistress as we know from *1 Henry VI*) that he is collaborating with the Cardinal and others only for the time being (I.iii.92–8):

> Although we fancy not the Cardinal,
> Yet must we join with him and with the lords
> Till we have brought Duke Humphrey in disgrace...
> So one by one we'll weed them all at last,
> And you yourself shall steer the happy helm.

(We know from Suffolk's soliloquy at the end of *1 Henry VI* that his real aim is to use Margaret as a means of wielding power himself.)

The Duchess of Gloucester is soon eliminated from the contest. In I.iv Buckingham and York, who presumably have been informed of the Duchess's activities, break in just after an evil spirit has been raised in the Duchess's presence to answer questions about the future. (The spirit's predictions, expressed somewhat enigmatically, turn out later to be true. According to the first prediction Henry will 'depose' Gloucester as Protector and eventually 'die a violent death' – this violent death occurs at the end of *3 Henry VI*. The other predictions concern the deaths of Suffolk and Somerset: these predictions are fulfilled later in this play, *2 Henry VI* – see IV.i.31–8 and V.ii.67–9.) The Duchess is duly denounced by Buckingham as 'Dealing with witches and with conjurers' (II.i.167), and Henry is obliged to sentence her to banishment in the Isle of Man (II.iii.9–13).

By now York has ceased to 'make a show of love' to Gloucester (his policy in I.i.236): we have seen him accompany Buckingham in the exposure of the Duchess's evil dealings, and in III.i it is clear that he has joined Suffolk, the Cardinal and Buckingham in working for Gloucester's destruction. (Gloucester is still regarded as powerful, even though in II.iii.22–4 he was called upon by the King to surrender his authority as Protector – as predicted by the evil spirit in I.iv.) These enemies of Gloucester seize upon the announcement that all English territory in France has been lost (III.i.84–5) as an excuse to have Gloucester arrested for treason (III.i.97), claiming that he had taken French bribes to weaken the defence of that territory (III.i.104–6 – the irony of this is that in the first scene of the play it was Gloucester who was distressed by Suffolk's cession of two areas of English territory in France because this would lead to the total loss of English territory there, I.i.140–1). Since, however, Henry has unshaken faith in Gloucester's 'honour, truth and loyalty' (III.i.203), it is agreed by Suffolk, Queen Margaret, the Cardinal and York that Gloucester should be murdered. The murder is soon performed – by men employed by Suffolk – and Suffolk reports to the King that Gloucester has been found dead in his bed: the Cardinal describes this death as 'God's secret judgment' (III.ii.31), and Queen Margaret, with supreme hypocrisy, says that Suffolk, despite having been treated as an enemy by Gloucester, 'most Christian-like, laments his death' (III.ii.58). It seems rather to be God's judgment that the Cardinal himself dies suddenly in his bed, stricken with terror as death approaches (III.iii) – Warwick's observation that 'So bad a death argues a monstrous life' (III.iii.30) meets with what is surely excessive charity on Henry's part (III.iii.31): 'Forbear to judge, for we are sinners all.' Suffolk's death follows soon after. Knowledge of his responsibility for Gloucester's murder quickly reaches the common people and in response to their outcry Henry sends Suffolk into exile (III.ii.242–97). In IV.i Suffolk and other passengers on the boat carrying him to France have become captives of officers from a warship who demand ransom money, but Suffolk is killed by one of these officers who knows about Suffolk's crimes.

At this point another contender for power appears in the person of the rebel leader Jack Cade – but Cade has been deliberately promoted by York for his own ends. York has gladly undertaken the task of suppressing a rebellion in Ireland in order to be given the command of a large army, and a rebellion led by Cade in England will prepare the way for York to return with his army from Ireland and take over the rebellion begun by Cade (III.i.348–81):

> Whiles I in Ireland nourish a mighty band
> I will stir up in England some black storm [that]
> Shall blow ten thousand souls to heaven or hell...
> I have seduced a headstrong Kentishman,
> Jack Cade of Ashford,
> To make commotion as full well he can...
> Say that he thrive, as 'tis great like he will,
> Why, then from Ireland come I with my strength
> And reap the harvest which that rascal sowed.

As for Cade himself, he is presented in a broad satirical vein – and is hardly to be taken as a true portrait of the real Jack Cade. York has persuaded Cade to pass himself off as a member of the Mortimer family, John Mortimer, who is now dead but whom Cade resembles in appearance (III.i.358–9, 372–3): York is keen to see how a contender for power with allegedly the same line of descent as himself will be generally received in England (III.i.374–5 – York's claim to the throne is based on his descent through the Mortimer family from the third son of Edward III, as was indicated in *1 Henry VI* II.v and is also stated in *2 Henry VI* II.ii.10–52). Cade gives free rein to his imagination by saying that he is heir to the throne because he is the hitherto unidentified son of a stolen elder twin in the Mortimer family (IV.ii.131–50). He tells his supporters that on becoming king he will institute a communist utopia: 'All the realm shall be in common...there shall be no money...' (IV.ii.67– ff.). Cade agrees with his friend Dick the butcher that the first thing to be done must be to 'kill all the lawyers' (IV.ii.72 +), and a classless society will be achieved by killing off all lords and gentlemen (IV.ii.179–80). Shakespeare's Cade is indeed a symbol of disorder, for as he himself says, 'then are we most in order when we are most out of order' (IV.ii.184–5).

York's plan works out wholly to his satisfaction. Cade is killed (IV.x) by a Kent landowner, Alexander Iden, shortly before York's return from Ireland. On his return York says to Henry (V.i.58–9) 'In all submission and humility/York doth present himself unto your Highness', but he then becomes defiant on the pretext that Somerset has exercised an evil influence over Henry and has not been removed. York's sons Edward and Richard arrive with forces to support him, and Salisbury and Warwick now come over to York's side, having been convinced of the legality of York's claim to the throne as expounded to them by York in II.ii. (On that occasion York must have displayed charm since Warwick addressed him as 'Sweet York', II.ii.7, and Salisbury and Warwick seem to be unaware of York's unscrupulous tactics since that occasion.) The play ends with York as sole contender for power and as victor in the battle fought at St Albans, the opening battle of the Wars of the Roses.

THE THIRD PART OF HENRY VI (c. 1591)

The theme of *3 Henry VI* is England in a state of utter lawlessness, the lawlessness of civil war.

The first two Parts of *Henry VI* showed that a root cause of conflict at this time was King Henry's questionable right to the throne, and it is with this question that *3 Henry VI* opens. When challenged by the Earl of Warwick to defend his right to the throne Henry in an 'aside' says to himself 'I know not what to say: my title's weak' (I.i.134), and the Duke of Exeter, one of Henry's loyal supporters, has to admit that the Duke of York has a rightful claim to the throne (I.i.150): 'My conscience tells me he is lawful king.' Henry comes to an agreement with York that the crown shall pass to York or York's heir on Henry's death but that Henry shall remain king for the rest of his life, without any further civil war on York's part – says York (I.i.204): 'Now York and Lancaster[20] are reconciled.' But this reconciliation ends almost immediately. As soon as Queen Margaret hears that her son is not to inherit the crown she rejects the agreement and leaves to raise an army against York. And York, even before hearing of the Queen's rejection of the agreement, is easily persuaded by his three sons to break his oath to Henry that war would cease – as his eldest son, Edward, says (I.ii.16): 'But for a kingdom any oath may be broken.' The civil war that was being waged at the beginning of the play (and had begun at the end of *2 Henry VI*) is resumed in earnest.

In *1 Henry VI* we were meant to sympathise with Talbot's fervent desire for revenge for the death of the Earl of Salisbury (an Earl of Salisbury previous to the one in *2 Henry VI*) at the hands of the French (*1 Henry VI* I.iv.104–5, I.v.34–5, II.ii.7–13). But *3 Henry VI* deplores the cycle of revenge and counter-revenge that occurs between the two sides in the civil war. In the first scene we hear that the Earl of Northumberland and Lord Clifford, because their fathers were killed in battle by the Duke of York, have vowed revenge not only on York but on 'his sons, his favourites, and his friends' (I.i.54–6). The first victim of Clifford's lust for revenge is York's young son, Rutland, a mere boy (described by his tutor as 'this innocent child', I.iii.8): ignoring the boy's appeal for 'pity', Clifford stabs him to death (I.iii.36–48). York himself is overwhelmingly defeated by Queen Margaret's army and, after wishing 'revenge upon you all' (I.iv.36), he is stabbed to death by Clifford and Queen Margaret. (So ends York, whose scheming for power seemed to promise success at the end of *2 Henry VI*.) The revenge York wished for soon follows. Warwick, hearing that his brother, killed in battle by Clifford, died appealing for revenge (II.iii.15–19), swears he will work tirelessly towards that end (II.iii.29–32), and York's son Richard pursues Clifford on the battlefield in revenge for the killings of Rutland and York (II.iv). Though Clifford escapes from Richard, he dies soon after of a wound he received, and immediately after Clifford's body has been identified Warwick orders that York's head, which Clifford had placed on the gates of the city of York, should be replaced by Clifford's own head, thus achieving 'measure for measure' (II.vi.52–5). In contrast to the revenge-seekers King Henry, though incapable of controlling the course of events, at least expresses pity for those killed on both sides: after seeing the body of a father unwittingly killed by his son (because they were fighting on opposite sides) and the body of a son unwittingly killed by his father, Henry pleads to heaven (II.v.96): 'O, pity, pity, gentle heaven, pity!' And he condemns both the red rose and the white rose as 'The fatal colours of our striving houses [families]' (II.v.97–8).

The scene of the deaths of Warwick's brother and of Clifford is the battlefield near Towton (in Yorkshire), and King Henry's description of this battle as being 'like a mighty sea' swayed this way and that by the tide (II.v.5–12) provides an image[21] that applies to the war in general, with victory swinging from one side to the other – as Henry says, 'So is the equal poise of this fell [cruel] war' (II.v.13). After York's death his eldest son, Edward, deposes Henry and so becomes King Edward (III.i.69); Henry is later restored (IV.iii.49–50), but is then again deposed (IV.viii.52–3). And allegiances shift. Warwick, who in *2 Henry VI* had transferred to York's side, now returns to Henry (III.iii.194 – Warwick feels dishonoured because King Edward has backed out of a marriage Warwick had arranged with the King of France's sister). The Duke of Clarence, Edward's brother, accompanied by the Duke of Somerset (son of the Somerset in *2 Henry VI*), joins Warwick on Henry's side (IV.i.123, IV.ii.6–7), but Clarence later returns to Edward (V.i.101–2). And the Marquis of Montague, Warwick's brother[22] (II.i.167), after vowing to be loyal to Edward (IV.i.143), fights for Henry (V.i.67). There is dramatic irony in a remark made by Lord Hastings during a discussion as to whether England needs to have France as an ally – Hastings says to Montague (IV.i.39–40):

> Why, knows not Montague that of itself
> England is safe, if true within itself?

While rightly stressing the need for England to be 'true within itself', this remark seems to show a blindness on Hastings's part to the fact that England at this time has failed to be 'true within itself' quite apart from any external alliance.

In the second half of the play another disruptive force emerges within the Yorkist ranks in the person of Richard, younger brother of Edward and Clarence, and created Duke of Gloucester as promised by Edward just before he became king (II.vi.103). Though earlier in the play Richard was loud in proclaiming a 'league inviolable' between himself and his brothers (II.i.30), Richard as Gloucester reveals in a long soliloquy at the end of III.ii that he will happily resort to murder and hypocrisy, and to being even more unscrupulous than Machiavelli, in order to win the crown for himself (III.ii,182-95):

> Why, I can smile, and murder whiles I smile...
> I can add colours to the chameleon,
> Change shapes with Proteus for advantages,
> And set the murderous Machiavel[23] to school.
> Can I do this, and cannot get a crown?
> Tut, were it farther off I'll pluck it down.

In the last Act, where Edward defeats Henry's supporters, Gloucester joins Edward and Clarence in stabbing Henry's son to death (V.v). He then makes his way to the Tower of London where the deposed Henry is confined and murders him (V.vi). Over Henry's dead body he proudly describes himself as possessing 'neither pity, love, nor fear' (V.vi.68) and as being wholly dedicated to the removal of those who stand between him and the throne (V.vi.89-90):

> King Henry and the Prince his son are gone.
> Clarence, thy turn is next, and then the rest...

This last line points forward to *Richard III*, where 'the rest' will include King Edward's son, another Edward, who in the last scene of *3 Henry VI* is a mere infant. In this scene King Edward congratulates himself an having made the throne safe for his son to inherit, but Gloucester in an 'aside' says 'I'll blast his harvest' (V.vii.21), and as he stoops to kiss his infant nephew he says in another aside 'To say the truth, so Judas kissed his master'

(V.vii.33). King Edward's hope as expressed in the last line of the play –

> For here, I hope, begins our lasting joy –

is thus belied by Gloucester's evil intentions.

Earlier in *3 Henry VI*, however, there is a pointer to what is to be the happy ending to the *Henry VI–Richard III* tetralogy as a whole: the ascent to the throne of Henry VII. In IV.vi of *3 Henry VI* King Henry encounters a certain young Henry, Earl of Richmond, and makes a supernaturally inspired prophecy (IV.vi.68–70):

> Come hither, England's hope. If secret powers
> Suggest but truth to my divining thoughts,
> This pretty lad will prove our country's bliss.

RICHARD III (c. 1591)

> Now is the winter of our discontent
> Made glorious summer by this sun of York,
> And all the clouds that loured [frowned] upon our house
> In the deep bosom of the ocean buried.

In these opening lines Richard celebrates the defeat of the Lancastrians by the Yorkists (as presented in the latter part of *3 Henry VI*), but it quickly becomes apparent (as we already know from the latter part of *3 Henry VI*) that Richard is concerned not with the predominance of the House of York but with the pursuit of power for himself. The theme of the play is the suffering of England – of Lancastrian and Yorkist alike – under the domination of one man, and this domination is related to a broad conception of the forces of good and evil at work in human nature and human life.

The plot of the play is largely taken up with the evil actions performed by Richard in order to make himself king and then to secure his position as king. After King Edward's two young sons the next in line to the throne is Richard's elder brother, George, Duke of Clarence. Since a wizard has made a prophecy that

Edward's heirs will be murdered by 'G', Richard persuades Edward that the 'G' applies to George, with the result that Clarence is imprisoned in the Tower of London (I.i.32–61). Richard then employs two murderers to stab Clarence to death (I.iii.339–56, I.iv). Following King Edward's death through illness (II.ii), Richard proceeds to isolate Edward's elder son, the heir to the throne, by parting him from the relatives of his mother, the widowed Queen Elizabeth (II.ii.145–52): Lord Rivers (Queen Elizabeth's brother) and Lord Grey (Elizabeth's son by her previous marriage) and also Sir Thomas Vaughan[24] are imprisoned in Pomfret Castle (II.iv.41–3), where they are led off to execution (III.iii). Richard puts it about that the dead king's two sons are illegitimate (III.v.72–5) and contrives to have himself declared king (III.vii.240–4). Having previously persuaded the two princes to take up residence in the Tower of London (III.i – allegedly for their own benefit!), Richard after his coronation employs a man called Tyrrel to murder them (IV.ii.66–81 – the wizard's prophecy in I.i about the murder of King Edward's heirs is thus fulfilled, the 'G' referring not to George, Duke of Clarence, but to Richard himself, then Duke of Gloucester). Before becoming king Richard ordered the execution of Lord Hastings (III.iv.78–80) because Hastings had emphatically refused to support the placing of Richard on the throne (III.ii.43–4,53–5), and after becoming king Richard turns against the Duke of Buckingham, his most energetic supporter, because Buckingham was unwilling to consent to the murder of the princes (IV.ii.18–26). Buckingham, hoping to escape Hastings's fate, leaves for Wales (IV.ii.120–1), but is later captured (IV.iv.533) and led off to execution (V.i). And yet another of Richard's victims is his wife Anne, whom he had persuaded to marry him (I.ii) even though she was the widow of Henry VI's son, stabbed to death by Richard and his brothers (*3 Henry VI* V.v). After he has become king Richard decides that it would help to secure his position if he were able to marry the late king's daughter (Richard's own niece), and so has it given out that Anne is gravely ill (IV.ii.49–50,55–60): though we are not told precisely how, Anne is driven to her death (IV.iii.39).

Richard's completely evil nature is stressed throughout the play. In his opening soliloquy he is shown as being determined to be evil ('I am determined to prove a villain', I.i.30) and as priding himself on being 'subtle, false and treacherous' (I.i.37). Anne, before she is won over by him, denounces Richard as a 'minister of hell' (I.ii.46 – this same phrase was applied to Joan of Arc in *1 Henry VI*, V.iv.93), a 'Foul devil' who 'knowest nor law of God nor man' (I.ii.50,70). And Queen Margaret, the surviving widow of Henry VI, denounces Richard even more vigorously – he is 'the son of hell' (I.iii.230), 'Sin, death and hell have set their marks on him' (I.iii.293), he is 'A hell-hound that doth hunt us all to death', 'That foul defacer of God's handiwork' (IV.iv.48,51). Especially notable – and what makes him one of Shakespeare's liveliest Machiavel characters – is Richard's unbounded delight in hypocrisy. In soliloquy he describes with great self-satisfaction how people are taken in when he is generously forgiving of crimes he attributes to others in order to cover up his own crimes (I.iii.334–8):

> But then I sigh, and with a piece of Scripture
> Tell them that God bids us do good for evil.
> And thus I clothe my naked villainy
> With odd old ends stolen forth of holy writ,
> And seem a saint when most I play the Devil.

And when the dying King Edward tries to promote friendship between rival factions in his palace (to make 'love of hate', II.i.50) Richard pronounces such an aim to be wholly in accord with his own feelings (II.i.60–1):

> 'Tis death to me to be at enmity.
> I hate it, and desire all good men's love.

There is heavy dramatic irony in the belief expressed by Lord Hastings that Richard is incapable of hypocrisy (III.iv.53–4):

> I think there's never a man in Christendom
> Can lesser hide his hate or love than he.

And this irony is all the greater in that Hastings makes this remark just before hearing Richard order his execution as a traitor. After his execution Hastings himself is condemned as a hypocrite by the very man he thought incapable of hypocrisy – Richard professes to be deeply hurt by the discovery of this fault in Hastings (III.v.24–9):

> So dear I loved the man that I must weep...
> So smooth he daubed his vice with show of virtue...

(A similar hypocritical condemnation of hypocrisy occurred earlier when Richard warned the young Prince of Wales against human deceitfulness, as especially to be found in 'false friends' such as the prince's uncles on his mother's side, III.i.7–15 :

> Sweet prince, the untainted virtue of your years
> Hath not yet dived into the world's deceit,
> Nor more can you distinguish of a man
> Than of his outward show...)

Richard's hypocrisy reaches its peak when he appears before the Lord Mayor and citizens of London as a holy man in the company of two bishops (III.vii.96–9):

> Two props of virtue for a Christian prince,
> To stay him from the fall of vanity,
> And, see, a book of prayer in his hand –
> True ornaments to know a holy man.

In the final Act of the play, on the night before he is killed in battle at Bosworth, Richard is visited in his sleep by the ghosts of his various victims who remind him of his crimes, and on waking he comes as near as he ever does to being disturbed by conscience – he is momentarily afflicted by what he calls 'coward conscience' (V.iii.179). Next morning, when addressing his troops, he has not the slightest hesitation in rejecting conscience as cowardly and says that all that matters is what can be achieved by force, even if one ends up in hell (V.iii.309–13):

Conscience is but a word that cowards use,
Devised at first to keep the strong in awe.
Our strong arms be our conscience, swords our law.
March on, join bravely, let us to it pell-mell,
If not to heaven, then hand in hand to hell.

In contrast to the evil that wholly consumes Richard, goodness, or at least repentance, is manifested by other characters. Tribute is paid, ironically by Richard himself, to the shining goodness of Henry VI's son, Prince Edward, killed by Richard and his brothers in *3 Henry VI* – Prince Edward is praised by Richard in soliloquy because he is maliciously pleased with himself at having persuaded Anne to marry him even though he had taken part in the killing of so fine a man as her husband (I.ii.242–5):

A sweeter and a lovelier gentleman,
Framed in the prodigality of Nature,
Young, valiant, wise, and no doubt right royal,
The spacious world cannot again afford [provide].

Anne is deceived by Richard's sham repentance (he promises to wet Henry VI's grave with 'repentant tears', I.ii.215), but Richard's sham repentance (later he claims to be repentant about his treatment of Henry VI's queen, Margaret, I.iii.307–8) contrasts with the genuine repentance of his brother Clarence. When imprisoned in the Tower Clarence is confronted in a dream by the ghost of the Earl of Warwick who complains bitterly of Clarence's 'perjury' (I.iv.48–51 – Clarence's desertion of Warwick in battle in *3 Henry VI* V.i.83–109) and by the ghost of Henry's Prince Edward whom Clarence had helped to murder (Prince Edward's ghost appears 'like an angel, with bright hair/ Dabbled in blood', I.iv.53–4): Clarence, overwhelmed by guilt, prays to God that if he is to be punished for his misdeeds his wife and children should at least be spared (I.iv.69–72). (Clarence is thus truly afflicted by conscience when visited by ghosts in a dream, in contrast to Richard's reaction to the ghosts in his sleep in the final Act.) The dying King Edward, who had also taken part in the murder of Henry VI's Prince Edward (Richard refers to this in I.ii.92), after trying to bring rival factions together in friendship, expresses at length his remorse for having given an order for Clarence's death (II.i.102–33) – '... Ah, poor Clarence!' Repentance displays itself even in those employed to carry out murder – in the second of the two murderers of Clarence ('I repent me that the Duke is slain', I.iv.276), and overwhelmingly in both murderers of the two young princes. Though Tyrrel undertook the murder of the princes, he arranged for it to be carried out by Dighton and Forrest who, despite being 'fleshed [hardened] villains, bloody dogs' (IV.iii.6), are overcome by 'conscience and remorse' (IV.iii.20), with Dighton saying of the murdered princes (IV.iii.17–19):

> We smothered
> The most replenished sweet work of Nature
> That from the prime creation e'er she framed.

(This kind of poetic language is similar to that used to describe Henry VI's Prince Edward in I.ii.242–5.) Henry VI's Queen Margaret, though she does not actually express repentance for her part in crimes committed in *2 and 3 Henry VI*, is in *Richard III* a changed woman: whereas in *2 Henry VI* (I.iii.53) she had spoken contemptuously of Henry's mind as being 'bent to holiness', she now sincerely describes him as 'holy Harry' (IV.iv.25), and, as one who laments the killing of her husband and son by Richard, she ranges herself with two Yorkist women, formerly enemies but now fellow victims of the evil Richard – the Duchess of York, mother of the murdered Clarence, and Queen Elizabeth, mother of the murdered princes (IV.iv.39–126). And Buckingham, who had done so much to help put Richard on the throne, when he is led to execution recognises that Richard's victims had suffered 'underhand, corrupted foul injustice' (V.i.6): Buckingham accepts that he deserves to be punished for his 'wrongs' (V.i.18–19).

In this play much is made of God as the supreme arbiter in human affairs. Clarence speaks of God as 'the great King of kings' (I.iv.191), King Edward's Queen Elizabeth speaks of 'All-seeing heaven' (II.i.82), and the third of the three London citizens in II.iii speaks of God as exercising final control over human life – 'leave it all to God' (II.iii.45). And Queen Margaret's phrase 'upright, just, and true-disposing God' (IV.iv.55) carries weight, even though her invocation of the Deity is linked with a craving for personal revenge ('I am hungry for revenge', IV.iv.61). From the Duchess of York we hear of 'God's just ordinance' (IV.iv.183), and Buckingham's description of God as 'That high All-Seer' (V.i.20) is a more emphatic variant of Queen Elizabeth's 'All-seeing heaven'. In the last Act the Earl of Richmond is clearly seen as the instrument of God's will. (Henry VI's prophecy in *3 Henry VI* IV.vi.68–74 that Richmond would one day become king is recalled in *Richard III* by Richard himself, IV.ii.94–5, and by Henry VI's ghost, V.iii.129.) Before the Bosworth battle between the forces of Richmond and Richard, Buckingham's ghost tells Richard in his sleep that 'God and good angels fight on Richmond's side' (V.iii.175), and Richmond, in addressing his troops, tells them that 'God and our good cause fight upon our side' (V.iii.240) against Richard as 'God's enemy' (V.iii.252,253). After personally killing Richard on the battlefield Richmond in the final speech of the play announces his intention of marrying Edward IV's daughter Elizabeth (whom Richard had sought to marry), thus bringing the Wars of the Roses to an end by a union of the Yorkist and Lancastrian claimants[25] to the throne, according to God's 'ordinance' (V.v.29–33):

> O now let Richmond and Elizabeth,
> The true succeeders of each royal house,
> By God's fair ordinance conjoin together,
> And let their heirs, God, if thy will be so,
> Enrich the time to come with smooth-faced peace...

TITUS ANDRONICUS (c. 1591)

Titus Andronicus is a Senecan play in that it contains horrific incidents of the kind to be found in *Thyestes* and other plays traditionally ascribed to the Roman philosopher Seneca (c. 4BC – AD65) – all these plays had been translated into English by 1581. In *Thyestes*, because Thyestes has seduced the wife of his brother Atreus and has tried to deprive Atreus of the right to rule as King of Argos, Atreus takes revenge by slaughtering Thyestes's sons and inviting Thyestes to a banquet where he is given his sons' flesh to eat and their blood to drink: Atreus then presents Thyestes with his sons' severed heads. A Senecan play that was very popular in Shakespeare's time was Kyd's *The Spanish Tragedy*, which probably preceded *Titus Andronicus*: Kyd's play concerns the revenge elaborately prepared by Hieronimo, Marshal of Spain, against the murderers of his son, and the play ends with numerous stabbings, including Hieronimo's stabbing of himself after biting out his tongue when ordered to say who his confederates were. So many brutal acts of revenge occur in *Titus Andronicus* that it becomes almost a caricature of the Senecan-type play, but in this play the acts of revenge are linked to a characteristically Shakespearean theme: the need for a properly ordered society. In this respect *Titus Andronicus* is similar to *3 Henry VI* where the acts of revenge and counter-revenge represent the breakdown of social order.

Titus Andronicus is set in a fairly late period of the Roman Empire when Rome had to contend with invading Goths (as actually happened from the 3rd century AD onwards). But, unlike the *Henry VI–Richard III* tetralogy, *Titus Andronicus* makes no pretence of being historical – its plot may have been based on a fictitious prose narrative now extant only in an 18th-century version.[26] In the opening scene we learn that in Rome there is moral degradation amongst leaders who profess high Roman virtues. Titus Andronicus, a Roman general who has achieved victory over the Goths, is described by his brother Marcus as having noble qualities as a man as well as being a brave soldier (I.i.25–6):

A nobler man, a braver warrior,
Lives not this day within the city walls.

And a Roman captain describes Titus as a 'Patron of virtue' (I.i.65). Yet on his triumphal return to Rome Titus readily accepts a suggestion that the deaths of his sons in battle should be avenged by sacrificing the life of a Gothic prisoner. Titus chooses for this purpose the eldest son of the Gothic queen, Tamora, who has been brought to Rome along with her sons and the other Gothic prisoners. Titus rejects Tamora's plea for mercy, even though she points out that 'Sweet mercy is nobility's true badge' (I.i.119), and her son is led away by Titus's four surviving sons to have his limbs lopped off and his entrails thrown into 'the sacrificing fire' (I.i.143–4). It is therefore ironic that Marcus should regard the Romans as being morally superior to the Goths by referring (earlier in the scene) to 'the barbarous Goths' (I.i.28). As a national hero Titus, after declining to stand as the common people's candidate for emperor,[27] is allowed to nominate the successor to the late emperor. He nominates Saturninus, the late emperor's eldest son, and is happy to grant Saturninus's request to marry his daughter Lavinia – but when Titus's four sons defend the right of Bassianus, Saturninus's brother, to marry Lavinia since Bassianus is already betrothed to her, Titus immediately stabs one of his sons (Mutius) to death. Though Titus praises Saturninus's 'virtues' and talks of him as being an emperor who will 'ripen justice in this commonweal' (I.i.225–7), we soon become aware of moral degradation in Saturninus. Saturninus gives way to Bassianus over Lavinia, but wants 'revenge' (I.i.433) against Titus's sons for defending Bassianus's right. Having become enamoured of Tamora to the point of announcing his intention to marry her, Saturninus immediately falls in with her suggested plan that he should pretend to be a friend of Titus's family while she takes it upon herself 'to massacre them all... The cruel father and his traitorous sons' (I.i.450–2). Tamora of course wants revenge against Titus on her own account for the killing of her eldest son (by now we see that her remark about 'mercy' being a noble virtue was hypocritical), but though Saturninus has no personal reason for wanting revenge against Titus he raises no objection to the inclusion of Titus in Tamora's proposed 'massacre'.

In the second Act we learn that Saturninus, in marrying Tamora and allowing her to exploit his desire for revenge, has in fact opened the way for Tamora as a Goth to work for revenge against the Roman state and Saturninus himself as the Roman emperor. This is revealed to us in a soliloquy by Aaron, Tamora's lover (who is actually a Moor, not a Goth, II.iii.51). Aaron in his soliloquy refers to Tamora as (II.i.23–4)

> This siren that will charm [bewitch] Rome's Saturnine
> And see his shipwreck and his commonweal's.

Aaron shows himself only too willing to assist Tamora in 'villainy and vengeance' (II.i.121), and, following incitement by Aaron and Tamora, Tamora's surviving sons, Demetrius and Chiron, murder Bassianus and drag Lavinia off to rape her (II.iii) – at the beginning of II.iv Lavinia appears with her hands cut off and her tongue cut out to prevent her from naming her assailants (by either the written word or the spoken word). And Aaron, having contrived that Titus's two sons Quintus and Martius fall into the pit where Bassianus's body has been thrown, brings Saturninus to the scene and convinces him that Bassianus was murdered by Titus's sons (II.iii). These sons are accordingly condemned to execution, and Aaron derives amusement from tricking Titus into having his hand cut off in the belief that if this hand is sent to Saturninus his sons will not be executed. In an aside Aaron tells us how this villainy fills him with pleasure (III.i.203–4):

> O, how this villainy
> Doth fat me with the very thoughts of it!

(We see that Aaron, unlike Richard III as a villain, is concerned with villainy for its own sake, not as a means of gaining power.) Titus soon learns that the execution has gone ahead – a messenger from Saturninus arrives to present Titus with the heads of his two sons and also his severed hand (III.i.237–8).

In IV.i Lavinia, writing in sand with a stick held in her mouth and between her two stumps, is able to indicate to Titus and his brother Marcus that she was raped by Demetrius and Chiron. Titus now lapses into madness (as does Hieronimo in *The Spanish Tragedy*), appealing to Jupiter and other gods, by means of messages attached to arrows, to send 'Justice' down to earth (IV.iii.50 ff.). Titus also sends a letter to Saturninus which is delivered by a simpleton, denoted in the stage directions as a 'Clown': on receiving this letter Saturninus, who has just been assuring the Roman 'lords' that he is an upholder of even-handed justice ('egal justice', IV.iv.4), gives orders for the Clown to be hanged because the letter complains that Titus's sons were wrongfully executed (IV.iv.45–55). So much for Saturninus as a promoter of 'justice' as recommended by Titus in the first scene (I.i.227)! But as regards Titus's mad appeal for divine justice, Shakespeare may be hinting that such justice is being enacted when very shortly afterwards it is announced that Titus's remaining son Lucius, who earlier left Rome to raise an army amongst the Goths (III.i.300–1), is marching on Rome (IV.iv.63–6) and we hear that Saturninus fears an uprising of the common people in favour of Lucius as emperor (IV.iv.72–80). (In V.i.1 Lucius addresses his Gothic soldiers as 'my faithful friends', so it turns out that not all Goths deserve to be described as 'barbarous', as they were in I.i.28.) Saturninus arranges to meet Lucius in Titus's house in order to reach a settlement (IV.iv.100–3, V.i.156–65), and Titus makes this meeting the occasion for his supreme act of revenge. Having cut the throats of Demetrius and Chiron to make a pie with their blood and bones (V.ii.197–201), Titus serves the pie to those attending the meeting between Saturninus and Lucius (V.iii). In his madness Titus, in front of Saturninus, kills Lavinia, his own daughter, to rid her of her 'shame', and then, after revealing that Tamora has been eating the flesh of her own sons,[28] kills her as the mother of the rapists. In quick succession Saturninus avenges Tamora by killing Titus, and Lucius avenges his father by killing Saturninus.

The rest of this final scene points the way to Rome's regeneration, as led by Titus's brother and son, Marcus and Lucius. After the break-up of the fatal meeting Marcus addresses the Roman people as follows (V.iii.67–72):

> You sad-faced men, people and sons of Rome,
> By uproars severed, as a flight of fowl
> Scattered by winds and high tempestuous gusts,
> O, let me teach you how to knit again
> This scattered corn into one mutual sheaf,
> These broken limbs again into one body.

Lucius is hailed as emperor (V.iii.141,146), and in thanking the Roman people he expresses his wish to be a healer of Rome's afflictions (V.iii.147–8):

> May I govern so
> To heal Rome's harms and wipe away her woe.

Aaron, who was captured earlier on by the Goths and who proudly boasted of his part in the crimes committed on Tamora's behalf and also of numerous other criminal activities (V.i.98–144), is sentenced to death by starvation – but he continues to boast of his total commitment to evil, his last words in the play being (V.iii.189–90):

> If one good deed in all my life I did,
> I do repent it from my very soul.

In the final speech[29] of the play Lucius says that, after seeing 'justice' done on Aaron (this is seen as true justice), the task must be to repair the damage done to the Roman state –

> to order well the state
> That like events may ne'er it ruinate.

THE COMEDY OF ERRORS (c. 1592)

Just as *Titus Andronicus* derives from Senecan tragedy, so *The Comedy of Errors* derives from Plautus (c. 254–184 BC), the Roman writer of comedy well known to the Elizabethans. In fact *The Comedy of Errors* derives more than certain kinds of incident from Plautus: its whole plot is based on that of one particular comedy – Plautus's *Menaechmi* (this title refers to two brothers, twins, both carrying the name Menaechmus). Plautus's play is a straight farce showing the misunderstandings that arise when identical twins are in the same town on the same day. (These twins were sons of a merchant in Syracuse, but at the age of seven one was lost and was then brought up by a merchant in Epidamnus. In early manhood the twin from Syracuse, who is searching for his lost brother, happens to arrive in Epidamnus.) And, just as in *Titus Andronicus* Shakespeare outdoes Seneca by increasing the number of horrific incidents in the one play, so in *The Comedy of Errors* he outdoes Plautus by increasing the number of misunderstandings in the one play (though these are still confined to one day, as in Plautus's play) – Shakespeare does this by having two pairs of identical twins: two young men who are twins are each attended by a servant, and the two servants are also twins. (This idea may have been suggested by another Plautus comedy, *Amphitruo*, where the god Jupiter, in order to sleep with Amphitryon's wife, takes on the human form of Amphitryon, thus becoming his double, and Jupiter is accompanied by the god Mercury who becomes the double of Amphitryon's servant. Amphitryon's actual servant thinks his double must be a twin, and later in the play he says that Amphitryon must also have a twin.) However, though the plot of *The Comedy of Errors* may derive from Plautus, the main theme of the play, like that of *Titus Andronicus*, is Shakespeare's own: in *The Comedy of Errors* the 'errors' become seriously symbolic of the confusions human beings have to face in earthly life. Shakespeare also introduces a Christian element into his play, whereas Plautus belonged to a pre-Christian era.

The play is set in Ephesus (in Asia Minor), and in the first scene Aegeon, a merchant from Syracuse (in Sicily), tells his story to the Duke of Ephesus. Some twenty-three years before, when Aegeon was on a trading mission to Epidamnum (i.e. Epidamnus, on the Adriatic coast, north-west of Greece), his wife who had joined him gave birth to twin boys, at a time when a woman in Epidamnum also gave birth to twin boys, and since this woman and her husband were very poor Aegeon took over these other twins to bring them up to attend on his own two boys. But the ship that was to have taken Aegeon, his wife and the two pairs of twins to Syracuse was wrecked in a storm, and a permanent separation resulted after the wife, one of her own twins and one of the adopted twins were rescued by one ship, and Aegeon and the other twins were rescued by another ship. It appears from I.i.128–9 that after Aegeon's return to Syracuse each of the two twins brought up by him there assumed the name of his lost twin brother (it was in this way that the twins in Plautus's *Menaechmi* came to have the same name, according to the Prologue of that play), and at the age of eighteen these Syracusan twins set off in search of their brothers, thereby becoming lost to Aegeon, whose five-year search for them has brought him to Ephesus at the beginning of the play. Aegeon's account is a moving one, showing him to be a loving man (he had 'lived in joy' with his wife, I.i.40, and he feels a strong 'love' for both his twin sons, I.i.131–2), a loving man who has been the victim of 'Fortune' (I.i.106). And to add to his misfortunes the Duke of Ephesus tells him that, because of the enmity between Ephesus and Syracuse, he must by Ephesian law be put to death unless before the end of the day he can raise the sum of a thousand marks to be paid as a fine.

In the second scene we find that, unbeknown to Aegeon, his son Antipholus and Antipholus's servant Dromio have also just arrived in Ephesus, with Antipholus lamenting his failure to find his mother and brother (I.ii.35–40):

> I to the world am like a drop of water
> That in the ocean seeks another drop...
> So I, to find a mother and a brother,
> In quest of them, unhappy, lose myself.

(We see here, as in Aegeon's account in the first scene, Shakespeare's affirmation of the importance of family bonds in human life.) From this scene onwards it becomes apparent that, though Antipholus and Dromio of Syracuse do not know it, the other Antipholus and Dromio are in fact resident in Ephesus (how this came about is not explained until the final scene of the play – V.i.348–67), and so errors about the identities of the two Antipholuses and Dromios proliferate.

An important moment of insight in the play arises out of Antipholus of Syracuse's encounter with Adriana, wife of Antipholus of Ephesus, and with her unmarried sister, Luciana. Unable to understand why he is regarded by Adriana as her husband and why Luciana urges him to show devotion to Adriana, Antipholus of Syracuse makes a passionate declaration of love to Luciana, a declaration in which love is seen to be a source of divine inspiration that can lift the human soul above the confusions ('errors') of earthly life (III.ii.33–40):

> Teach me, dear creature, how to think and speak.
> Lay open to my earthy gross conceit [power of understanding],
> Smothered in errors, feeble, shallow, weak,
> The folded [hidden] meaning of your words' deceit...
> Are you a god? Would you create me new?
> Transform me, then, and to your power I'll yield.

Antipholus describes Luciana as 'more than earth, divine' (III.ii.32), 'My sole earth's heaven' (III.ii.64).[30]

As regards the confusions that Antipholus of Syracuse and his Dromio encounter at every cut and turn in Ephesus, Antipholus as a Christian (he refers to himself as such in I.ii.77) can only conclude (as would not have been uncommon for Christians in Shakespeare's time to do) that witches are at work: 'There's none but witches do inhabit here' (III.ii.154) – apart, that is, from Luciana who is 'Possessed with such a gentle sovereign grace' (III.ii.158). (Previously Dromio of Syracuse wished he had his rosary with him – 'O for my beads!' – so that he could pray for protection against evil spirits, II.ii.187–91.)

Antipholus fervently wishes that some divine power would come to the rescue (IV.iii.38–9):

> And here we wander in illusions.
> Some blessed power deliver us from hence!

Shakespeare seems to imply that, following this plea for divine help, it is divine intervention that enables all the confusions of the play to be resolved in the final scene.

In the final scene (V.i) officers, with the Duke in attendance, are leading Aegeon to a place of public execution (since so far he has not been able to raise the money for his fine), and on the way there is a priory where Antipholus of Syracuse and his Dromio have taken refuge. The abbess in charge of this priory (symbol of a Christian presence in the play) turns out to be Aegeon's lost wife Aemilia, who explains that soon after being rescued at sea (in the circumstances described by Aegeon in the first scene) the two different twins who had been with her were taken from her and she then became a nun. In this final scene both pairs of twins come together for the first time, and Antipholus of Ephesus and his Dromio reveal that they were brought to Ephesus by the Duke's uncle. With the identities of the characters now clearly established Antipholus of Syracuse is free to marry Luciana and Aegeon is spared both the execution and the fine. The play ends on a Christian note: Aemilia wishes to proceed (belatedly) with a christening ceremony (which is what is meant by a 'gossips' feast', V.i.404), and she invites the Duke and all concerned to attend this ceremony in the priory.

THE TAMING OF THE SHREW (c. 1592)

In *The Comedy of Errors* love appears as an important aspect of the main theme, but in *The Taming of the Shrew* love becomes the central theme of the whole play: more precisely, the central theme is the quality of the love relationship as a basis for marriage. This theme is developed in connection with the wooing of three women, though the wooing of the third woman is dealt with only briefly and is not introduced until the fourth Act.

Before the beginning of the play proper there is an 'Induction' in two scenes. This Induction concerns a practical joke played by a lord on a drunken tinker, Christopher Sly. Sly is to be taken to a luxurious bedchamber in the lord's house, waited on by servants, and told that he is really a lord himself who has been suffering from mental disorder. In particular he is to be attended by a page who, dressed as an attractive young woman, is to be presented to Sly as his wife. It is here that the marriage theme is brought in. The page is to ask Sly 'Wherein your lady and your humble wife/May show her duty and make known her love' (Induction, i.114–15), and when the page does put this question to Sly his reply is 'Madam, undress you and come now to bed' (Induction, ii.115). Sly's attitude to marriage is clearly sensual. The play proper is supposed to be presented for Sly's entertainment, but by the end of the first scene he is already bored and wishes the play were over ('Would 'twere done!', I.i.247): the play's approach to the subject of courtship and marriage is beyond Sly's level of response.

In the first scene of the play proper we hear that Baptista Minola, a rich gentleman of Padua, refuses to allow suitors to approach his younger daughter, Bianca, until a husband has been found for his elder daughter, the shrewish Katherina. Bianca already has two would-be suitors, Hortensio and Gremio, and now in this first scene the young Lucentio, who has just arrived in Padua to study at the university there, is also attracted to Bianca. On the suggestion of his servant Tranio Lucentio decides to gain access to Bianca in the guise of a private tutor, during which time Tranio is to pass himself off as his master. As regards the finding of a husband for Katherina, a chance of solving this problem presents itself when Hortensio's friend Petruchio arrives from Verona in search of a wealthy wife and is easily persuaded by Hortensio to offer himself as a wooer of Katherina. In the first part of the play Lucentio contrasts with Petruchio, to Petruchio's disadvantage. Lucentio wishes to marry Bianca as the result of falling passionately in love with her at first sight – on first seeing her he tells Tranio (I.i.150–1):

> Tranio, I burn, I pine, I perish, Tranio,
> If I achieve not this young modest girl.

Petruchio, on the other hand, frankly admits that he wants to marry for money (I.ii.73-4):

> I come to wive it wealthily in Padua:
> If wealthily, then happily in Padua.

And in the next scene, having introduced himself to Baptista, Petruchio wastes no time in raising the question of a dowry (II.i.118–19):

> Then tell me, if I get your daughter's love,
> What dowry shall I have with her to wife?

As the play proceeds, however, we see that out of the Petruchio–Katherina relationship true love gradually emerges. Just before his first meeting with Katherina Petruchio says in soliloquy that he will 'woo her with some spirit' (II.i.168) and that he will adopt the tactic of lavishing praise on her however badly she treats him (II.i.169–75). In the actual encounter he puts this tactic into operation with farcical extravagance, but in his praise of her beauty there enters a note of true feeling (II.i.246–8 and 265–7):

>   Kate, like the hazel twig,
> Is straight and slender, and as brown in hue
> As hazel nuts and sweeter than the kernels

and

> For by this light, whereby I see thy beauty,
> Thy beauty that doth make me like thee well,
> Thou must be married to no man but me.

Unabashed by Katherina's rejection of him as one who is 'half lunatic' (II.i.279), Petruchio gives Baptista and others an absurdly untrue account of his encounter with Katherina, claiming that, despite her behaviour in public, privately she is deeply in love with him (II.i.298–302):

> I tell you, 'tis incredible to believe
> How much she loves me. O, the kindest Kate!
> She hung about my neck...

Baptista, it seems, prefers not to question the truth of this account, since he immediately gives his consent for the marriage to go ahead. On the appointed wedding day there is doubt as to whether Petruchio has any intention of coming, but in Petruchio's defence we are meant to take note of what Lucentio's Tranio says of him (III.ii.22–5):

> Upon my life, Petruchio means but well...
> Though he be merry, yet withal he's honest [honourable].

Petruchio does indeed employ outrageous tactics in order to shock Katherina into submission. When he does arrive for the wedding he appears in worn-cut clothes, riding a disease-ridden horse (III.ii.41ff.), and in the church he browbeats the priest who is performing the marriage ceremony (III.ii.154–60). Then, having brought Katherina to his country home, he makes a great show of bullying his servants (IV.i.108–39), and later he prevents Katherina from eating by hurling her food at the servants on the pretext that it is unfit to eat (IV.i.144–9), and he prevents her from accepting a cap and a gown that have been made for her by finding fault with them (IV.iii.64–114). But in IV.v we see that the point has been reached where Petruchio's assertiveness has become a game that is affectionately played between the two of them. Katherina light-heartedly concedes Petruchio's right to say that the moon, not the sun, shines in the daytime and also his right to change his mind in favour of the sun shining at that time (IV.v.19–20):

> sun it is not when you say it is not,
> And the moon changes even as your mind.

Similarly she pretends to agree unreservedly when Petruchio

describes an elderly man (actually Lucentio's father) who is walking towards them as an attractive young woman (IV.v.28–40), whereupon Petruchio says that Katherina is making a foolish mistake and she apologises for her 'mad mistaking' (IV.v.41–8). And at the end of the next scene Petruchio is given a kiss by his 'sweet Kate' (V.i.133–4).

As regards the wooing of Bianca, Lucentio becomes the successful contestant. In II.i, after it is settled that Petruchio will marry Katherina, the way is clear for Bianca's suitors to come forward. Since Lucentio, earlier in II.i, has been received into Baptista's household as a languages tutor under the name of 'Cambio', his servant Tranio, posing as Lucentio, proceeds to outbid Gremio as a rival suitor by saying that Lucentio's father will make over even more wealth to Lucentio as a husband to Bianca than is offered by Gremio (II.i.355–62). Hortensio, as the other would-be suitor, also early in II.i gains admittance to Baptista's household as a tutor (as a music tutor under the name of 'Licio'), but he loses interest when he sees himself outdone by Lucentio as 'Cambio' in their competing attempts to win a favourable response from Bianca (III.i). Though Gremio is outbidden, Baptista's acceptance of Lucentio as a husband for Bianca is conditional on an assurance being given personally to Baptista by Lucentio's father as to the wealth to be made available (II.i.378–80), and Tranio takes it upon himself to persuade a 'pedant' (teacher), who is on a visit to Padua, to impersonate Lucentio's father (IV.ii). After this pedant has given Baptista the required assurance (IV.iv), Lucentio's real father, Vincentio, arrives (IV.v), and Tranio in the presence of Baptista calls for an officer to take Vincentio to prison as a mad impostor (V.i.80–1), whereupon Lucentio has to acknowledge his true father and confess to Baptista that he, and not Tranio, is Lucentio. It is at the end of this scene in which the subterfuges of Lucentio and his servant have been exposed that Petruchio, who has been far more open in his relations with Katherina, receives a loving kiss from her.

Another relationship which also compares unfavourably with that between Petruchio and Katherina is brought briefly to our attention in Act IV. Hortensio, after assuring Tranio that he no longer has any intention of being a suitor to Bianca, informs Tranio that he is about to marry a wealthy widow who has been in love with him for some time, a woman in whom he can find 'kindness' rather than 'beauteous looks' (IV.ii.41). Tranio also learns that Hortensio proposes to apply Petruchio's method of taming to the widow – Hortensio has become a pupil at Petruchio's 'taming-school' (IV.ii.53–8). At the end of Act IV Hortensio concludes that the lesson to be drawn from Petruchio's success with Katherina is that he should be prepared for his widow to be antagonistic ('froward') towards him and that he must then be antagonistic ('untoward') towards her (IV.v.76–8):

> Well, Petruchio, this [Petruchio's success] has put me in heart.
> Have to [I'll set about] my widow, and if she be froward
> Then hast thou taught Hortensio to be untoward.

In view of what Hortensio said earlier about his widow's 'kindness', it is hardly appropriate that he should think of her as needing to be treated in this way.

In the final scene (V.ii) all three couples are by now married and are dining at Lucentio's house. When the wives are out of the room Petruchio, in reply to taunts that he has married a shrew, proposes a bet whereby the three husbands send for their wives and the one whose wife arrives first shall receive a sum of money (the sum of a hundred crowns is agreed upon) to be paid by the other two husbands. Only Katherina comes – and the other two wives have to be fetched by her. The reformed Katherina then makes a speech in which she says that a wife should obey a husband as a subject should obey a ruler (V.ii.155–6):

> Such a duty as the subject owes the prince,
> Even such a woman oweth to her husband.

And she refers to the pledge made in the Church of England marriage service by saying that wives 'are bound to serve, love, and obey'[31] (V.ii.164). But she indicates that the husband who commands such obedience should be honourable and loving – the wife should be obedient to her husband's 'honest will', 'to her loving lord'[32] (V.ii.158,160). (Katherina's speech should be compared with Luciana's remarks in *The Comedy of Errors* at the beginning of II.i. Talking to her sister about husbands, Luciana says of herself as a possible future wife, II.i.29: 'Ere I learn love I'll practise to obey.' She admits that she has remained unmarried so far because of 'troubles of the marriage bed', II.i.27. We may therefore take it that she will marry and obey a man who can be depended on to be faithful to her.)

Though Shakespeare's prescription for marital harmony may not be generally acceptable today, we may at least be able to respond emotionally to the emergence in *The Taming of the Shrew* of true love from unpromising beginnings – and so find ourselves saying with Lucentio about what has been achieved in the marriage between Petruchio and Katherina: 'Here is a wonder', ' 'Tis a wonder' (V.ii.106,189).

THE SONNETS (c. 1592–3)

Though Shakespeare's Sonnets were not published until 1609, it seems likely that they were written in the 1590s, when sonnet writing was much in vogue, and they may well have been written when theatrical activity was curtailed by plague in 1592–4. (Slightly different versions of Sonnets 138 and 144 were published in *The Passionate Pilgrim*, 1599, a collection of various short poems all attributed by the publisher to Shakespeare, though some of these are known to have been written by other poets.) The Sonnets appear not to have been prepared for publication by Shakespeare himself in 1609: the 154 sonnets present a narrative situation, yet many of the sonnets are clearly out of sequence. There is also a great deal of repetition, as though many re-workings of the same idea have been included without any attempt to make a final selection. As regards the narrative situation,[33] a poet (Sonnet 17) is in love with a handsome young man (2) of high birth and of wealth (37), though this love is not physical (20). The poet has to face the fact that his friend has seduced his (the poet's) mistress (35,

40, 41, 42, 92, 134, 144 – Sonnet 92 refers to the friend's 'revolt', i.e. betrayal), but the poet is ashamed of his own lust for his mistress (both he and she are married, 152), so that he has to admit that his friend's 'trespass' is matched by his own (120).

The predominant theme to emerge from all this is the nature of true love, seen as transcending time and the flesh. These two aspects of true love are especially brought out in Sonnets 116 and 151. Sonnet 116 proclaims that love should be a union of minds eternally faithful to each other despite changing circumstances:

> Let me not to the marriage of true minds
> Admit impediments. Love is not love
> Which alters when it alteration finds...

True love is not subject to destruction by Time, as is youthful beauty:

> Love's not Time's fool, though rosy lips and cheeks
> Within his bending sickle's compass come.

And in Sonnet 151 the poet condemns himself for letting his soul be betrayed by his body – his soul speaks of the exultation to be experienced through love, but his body seeks only the satisfaction of physical sex with his mistress, and so becomes a mere 'drudge':

>   I do betray
> My nobler part to my gross body's treason.
> My soul doth tell my body that he may
> Triumph in love. Flesh stays no farther reason,
> But, rising at thy name, doth point out thee
> As his triumphant prize. Proud of this pride,
> He is contented thy poor drudge to be...

Now let us look at the themes of the Sonnets in more detail. Early on in the Sonnets as published the Poet celebrates the beauty of a young person such as his friend. Such beauty should be immortalised by human reproduction, as stated in Sonnet 1:

> From fairest creatures we desire increase,
> That thereby beauty's rose might never die...

(This theme is repeated in Sonnets 12 and 13.) Such beauty may also be immortalised by its description in verse (Sonnets 18, 60, 63, 65). Sonnet 18 speaks of the Friend's 'fair' (used here as a noun to mean beauty) by comparing it with the beauty of a summer's day:

> Shall I compare thee to a summer's day?
> ... thy eternal summer shall not fade
> Nor lose possession of that fair thou ow'st [that beauty you possess]...
> So long as men can breathe or eyes can see,
> So long lives this [this verse], and this gives life to thee.

But physical beauty needs to be accompanied by 'constancy' or 'truth', meaning fidelity in love. In Sonnets 14, 53, 54, 101 and 105 the Poet is confident that his friend does in fact combine beauty with constancy. Sonnet 14 says of the Friend:

> truth and beauty shall together thrive
> If from thy self to store thou wouldst convert.

(The second line here means 'If you would turn your attention to the business of having children'.) In the closing lines of Sonnet 53 the Friend is applauded:

> In all external grace you have some part,
> But you like none, none you, for constant heart.

Sonnet 54 exclaims with reference to the Friend:

> O how much more doth beauty beauteous seem
> By that sweet ornament which truth doth give!

And in Sonnet 105 the Friend is described as 'Fair, kind, and true'. But Sonnets 69, 94 and 95 show the Poet's confidence to be ill-founded – the Friend is discovered to be false. Sonnet 69 tells us that when people look beyond the Friend's outward beauty in search of 'the beauty of thy mind'[34] they find that his 'fair flower' is contaminated by 'the rank smell of weeds'. Similarly, in connection with the Friend's falsity, Sonnet 94 speaks of festering lilies ('Lillies that fester smell far worse than weeds'), and Sonnet 95 speaks of a cankered rose (whereas in Sonnet 54 the Friend's beauty had been confidently compared to a rose that was free of canker). Sonnets 123 and 124 proclaim the Poet's undying love for his friend (the Poet's love will never be destroyed by 'Time'), and it may be that we are meant to take this as being so even after the Poet has been betrayed by the Friend. But this undying love is one-sided: the relation between the Poet and the Friend fails to match up to the description of love in Sonnet 116 as 'the marriage of true minds' – a marriage of minds *both* of which are 'true'.[35]

We have already noted that in Sonnet 151 the Poet refers to his relationship with his mistress as a betrayal of his soul by his body. Other sonnets about the Dark Lady (as the mistress has come to be known, following the description of her in Sonnets 127, 130 and 132) elaborate on this theme. Sonnet 129 dwells on the shamefulness and irrationality[36] of 'lust':

Past reason hunted, and, no sooner had,
Past reason hated as a swallowed bait...

The victim of lust fails to see that what in anticipation appears to be 'bliss' results in misery – there is a failure 'To shun the heaven that leads men to this hell.' (This last point may explain why in the previous sonnet, 128, the Dark Lady is presented attractively: the Poet longs to kiss her as she plays on the virginals.) Sonnet 147 describes the Poet's love for his mistress as 'a fever', now incurable because of his rejection of reason:

Past cure I am, now reason is past care...

Several sonnets (137, 148, 149, 150) speak of the blindness[37] of the Poet's love, a blindness which undermines his judgment –

Sonnet 137 begins: 'Thou blind fool, Love'. (This blindness contrasts with an acceptable form of blindness in Sonnet 113, where the Poet's mind is so dominated by the image of the loved one – his Friend – that it distorts everything around him.) And the Poet's infatuation is also seen as a form of slavery: he is his mistress's 'slave and vassal wretch' (Sonnet 141 – 'vassal' is here used as an adjective), his 'mistress' thrall' (Sonnet 154). (This slavery, however, like the Poet's blindness, contrasts with a favourable form: in connection with his Friend, 'vassalage' in Sonnet 26 and 'your slave' in Sonnets 57 and 58 express love's devotion rather than enslavement to lust.) Finally, mention must be made of Sonnet 146 which describes the soul's imprisonment in the flesh:

> Poor soul, the centre of my sinful earth,
> Fooled by[38] these rebel powers that thee array [are ranged against you]...

Here 'rebel powers' certainly includes lust.[39]

In Shakespeare's Sonnets as a whole, therefore, we see that the Poet's love for his Friend belongs to an essentially spiritual order, in contrast to his 'love' for his mistress, which represents enslavement to the flesh.

VENUS AND ADONIS (1593)

Shakespeare's narrative poem *Venus and Adonis* is based on the brief account given in Book X of Ovid's *Metamorphoses* of Venus's love for the beautiful youth Adonis who went hunting and was killed by a wild boar, after Venus had pleaded with him not to hunt dangerous animals. Shakespeare's account is much longer – his poem runs to 1194 lines – and in spirit is the opposite of Ovid. Ovid delights in sensuality, but Shakespeare's poem, while giving a vivid description of sensual feeling, is a condemnation of 'desire' and 'lust': it is thus written in the spirit of the Dark Lady sonnets.

Venus is introduced as being 'Sick-thoughted' (line 5), meaning that she is love-sick – later she is actually described as 'love-sick' (line 175) and her infatuation with Adonis is described as 'love-sick love' (line 328). At the beginning of the story it is 'desire' that impels her to pull Adonis down from his horse (line 29). Shakespeare allows her to give lyrical expression to sensual feeling in her attempts to seduce Adonis, as in lines 145–50:

> 'Bid me discourse, I will enchant thine ear,
> Or like a fairy trip upon the green,
> Or like a nymph with long dishevelled hair
> Dance on the sands and yet no footing seen.
>   Love is a spirit all compact of fire,
>   Not gross to sink, but light and will aspire.'

But the poem proceeds to draw a parallel between Venus's desire for Adonis and the 'high desire' (line 276) of Adonis's horse for a young mare that rushes out from a copse. Venus applauds the horse's response to 'sweet desire' (386) and sees the horse's behaviour as showing that 'deep desire' is a force that cannot be restrained (389): she urges Adonis to follow his horse's example ('learn of him, I heartily beseech thee', 404). Adonis, who all along has tried to resist Venus's advances, insists that he is not yet ready for love (524–5):

> 'Measure my strangeness [aloofness] with my unripe years.
> Before I know myself, seek not to know me.'

But Venus is driven on by 'quick desire' (547), by 'careless [reckless] lust', 'beating reason back' (556–7: compare Sonnet 129 where the kind of pleasure sought by a lustful person leaves reason[40] behind – 'Past reason hunted') .

It becomes clear that it is Adonis's view of 'desire' that the poem asks us to accept. With the coming of darkness Venus says 'In night desire sees best of all' (720), but Adonis regards 'black-faced night' as being 'desire's foul nurse' (773). Earlier in the poem Venus had argued that as a beautiful young man Adonis should beget beauty (167–74 – 'By the law of nature thou art bound to breed'), and when she repeats this point by saying that in contrast to the 'fruitless chastity' of nuns Adonis should be 'prodigal' (751–5) his answer is that such reasoning 'is the bawd to lust's abuse' (792). Venus's argument is similar to that of the Poet in the Sonnets when he asks his beautiful young friend to immortalise his beauty by having children (Sonnets 1, 12, 13), but the difference is that the Poet is referring to procreation within marriage – in Sonnets 3 and 8 he appeals to his friend not to remain 'single'. Adonis condemns Venus's conception of love as sanctioning promiscuity (789–90):

> 'I hate not love but your device in love [way of thinking about love],
> That lends embracements unto every stranger.'

And he proclaims the positive viewpoint of the poem by distinguishing between lust and true love (799–804):

> 'Love comforteth like sunshine after rain,
> But lust's effect is tempest after sun.
> Love's gentle spring doth always fresh remain,
> Lust's winter comes ere summer half be done.
>   Love surfeits not, lust like a glutton dies.
>   Love is all truth, lust full of forgèd lies.'

Soon follows Adonis's fatal encounter with the wild boar. Fearing Adonis's death and then discovering his actual death, Venus bitterly laments the destruction of 'beauty' (931–6, 1080, 1105–7 – we see here that Venus appreciates only physical beauty, whereas Sonnet 69 stresses the importance of beauty of the 'mind'). Venus then makes a prophecy about love in the future which really amounts to a curse (1135–64): love is to be subject to sorrow, jealousy, deception, folly, instability, and strife, so that

> 'They that love best their loves shall not enjoy.'

Because Venus has suffered all lovers must suffer! And, 'weary of the world' (1189), she departs.

The poem allows some sympathy for Venus but leaves us in no doubt about the limitations of her conception of love, and the curse she pronounces at the end of the poem shows her to be completely destructive of true love.

THE TWO GENTLEMEN OF VERONA (c. 1593)

The Two Gentlemen of Verona proclaims the ideal of constancy, and deplores inconstancy, in love and friendship. The two gentlemen of Verona are the two young friends Proteus and Valentine, and Proteus, having won the love of Julia, betrays both Julia and his friend by trying to seduce Silvia, with whom Valentine is in love. The theme of the play is close to that of the Sonnets, except that the friendship between the two young men in the play has not the emotional intensity of the relationship between the Poet and Friend in the Sonnets, so that as regards love the play is concerned primarily with constancy in heterosexual love.

The early part of the play brings out an aspect of love which reappears in two later plays (*Romeo and Juliet* and *A Midsummer Night's Dream*): irrational behaviour as a characteristic even of true love in its early stages[41] – behaviour that is akin to the lover's 'partly blind' view of the surrounding world, as described in Sonnet 113. When Julia's female attendant, Lucetta, brings in a love letter from Proteus, Julia refuses to read it and asks for it to be returned – but then, in soliloquy, condemns herself (I.ii.57ff.): 'Fie, fie, how wayward is this foolish love...' And when Lucetta picks up the letter after dropping it Julia tears it to pieces – but gathers the pieces together after Lucetta has left. Valentine falls in love with Silvia, daughter of the Duke of Milan, during a long stay at the Duke's court (there is textual inconsistency in that this court is referred to as the Emperor's court in I.iii), and he is recognised as being in love by his servant Speed on account of certain 'special marks' (II.i.16), such as wandering about alone, sighing, weeping, and being off his food: Speed, who is on easy terms with his master, taunts him for having a false conception of Silvia's beauty 'because love is blind' (II.i.63). (It is ironical that in the first scene of the play, when Proteus is in love with Julia but Valentine has not yet fallen in love, it is Valentine himself who mocks the 'folly' induced by love – 'by love the young and tender wit [mind]/Is turned to folly', I.i.47–8.) And Silvia herself behaves foolishly towards Valentine, who at her request has written a letter for her to send to an unnamed friend: she hands the letter back to Valentine on the grounds that he wrote the letter 'unwillingly' (II.i.112), thus pouncing unfairly on a remark made by Valentine that he had been 'unwilling' (II.i.95) to proceed with this letter in so far as it was difficult to write to an unknown person – by which he certainly did not mean that he was unwilling to assist Silvia, for whom he would, he assures her, write 'a thousand times as much' (II.i.103).

As regards the main theme, Proteus at the beginning of the play is deeply in love with Julia. He describes himself as 'metamorphosed' by her (I.i.66 – the same word is later used by Speed, II.i.30 – , to describe the effect Silvia has on Valentine). When Proteus takes leave of Julia because his father has insisted that for the sake of his general education he should join Valentine at the Duke of Milan's court, he exchanges rings with Julia and says 'Here is my hand for my true constancy' (II.ii.8). But on arriving in Milan he immediately becomes infatuated with Silvia (Proteus's changeableness is suggested by his name, since in Greek myth Proteus was a sea god who often changed his shape). He knows he is submitting to a passion that is blind to reason – 'There is no reason but I shall be blind' (II.iv.208) – and this kind of blindness is far more damaging than the blindness attributed to Valentine by his servant. Proteus's blindness is in fact the same as that of the Poet in the Dark Lady sonnets (compare, for instance, Sonnet 152, while allowing for the moral difference between Silvia and the Dark Lady: 'In loving thee thou know'st I am forsworn... gave eyes to blindness...'). In his soliloquy at the beginning of II.vi Proteus shows a full awareness of his guilt:

> To leave my Julia shall I be forsworn.
> To love fair Silvia shall I be forsworn.
> To wrong my friend I shall be much forsworn...

But this does not deter him from being even more treacherous to his friend by informing Silvia's father (in III.i) that Silvia is about to elope with Valentine (as Proteus had been told by Valentine in confidence in II.iv.175–9) in order to avoid marrying Thurio, a man favoured by the Duke because of his wealth. And (in III.ii) Proteus actually undertakes to assist the Duke by slandering Valentine with the intention, so the Duke thinks, of encouraging Silvia to love Thurio. Here there is heavy irony in the Duke's belief that because Proteus's heart is engaged elsewhere he may safely be given full access to Silvia (III.ii.56–61):

> And, Proteus we dare trust you in this kind
> Because we know, on Valentine's report,
> You are already love's firm votary,
> And cannot soon revolt and change your mind.
> Upon this warrant shall you have access
> Where you with Silvia may confer at large.

In contrast to Proteus Julia is a shining example of constancy (despite her foolish behaviour earlier on), and constancy is also exemplified by Silvia (again, despite foolish behaviour earlier). After the exchange of rings just before Proteus leaves for Milan, Julia asks that they 'seal the bargain with a holy kiss' (II.ii.7), and while Proteus pledges his 'true constancy' at some length verbally (II.ii.8–16) Julia disappears, too moved to speak. As Proteus realises, for Julia deeds are more important than words (II.ii.17–18):

> Ay, so true love should do. It cannot speak,
> For truth [constancy] hath better deeds than words to grace it.

Julia so longs to be with Proteus that soon afterwards she decides to travel alone to Milan, disguised (to avoid the attentions of other men) as a page. It is symbolically appropriate that she speaks of tying her hair in twenty 'true-love knots' (II.vii.46), and her devotion to Proteus is reflected in her complete faith in his constancy to her (II.vii.75–6):

> His words are bonds, his oaths are oracles,
> His love sincere, his thoughts immaculate.

She is tragically disillusioned when, after arriving in Milan, she sees Proteus making advances to Silvia (IV.ii). In this situation Julia decides to remain in her male disguise, and, calling herself 'Sebastian', she gains employment with Proteus who uses her as a messenger in his amorous pursuit of Silvia (IV.iv). As for Silvia, since she knows about Proteus's commitment to Julia, she denounces his advances to her, calling him a 'perjured, false, disloyal man' (IV.ii.91). (Incidentally, when Silvia heard from Valentine about Proteus's love for Julia and Julia's love for him, she said 'Nay, then, he should be blind', II.iv.89 – here, as with Valentine when Speed said of him 'love is blind', blindness denotes rapt devotion, not reckless folly.) And after the Duke of Milan's banishment of Valentine, following Proteus's treacherous revelation of the planned elopement, Silvia shows her devotion to Valentine by setting off in the company of a trusted male friend to seek Valentine out (V.i).

All is resolved in the last Act. After his banishment Valentine (in IV.i) encountered a band of outlaws, among whom were several 'gentlemen', victims, like Valentine, of high-handed banishment, and these outlaws made Valentine their leader. After Silvia's departure from Milan to go in search of Valentine Proteus goes off in search of Silvia. It happens that Proteus finds Silvia just after she has fallen in with the outlaws now led by Valentine, and Proteus, according to his own view of his action, rescues (V.iv.21) Silvia from the outlaws: then, in the hidden presence of Valentine, he threatens Silvia with force to make her submit to him. When confronted by Valentine Proteus becomes so genuinely repentant that Valentine immediately forgives him, adding (V.iv.82–3):

> And, that my love may appear plain and free [generous],
> All that was mine in Silvia I give thee.

These words would appear to mean that Valentine is prepared to sacrifice Silvia to Proteus – which would be grossly unfair to Silvia – but the words are best taken to mean that Valentine in his forgiveness extends to Proteus love of the quality that he already has for Silvia.[42] At this moment Julia, who is in attendance as 'Sebastian', swoons – it seems that the strain she has been under has reached breaking-point – and her true identity becomes apparent. Proteus, moved by Julia's devotion, finds his love for her restored, and he laments his own inconstancy as a man (V.iv.110–12):

> O heaven, were man
> But constant, he were perfect! That one error
> Fills him with faults.

When the Duke and Thurio arrive on the scene (they also have set out in search of Silvia), Thurio, realising the folly of trying to marry a woman who does not love him, leaves the way clear for Valentine to marry Silvia, and the Duke now consents to this marriage. The play ends with Valentine's proposal that Proteus's marriage to Julia should be jointly celebrated with his own marriage to Silvia:

> our day of marriage shall be yours,
> One feast, one house, one mutual happiness.

A LOVER'S COMPLAINT (c. 1593)

A Lover's Complaint, a fairly short narrative poem (329 lines in length), was first published along with the Sonnets in 1609, and though the publisher (Thomas Thorpe) ascribed it to Shakespeare some doubts have been cast on this claim. The poem is written in rhyme royal stanzas (with the rhyme scheme *ababbcc*), as in Shakespeare's *The Rape of Lucrece*, which we shall be looking at next. *A Lover's Complaint* may have been suggested by Samuel Daniel's poem *The Complaint of Rosamond*, published in 1592, which was also written in rhyme royal (and the word 'complaint', meaning lament, occurs in both titles). In Daniel's poem Rosamond laments her fall from virtue through becoming the mistress of King Henry II. In *A Lover's Complaint* a woman laments her seduction by an unscrupulous young man: she tells an elderly countryman (in his younger days a courtier) how she succumbed to the wiles of a man who claimed to be the idol of many other women, including even a nun, but assured the young woman (the narrator) that she was the only one he really loved: he talked of handing over to her all the jewels allegedly given him by his besotted female admirers.

In theme *A Lover's Complaint* certainly has something in common with Shakespeare's Sonnets. In this poem the word 'appetite' is the equivalent of 'lust' in the Sonnets – in the Sonnets the Poet submits to 'lust' (Sonnet 129), and in *A Lover's Complaint* the woman submits to 'appetite' (line 166). It is its main theme, the lamentable rejection of 'reason', that brings the poem close to the Dark Lady sonnets. Just as the Poet (in Sonnets 129 and 147) refuses to listen to 'reason', so the young woman wants to distance herself from 'judgment' and 'reason' when she is in the grip of appetite (lines 166–8):

> O appetite, from judgment stand aloof!
> The one [appetite] a palate hath that needs will taste,
> Though reason weep and cry 'It is thy last'.

And near the end of the poem the woman says of her seduction (lines 295–7):

> For lo, his passion, but an art of craft,
> Even there resolved my reason into tears.
> There my white stole [robe] of chastity I daffed [doffed].

The woman admits that her folly was all the more inexcusable in that she knew the man was not to be trusted (lines 169–70):

> For further I could say 'This man's untrue',
> And knew the patterns of his foul beguiling.

Such an attitude is similar to that of the Poet towards the Dark Lady in Sonnet 138:

> When my love swears that she is made of truth
> I do believe her, though I know she lies.

Another parallel with the Sonnets is to be found in the character of the seducer in the poem. The seducer, like the Poet's Friend in the Sonnets, is a handsome young man whose outward appearance belies his inner failings – the seducer is described as 'one by nature's outwards so commended' (line 80), and Sonnet 69 says of the Friend 'Thy outward thus with outward praise is crowned'.

It should also be noted that the seducer is predominantly a Machiavel character. In this respect he is more akin to Shakespeare's Richard III than to the Friend in the Sonnets. He is the wholly evil hypocrite who sheds false tears and professes to uphold a moral ideal that he himself violates. The woman says of him (lines 288–9):

> what a hell of witchcraft lies
> In the small orb of one particular tear!

And a little later (lines 313–17) she adds:

> Against the thing he sought he would exclaim.
> When he most burned in heart-wished luxury [lust],
> He preached pure maid and praised cold chastity.
>
> Thus merely [entirely] with the garment of a grace
> The naked and concealèd fiend he covered.

THE RAPE OF LUCRECE (1594)

The theme of *The Rape of Lucrece*, a narrative poem running to 1855 lines and so longer than *Venus and Adonis*, is the evil of lust: in *Venus and Adonis* the word 'lust' was secondary to the word 'desire', but, though 'desire' also appears in *The Rape of Lucrece*, 'lust' is primary. ('Appetite', the key word in *A Lover's Complaint*, occurs twice in *The Rape of Lucrece*, in lines 9 and 546.) *The Rape of Lucrece* may in fact be regarded as a lengthy elaboration of what is said about lust in Sonnet 129. The poem tells the story of the rape of Lucretia, chaste wife of the Roman Collatinus, by Sextus Tarquinius, son of the last Roman king – a story recounted by the Roman historian Livy, by Ovid (in 132 lines) in his poem *Fasti* (*The Calendar*), and by Chaucer (in 206 lines) in his *The Legend of Good Women* ('Lucrece', as spelt by Shakespeare, is close to Chaucer's spelling, 'Lucresse'). References to Lucrece as a byword for chastity had already been made by Shakespeare in *Titus Andronicus* (II.i.108) and *The Taming of the Shrew* (II.i.288), and the rape of Lucrece was referred to in a later scene of *Titus Andronicus* (IV.i.64–5).

The opening stanza of *The Rape of Lucrece* draws a contrast between the 'Lust-breathèd Tarquin' (line 3) and 'Lucrece the chaste' (7). Lucrece is remarkable for her combination of 'beauty' and 'virtue' (52–70) – like the combination of 'truth' (constancy) and 'beauty' that is praised in Sonnets 14 and 101. In due course Lucrece and Tarquin are contrasted even more emphatically as being at the opposite poles of good and evil – Lucrece is an 'earthly saint', Tarquin a 'devil' (85).

Tarquin, however, is not entirely without conscience – in fact he is an early example in Shakespeare of an evil character in whom a struggle between good and evil occurs. Before he commits the act of rape, 'in his inward mind he doth debate' (185). Such an act, he realises, will bring shame to his social position as a member of a royal family ('O shame to knighthood...O foul dishonour to my household's grave', 197–8), and he reflects that Lucrece's husband is his close friend ('as he is my kinsman, my dear friend,/The shame and fault finds no excuse nor end', 237–8) – here we have a similarity to Proteus's sin against his friend in *The Two Gentlemen of Verona*. But Tarquin refuses to let 'reason' stand in the way of his 'will' (lustful desire): 'My will is strong, past reason's weak removing' (243 – compare the similar rejection of 'reason' in Sonnets 129 and 147 and in *Venus and Adonis*, line 557). His 'frozen conscience' yields to his 'hot-burning will' (246–52): 'Affection [desire] is my captain' (271), 'Desire my pilot is' (279). When Tarquin enters Lucrece's bedchamber and clearly indicates his intentions, she tries to restrain him by appealing to the very principles that we know he had already considered in his own 'inward debate': she pleads with him to respect the moral code of 'knighthood'[43] (569) and to remember 'My husband is thy friend' (582). But all to no avail. When he departs after his act of rape Tarquin does, however, feel shame: 'This hot desire converts to cold disdain' (691), and he 'hates himself for his offence' (738) – compare what is said about acts of lust in Sonnet 129: 'Enjoyed no sooner but despisèd straight.'

Much of the rest of the poem is taken up by Lucrece's grim reflections. She reflects on evil as represented by night in contrast to day ('O comfort-killing Night, image of hell... Vast sin-concealing chaos', 764–7) and on human subjection to the reverses of Time ('injurious, shifting Time', 930) and Fortune ('the giddy round of Fortune's wheel', 952). Because she has been defiled ('my foul defilèd blood', 1029) and to avoid bearing an illegitimate child ('This bastard graff [graft] shall never come to growth', 1062), she resolves to control her fate ('I am the mistress of my fate', 1069) by taking her own life. She compares herself (1128–34) to Philomel, raped by her brother-in-law Tereus (this story was referred to in *Titus Andronicus*, V.ii.195–6, in connection with the rape of Titus's daughter Lavinia), and, calling to mind a painting that depicts the Trojan War, she dwells on the miseries of that war caused by the abduction of the Greek Helen ('Helen's rape', 1369) by Paris, son of the King of Troy, in the 'heat of lust' (1473). When her husband and her father arrive on the scene she tells them what has happened, and then she stabs herself with a knife in order to release her soul from 'that polluted prison where it breathed' (1726 – compare 'Poor soul, the centre of my sinful earth', Sonnet 146, though Lucrece's body, of course, is not polluted by her own sinfulness).

Before killing herself Lucrece asks that revenge should immediately be taken against her attacker ('Be suddenly revengèd on my foe', 1683). This revenge is to be distinguished from the cycle of revenge and counter-revenge condemned in *3 Henry VI*. Lucrece is asking for revenge in the sense of just punishment (1686–7):

> let the traitor die,
> For sparing justice feeds iniquity.

Attending Lucrece's husband and father is one Brutus (an

earlier Brutus than the one who appears in Shakespeare's *Julius Caesar*), and this Brutus proceeds to rouse the Roman people against Tarquin, who is duly condemned to 'everlasting banishment' (1855).

LOVE'S LABOUR'S LOST (c. 1594)

The theme of *Love's Labour's Lost* is the place to be assigned in human life, or more specifically in the life of a courtier, to 'Cupid' or sexual attraction. (In Sonnet 154, the last of the Sonnets as published in 1609, Cupid is associated with 'hot desire'. In *Love's Labour's Lost* Cupid denotes strong emotional attraction as well as physical desire.) As the play proceeds Cupid is accepted as having an important place in human life, but in the last scene the subjection of Cupid to moral discipline is called for.[44]

In the opening scene we hear that the King of Navarre[45] and three of his courtiers, Berowne, Longaville and Dumain, have agreed to devote three years to study (to the study of 'philosophy', I.i.32), in opposition to worldly distractions ('the huge army of the world's desires', I.i.10). Berowne (this is his name according to the Quarto edition of the play – in the Folio edition he is called Biron) protests, however, against the laying down of certain rules, rules about not seeing women, fasting, and the severe restriction of time for sleep (I.i.36–48). The King wants to ensure that 'our intellects' are not seduced by 'vain delight' (I.i.70–1), but Berowne insists that a pursuit of enlightenment that is limited to book learning detracts from enlightenment – that in such a situation 'Light, seeking light, doth light of light beguile [deprive]' (I.i.77) – and in particular he claims that the company of women can be a valuable source of enlightenment[46] (I.i.80–3). He then reminds the King that the French king's daughter is due to visit the Navarre court to discuss the surrender of territory to France: the King confesses that he had forgotten about this visit and he immediately concedes that for the period of the visit the rule against the presence of women will have to be suspended of 'necessity'

(I.i.145–6). Berowne points out that only men specially endowed with divine grace can be expected to be celibate (I.i.149–50):

> For every man with his affects [natural inclinations] is born,
> Not by might mastered, but by special grace.

Berowne puts his signature to the agreement to abide by the rules, but observes that the King's word 'necessity' provides a convenient excuse for breaking the rule against women (I.i.151–2), and he declares his belief that at least he will be able to stand by this rule longer than the others (I.i.157–8).

The King's court has for some time been attended by a bombastic Spaniard called Armado (Don Adriano de Armado), and in the first scene Costard, a young countryman (a 'swain' I.i.177), appears in the company of a constable, constable Dull, to deliver a letter to the King in which Armado reports having seen Costard consorting with a female, Jaquenetta, in the grounds of the palace, 'contrary to thy established proclaimed edict' (I.i.245–6) – punishment, says Armado, can be administered by the constable. Yet in the second scene we hear that Armado, who had 'promised to study three years with the Duke' (I.ii.35–6), has difficulty in resisting 'Desire' or 'Cupid' (I.ii.63–), since he himself has fallen in love with Jaquenetta. By the end of this scene Armado has decided he cannot help but to submit to Cupid's 'butt-shaft' (arrow, I.ii.157+).

Armado's submission to Cupid is the forerunner of other such submissions. Not long after the French princess's arrival, in the company of three attendants, Rosaline, Maria and Katherine, Berowne is angry with himself for falling in love with Rosaline, for falling so soon under the spell of Cupid (he refers twice to Cupid, III.i.170, 192, in his soliloquy at the end of III.i) – he had, after all, declared he would not break the rule about not associating with women before the others had done so (I.i.157–8). After hearing in IV.i the contents of a love letter sent by Armado to Jaquenetta, we hear in IV.ii about a love sonnet addressed by Berowne to Rosaline in a letter that was wrongly delivered by Costard to Jaquenetta. But in the next scene, IV.iii,

Berowne discovers that the King has also been 'shot' by Cupid's arrow (IV.iii.19–21) – Berowne overhears the King reading aloud a love poem which is clearly addressed to the Princess. And Berowne then overhears Longaville and Dumain reading out love poems addressed to Maria and Katherine respectively. Just after he has confronted the King and the other two scholars with their breach of the rule against relations with women Berowne's own guilt comes to light – Jaquenetta arrives at court and presents the King with Berowne's love letter that was wrongly delivered to her. Now that the breaking of this rule by all four of the men has been exposed, Berowne makes an eloquent speech in praise of love (IV.iii.285–361). Even more than books, he says, a woman's eyes are a source of true inspiration:

> They are the ground, the books, the academes,
> From whence doth spring the true Promethean fire...
> For where is any author in the world
> Teaches such beauty as a woman's eye?[47]

Berowne's speech reaches a climax in the lines:

> And when Love speaks the voice of all the gods
> Makes heaven drowsy with the harmony.[48]

And after hearing this speech the King is moved to proclaim allegiance to 'Saint Cupid' (IV.iii.362).

Entertainment is provided for the ladies, entertainment which includes a ridiculous pageant about the Nine Worthies (such characters as Pompey the Great, Alexander the Great, and Hercules) – in actual fact the King and his fellow scholars and the Princess and her ladies find entertainment in making fun of this pageant. The pageant was devised by a schoolmaster, Holofernes, and a parson, Nathaniel, described by Dull the constable as 'book-men' (IV.ii.32): these two, who quite unjustifiably regard themselves as being men 'of taste and feeling' (IV.ii.27), may be intended to represent somewhat extreme examples of Berowne's point about the inadequacy of learning limited to books. The pageant of the Worthies is brought to a sudden halt by the entry of a messenger bearing the news that the Princess's father, the King of France, has died. The Princess decides to leave immediately, but the King asks that before they go the ladies should make some favourable response to the men's courting of them. The Princess tells the King that she will become his wife on condition that he first spends a year at some hermitage 'Remote from all the pleasures of the world' (V.ii.784) – to ensure that his love endures beyond an 'offer made in heat of blood' (V.ii.788). The three other ladies also require their suitors to wait a year (Rosaline requires Berowne to visit the sick during that year). To this extent love's labour's lost, but this needs to be so only for a year and a day, as the King points out (V.ii.865).

In this last scene we hear that Armado's love is also to be put to the test: according to Armado himself (V.ii.869+), he has vowed to work at the plough for three years before marrying Jaquenetta (who is a country girl). But now, in the last few moments of the play, Armado's concern is to persuade the King to listen to the song that 'the two learned men' had composed to be sung at the end of the pageant, a song written 'in praise of the owl and the cuckoo' (V.ii.869+ ff.): the King agrees briefly to listen. In the first part of this song the cuckoo in spring 'Mocks married men', the reference here being to adultery or cuckoldry (the word 'cuckold' derives from 'cuckoo', in connection with the cuckoo as an intruder in other birds' nests). In the second part of the song the owl in winter is cheerful while human beings suffer from the cold, and there is particular stress on the owl's uttering of 'a merry note/While greasy Joan doth keel [cool] the pot' – here we have a drab picture of human domestic, perhaps married, life. Since Armado is so keen to promote this song, which in the first part, if not in the second part, expresses a disenchanted view of marriage, doubt may well be cast on the likelihood of Armado's ever being married to Jaquenetta. At the end of the play comes the comment: 'The words of Mercury are harsh after the songs of Apollo.' In the First Folio edition of the play this comment is attributed to Armado, though in the Quarto edition the speaker is not indicated. If we take the comment as being Armado's, it seems that, since Mercury was the messenger of the gods, Armado is recalling with characteristic literary affectation the arrival of the messenger whose grim news has brought to an end the entertainment provided for the lady guests. And it seems that Armado, in speaking of 'the songs of Apollo' (Apollo being the god of music), has in mind the song of the owl and the cuckoo that has just been sung. If so, there is a glaring contrast between this reference to Apollo, in connection with a basically cynical song, and Berowne's earlier association of Apollo with love as a truly inspiring force – 'Love... sweet and musical/As bright Apollo's lute' (IV.iii.336–9).

KING JOHN (c. 1594)

In *King John* the concern that Shakespeare shows in the Sonnets and *Two Gentlemen of Verona* for 'constancy' and 'truth' in love relationships is carried over into politics. In the *Henry VI–Richard III* tetralogy the overall theme had been the need for social order: in *King John* the stress falls on the need for moral integrity – 'truth' – in political leaders.

In the opening scene of *King John* there is certainly a similarity to the *Henry VI* plays as regards the disputed legality of the reigning king's claim to the throne. 'My title's weak' was the admission of King Henry (*3 Henry VI* I.i.134), and King John's mother, Queen Elinor, privately admits that John's claim to the throne depends on 'possession' rather than 'right' (I.i.40). But, whereas the weakness of Henry VI's title was the result of an earlier king (Richard II) having been deposed (by Henry IV), in *King John* John is himself a usurper[49] since, as the French ambassador Chatillon insists, the lawful heir to the English throne is Arthur, son of John's deceased brother Geffrey (I.i.7–15 – in the following scene it is made clear that Geffrey was John's 'elder' brother, II.i.104). The rest of the first scene introduces us to the 'Bastard', Philip Faulconbridge, who is the illegitimate son of the previous king, Richard I, and is proud of being so – but Richard was, after all, responsible for the moral confusion of leaving an illegitimate son rather than a legitimate one: when John's (and Richard's) mother acknowledges the Bastard as a grandson he replies 'Madam, by chance, but not by truth' (I.i.169).

When in the first scene the French king, Philip, threatens through his ambassador to go to war against John if he does not give up the English throne to Prince Arthur, John's answer is that he will offer 'war for war' (I.i.19), and in the next scene (II.i), which is set in France where the war is being fought, King Philip and also the Duke of Austria promise, in the presence of Arthur's mother Constance, to continue the fight against England until Arthur is made king – the Duke of Austria talks of fighting 'a just and charitable war' (II.i.36), and King Philip claims to be acting on the authority of God ('that supernal [heavenly] judge', II.i.112). But Philip and John are quick to accept a suggestion made by a citizen of Angiers (i.e. Angers in Anjou) that the two kings should cease fighting and come to an agreement based on a marriage between the Dauphin (Philip's son Lewis – i.e. Louis) and John's niece, Blanch. An agreement is reached whereby John is left in possession of the English throne but cedes as a dowry for Blanch certain English territories in France – the Dauphin, to clinch the agreement, transacts a quick courtship of Blanch (who is present with her uncle in France), a courtship which takes the form of extravagant flattery (II.i.496–503). The Bastard (who is also present, having been invited in I.i to take part in the war in France) describes the Dauphin as 'a lout' (II.i.509), and at the end of the scene delivers a long soliloquy (II.i.561–98) deploring the way in which the two kings have been motivated by 'commodity' (opportunism or self-interest, II.i.573–4):

> John, to stop Arthur's title in the whole,
> Hath willingly departed with a part,

and Philip has withdrawn

> From a resolved and honourable war
> To a most base and vile-concluded peace.

And in the next scene (III.i) Arthur's mother Constance bitterly condemns both King Philip and the Duke of Austria for being 'forsworn' (III.i.101) and 'perjured' (III.i.111,120) – these are the words used in connection with love relationships in Sonnet 152 and in *The Two Gentlemen of Verona* (II.vi.1–3, IV.ii.91).

The situation changes again with the arrival in France of Pandulph, the Pope's legate. When John refuses to yield to the Pope in a dispute about who should be appointed Archbishop of Canterbury, Pandulph calls upon Philip to support the Pope by resuming the war against England. In answer to Philip's protest that his agreement with John was a matter of 'deep-sworn faith' (III.i.231) Pandulph argues in a long speech of twisted logic that the Church must come first and therefore in Philip's situation 'truth' (honourable conduct) requires that he should *not* abide by his agreement with John (III.i.273): if he abides by that agreement he will be 'forsworn' by not obeying the Church (III.i.286–7). Bowing to the pressure from Pandulph Philip resumes the war, and soon afterwards Arthur is taken prisoner and is handed over by John to one of his followers, Hubert, whom John has persuaded to put Arthur to death. (In handing Arthur over to Hubert John hypocritically assures Arthur that Hubert will attend him 'With all true duty', III.iii.73.) After Arthur has been taken prisoner Pandulph gives worldly encouragement to the Dauphin by telling him that 'Fortune' (III.iv.119) is favourably inclined towards him, since John will almost certainly kill Arthur and the Dauphin can then through his wife Blanch lay claim to the English throne (III.iv.131–43) – it is significant that the worldly Pandulph talks here entirely in terms of Fortune without any reference to the supreme power of God in human affairs (such as we see in *Richard III*).

Arthur, as it happens, is not killed by Hubert since at the end of IV.i Hubert gives way to 'mercy' (IV.i.26,120) and 'compassion' (IV.i.89), but in IV.iii Arthur, in attempting to escape, is killed after leaping from the wall of the castle where he has been imprisoned. The Bastard's reaction on discovering the dead Arthur is to proclaim (IV.iii.143–5):

> From forth this morsel of dead royalty
> The life, the right, and truth of all this realm
> Is fled to heaven.

The Bastard foresees that Arthur's death will cause so much discontent in England that the result will be 'vast confusion' (IV.iii.152).

The Bastard is right in his prediction. In V.i we hear him reporting to John that England has been invaded by French troops led by the Dauphin and that these troops are actually welcomed by the English nobles (V.i.31–4):

>   London hath received,
> Like a kind host, the Dauphin and his powers [forces].
> Your nobles will not hear you, but are gone
> To offer service to your enemy.

The Bastard's reaction to this situation is to be blindly loyal to his king and country. Having accepted Hubert's word that he did not kill Arthur (V.i.43), the Bastard does not even question whether John was responsible for an attempted murder of Arthur. His first concern is to see that John gives an effective lead in resisting the French, and to that end he immediately seeks to boost John's morale by deliberate flattery (V.i.44–5):

> But wherefore do you droop? Why look you sad?
> Be great in act as you have been in thought.

And when John says that he has just made his peace with the Pope in return for a promise by Pandulph to call upon the Dauphin to lay down his arms, the Bastard opposes any tame submission to France and is sceptical of Pandulph's ability to bring about peace. In V.ii the Dauphin does in fact refuse Pandulph's appeal to make peace, and in this scene the two of them are confronted by the Bastard who gives them a jingoistic description of John as an invincible soldier (V.ii.148–50):

> Know the gallant monarch is in arms,
> And, like an eagle, o'er his aery towers [soars over his nest]
> To souse [swoop down upon] annoyance that comes near his nest.

Though this description of John may be regarded as militarist propaganda, at the end of the play the Bastard's loyalty seems to have reached the point of complete self-deception – when John dies as the result of being poisoned by a monk (V.vi.23), the Bastard professes to be in no doubt that John will be in heaven (V.vii.72–3):

> my soul shall wait on thee [go as your servant] to heaven,
> As it on earth hath been thy servant still [always].

Whereas the Bastard after Arthur's death is driven towards blind loyalty, Salisbury, Pembroke and Bigot are examples of nobles who feel they have no choice but to desert their king ('such is the infection of the time', V.ii.20). They enter into a mutually binding alliance with the Dauphin, who talks of 'our faiths firm and inviolable' (V.ii.7). On the Dauphin's part this soon proves to be yet another false pledge in the play. These three English nobles are warned by the French Count Melun, as he is dying of battle wounds, that they will be beheaded if the Dauphin achieves victory (V.iv.10–20). The three nobles therefore decide to return to the king whom Salisbury now describes as 'our great King John' (V.iv.57) – this description suggests that in their reaction against the Dauphin (and also perhaps to appease their guilt as deserters) these nobles have now, like the Bastard, have become blind to John's faults.

John's death, however, brings to an end the moral dilemmas he has inflicted on his subjects. Since Arthur is also dead John's son Henry is the undisputed heir to the throne: in the Bastard's words, in him is invested 'The lineal state and glory of the land' (V.vii.102). And in the final speech of the play the Bastard proudly asserts that England need have no fear of being conquered 'If England to itself do rest but true' – this last word thus underlining the main theme of the whole play.

ROMEO AND JULIET (c. 1595)

Romeo and Juliet is about true love, but it is also about social disorder. The love between Romeo and Juliet is destroyed by the feud between two families, the Montagues and the Capulets, in the state of Verona, a feud that could be regarded as a parallel in miniature of the civil war between Yorkists and Lancastrians in *3 Henry VI*. Stated in full, therefore, the main theme of *Romeo and Juliet* is the tragic destruction of love by civil strife. This theme is clearly indicated in the opening Prologue (which is in the form of a sonnet) – as the result of enmity between two families in Verona, the Prologue tells us, 'civil blood makes civil hands unclean', and the Prologue goes on:

> From forth the fatal loins of these two foes
> A pair of star-crossed lovers take their life,
> Whose misadventured piteous overthrows
> Doth with their death bury their parents' strife.

Civil strife is the keynote of the first scene. Fighting breaks out between the servants and members of the Capulet and Montague families, and citizens join in to oppose the fighting on both sides (I.i.71): 'Clubs, bills and partisans [axes and spears]! Strike! Beat them down!' The rioters are called to account by the Prince of Verona who addresses them as 'Rebellious subjects, enemies to peace' (I.i.79) and warns them that repetition of such behaviour will be punished by death. This brawling is rooted in 'hate', as we see from what is said by Tybalt (Capulet) to Benvolio (Montague) about 'talk of peace' (I.i.68–9):

> ... talk of peace? I hate the word,
> As I hate hell, all Montagues, and thee.

And the Prince in his speech condemns the 'cankered hate' (I.i.93) that exists between the two families.

It is against this hate that love has to struggle, and Romeo is introduced as the embodiment of such a struggle. As son of the head of the Montague family he is expected to hate the

Capulets, yet he is in love, at the beginning of the play, with 'the fair Rosaline' (I.ii.83), niece of the head of the Capulet family (I.ii.70–). Romeo is in a state of mental confusion (I.i.173–4):

> Here's much to do with hate, but more with love.
> Why then, O brawling love, O loving hate...

Romeo is persuaded by his cousin Benvolio to attend a public feast to be given in the Capulet household, where, Benvolio says, Romeo will discover that Rosaline's beauty is not superior to that of other young ladies. Romeo goes to the feast wearing a mask, as do several others, and there his love for Rosaline, who does not return his love, is instantly replaced by a passionate love for Juliet, Capulet's young daughter (who is not yet fourteen years old). After hearing Romeo's declaration of love for her Juliet finds herself in love with him, but when she learns from her nurse that Romeo is a Montague she, like Romeo before her, is caught up in a conflict between love and hate (I.v.136): 'My only love sprung up from my only hate!'

The conflict between love and hate continues throughout the play. At the beginning of II.iii the good Friar Lawrence reflects on the creative and destructive forces in the natural world, and compares the medicinal and poisonous qualities of herbs with opposed forces in human nature (II.iii.27–8):

> Two such opposèd kings encamp them still [always]
> In man as well as herbs – grace and rude will.

And in this play 'grace' is clearly to be associated with the goodness of love and 'rude will' with an obstinate determination to foster hatred. When Romeo asks the Friar to perform the marriage ceremony between Juliet and himself, the Friar sees a chance here of converting the hatred between Montague and Capulet into love (II.iii.91–2):

> For this alliance may so happy prove
> To turn your households' rancour to pure love.

But the Friar's optimism is soon confounded. After the marriage ceremony has been performed in secret Romeo does indeed feel love towards the Capulets as being his wife's family – when he encounters Tybalt, who as a Capulet tries to provoke a fight, Romeo answers (III.i.66–70):

> I ... love thee better than thou canst devise [imagine]
> Till thou shalt know the reason of my love.
> And so, good Capulet – which name I tender [value]
> As dearly as mine own – be satisfied.

But when Tybalt kills Romeo's friend Mercutio Romeo feels obliged to attack Tybalt: Tybalt is killed, and Romeo is duly banished from Verona by the Prince. Juliet is grief-stricken, but she has to pretend to her mother that the cause of her grief is the death of Tybalt, her cousin, and she has to pretend to 'hate' Romeo as the killer of Tybalt (III.v.122). When Juliet's father, not knowing of her secret marriage to Romeo, arranges for her to marry Paris, a young nobleman, Friar Lawrence puts into operation a plan to reunite Romeo and Juliet. He gives Juliet a drug that will make her appear dead for forty-two hours, so that when she wakes in the family vault Romeo will be there to take her away with him. But a letter from the Friar informing Romeo of this plan is never delivered. Romeo, hearing from his servant that Juliet is dead, goes to the Capulet vault and swallows poison in order to lie dead beside Juliet: when Juliet wakes to find Romeo dead she joins him in death by stabbing herself. Just before taking his life Romeo shows himself to be free of hatred. He was provoked into fighting – and killing – Paris who came upon him in the vault and tried to arrest him so that he might be put to death as the 'vile Montague' (V.iii.54) who killed Tybalt: Romeo reverently carries out Paris's dying request to be laid in Juliet's tomb (Romeo recalls being told by his servant about the intended marriage between Paris and Juliet). And then, seeing Tybalt's body in the vault, Romeo feels remorse for having killed him. The taking of his own life, he says, will make amends for Tybalt's death and, since Tybalt was Juliet's cousin, Romeo refers to Tybalt as his own cousin (V.iii.98–101):

> O, what more favour can I do to thee
> Than with that hand that cut thy youth in twain
> To sunder his that was thine enemy?
> Forgive me, cousin.

At the end of the play hatred between the Montagues and Capulets is at last overcome as the heads of the two families come together in friendship – a reconciliation that it has taken the deaths of Romeo and Juliet to bring about.

Apart from the conflict between love and hate there are two other aspects of the play that are worth noting in some detail: the love between Romeo and Juliet as representing Shakespeare's conception of true love, and the role of 'heaven' (God) in relation to 'fortune'.

In *Romeo and Juliet*, as in *The Two Gentlemen of Verona*, irrational behaviour is accepted as an early stage in true love. Romeo, when in love with 'the fair Rosaline' weeps and sighs and shuts himself up in his chamber during daylight hours (I.i.129–38 – sighing and weeping were among the 'special marks' of love identified by Valentine's servant in *The Two Gentlemen of Verona*, II.i.16 ff.). And when Romeo falls in love with Juliet his behaviour draws from his friend Mercutio the cry 'Romeo! Humours! Madman! Passion! Lover!' (II.i.7). The love between Romeo and Juliet is indeed 'passion' ('passion lends them power', Prologue to Act II), and it is a passion that is immediately associated with marriage. When Romeo asks Juliet for 'The exchange of thy love's faithful vow for mine' (II.ii.127), she replies (II.ii.143–8):

> If that thy bent [aim] be honourable,
> Thy purpose marriage, send me word tomorrow...
> And all my fortunes at thy foot I'll lay
> And follow thee, my lord, throughout the world.

(In the last line we have an echo of Katherina's whole-hearted advocacy of a wife's obedience to her 'loving lord' at the end of *The Taming of the Shrew*.) The physical side of marriage is important, for Juliet after the secret marriage ceremony longs for Romeo to come to her so that they may perform their 'amorous rites' (III.ii.8) – rites that should follow pre-marital chastity: marriage is described by Juliet as a 'match/Played for a pair of stainless maidenheads' (III.ii.12–13). But Juliet's nurse is satirised in the play for not being able to see beyond the physical side of marriage: bearing Romeo's message that Juliet should attend Friar Lawrence's cell for the marriage ceremony, the Nurse talks about this marriage in terms of 'wanton blood' (II.v.70) and says to Juliet 'you shall bear the burden soon at night' (II.v.76). And there is no conception of any personal commitment: when Juliet's father (not knowing about the marriage to Romeo) insists that Juliet should marry the Count Paris, the Nurse is enthusiastic, saying to Juliet 'O, he's a lovely gentleman! Romeo's a dishclout to him' (III.v.219–20), and she shows no concern about Juliet committing bigamy – since Romeo has been banished he is as good as 'dead' (III.v.225).

In *Romeo and Juliet* stress is put on the dominance of Fortune in human life – Fortune had already figured in the Sonnets where the Poet speaks of himself as being out of favour with Fortune (in Sonnets 25, 29 and 37 – Sonnet 25 also refers to the stars, regarded as influencing fortune), and in *The Rape of Lucrece* Lucrece links 'the giddy round of Fortune's wheel' (line 952) with the changes brought about Time. In *Romeo and Juliet* the Prologue to Act I talks of Romeo and Juliet as being 'star-crossed', Juliet talks of Fortune as being 'fickle' (III.v.60), and Romeo sees himself as the victim of Fortune – he is 'Fortune's fool' (III.i.133), and in his final speech he feels sorry for Paris as having been, like himself, 'in sour misfortune's book' (V.iii.82): also in his final speech Romeo sees the death he is about to inflict upon himself as a liberation of his 'world-wearied flesh' from subjection to 'inauspicious stars' (V.iii.111–12). But *Romeo and Juliet* also assigns a major role to God or Heaven. Early on in the play Romeo has a premonition of his 'untimely death' as 'hanging in the stars' (I.iv.111,107), but he then goes on (I.iv.112–13):

> But He [God] that hath the steerage of my course
> Direct my sail!

This seems clearly to imply that the power of the stars over human life is subject to a greater power – the power of God. (I have already suggested that in *King John*, III.iv.119, the reference made to Fortune by the Papal legate Pandulph without any reference to the supreme power of God is indicative of Pandulph's worldliness.) In *Richard III* it is made clear that God intervenes to put an end to the evils of civil war and a tyrannical monarch, and in *Titus Andronicus* and *The Comedy of Errors* it is at least hinted that there is a positive response from above to Titus's plea (IV.iii.50-1) that 'heaven' should send down 'Justice' to earth, and to Antipholus of Syracuse's prayer (IV.iii.38-9) that 'Some blessed power' should bring relief from confusion. In *Romeo and Juliet* heaven's involvement does not take the form of coming to the aid of the two lovers. When Friar Lawrence is about to join the lovers in marriage he hopes that their marriage will be blessed by heaven ('So smile the heavens upon this holy act', II.vi.1). But when in the last scene the Friar finds Romeo dead he realises that his plan to reunite Romeo and Juliet has not received heavenly support (V.iii.153-4 – he is here addressing Juliet just before she takes her own life):

> A greater power than we can contradict
> Hath thwarted our intents.

It is the Prince who at the end of the play tells the heads of the Montague and Capulet families that the deaths of Romeo and Juliet as lovers have been heaven's means of resolving the hatred between the two families (V.ii.292-3):

> See what a scourge is laid upon your hate
> That heaven finds means to kill your joys [Romeo and Juliet] with love.

Capulet, now reconciled to Montague, acknowledges that Romeo and Juliet have been the 'Poor sacrifices of our enmity' (V.iii.303).

It may well seem to be cruelty on the part of heaven to allow the lives of Romeo and Juliet to be sacrificed. But there is the suggestion in this play that they are rewarded after their earthly deaths. Before Juliet's actual death Romeo's servant Balthasar, in reporting what at that time was believed to be her death, says to Romeo (V.i.17–19):

> she is well and nothing can be ill
> ... her immortal part with angels lives.

And Balthasar's report follows immediately after Romeo's description of a dream he has had in which after his death new life is breathed into him by Juliet (V.i.6–9).

RICHARD II (c. 1595)

In the *Henry VI* plays and *King John* Shakespeare showed that trouble arose out of doubts as to the legitimacy of the ruling king's claim to the throne, and Richard III was clearly an evil usurper. In *Richard II* there are no doubts about Richard's legitimacy as king, but he is shown to be evil enough to deserve to be deposed by his cousin Bolingbroke, who becomes Henry IV. The theme is the need for a king as the holder of a divinely appointed position in human society to live up to his responsibilities: he cannot expect divine protection if he betrays those responsibilities.

The play opens with charges of corruption brought before King Richard by Henry Bolingbroke, Duke of Hereford, against Thomas Mowbray, Duke of Norfolk: the most serious of these charges is that Mowbray was responsible for the murder of the Duke of Gloucester, uncle of both Richard and Bolingbroke. Mowbray rejects these charges, and Richard, having declared his determination to be 'impartial' (I.i.115) even though Bolingbroke is his cousin (he will not allow kinship to sway 'The unstooping firmness of my upright soul', I.i.121), announces that 'justice' (I.i.203) must be determined by a trial by combat to take place at a specified later date. Richard's presentation of himself in the first scene as a virtuous king is exposed as a sham in the second scene, where we learn that it was Richard himself who was responsible for Gloucester's death (Gloucester in this scene is referred to as Woodstock, since he was also known as Thomas of Woodstock): Bolingbroke's father, John of Gaunt and Duke of Lancaster, tells Gloucester's widow that it was Richard who 'caused his death'[50] (I.ii.39). (This revelation gives a fuller meaning to Mowbray's assertion in the first scene, I.i.132–4:

> For Gloucester's death,
> I slew him not, but to my own disgrace
> Neglected my sworn duty in that case.

Here Mowbray seems to be admitting that he was guilty of negligence when it was his 'duty' to protect Gloucester, but he may also have been privately reminding the King of the 'duty' the King sought to impose on him of murdering Gloucester. Gaunt's revelation would also suggest that in the first scene, where Gaunt actually presented his son Bolingbroke to the King, Bolingbroke already knew from his father of Richard's involvement in Gloucester's murder but at this stage wished to establish who carried out the murder.) In I.ii Gaunt is taunted by Gloucester's widow for making no effort to avenge Gloucester's death (Gloucester being Gaunt's own brother), but Gaunt says that such punishment should be left to heaven (I.ii.6–8):

> Put we our quarrel to the will of heaven,
> Who, when they [the heavenly powers] see the hours ripe on earth,
> Will rain hot vengeance on offenders' heads.

And he repeats this point: 'Let heaven revenge' (I.ii.40). In the third scene of the play all arrangements have been made for the combat between Bolingbroke and Mowbray to proceed when Richard suddenly stops the combat and sentences both combatants to banishment – from this action it may be inferred that Richard wishes to hush up his own responsibility for Gloucester's murder: he now makes no attempt to dispense the 'justice' he spoke of in the first scene (I.i.203). Soon after

Bolingbroke's banishment Gaunt is near the point of death, and before his death he makes the now famous speech that laments England's degeneration under Richard's rule: 'This royal throne of kings, this sceptered isle[51]...is now bound in with shame' (II.i.40–63). He accuses Richard to his face of Gloucester's murder – 'thou respect'st not [you care nothing about] spilling Edward's blood' (II.i.131 – he is referring to Gloucester as one of the sons of King Edward III), and in his last words Gaunt says Richard deserves to be cursed by shame for the rest of his life – life is to be enjoyed only by those who have love and honour (II.i.138): 'Love they to live that love and honour have.'

Immediately after being told that Gaunt is dead Richard announces his intention of seizing Gaunt's estates (which legally should pass to Bolingbroke) in order to pay the cost of crushing rebels in Ireland. He ignores the warning of the Duke of York, another of his uncles, that a vast number of his subjects will be alienated by this illegal act (II.i.201–6), and when the King is no longer present we hear from other nobles (II.i.246–61) that he has squandered money extorted from both commoners and nobles so that he has no money left for military purposes. Before leaving for Ireland Richard makes the Duke of York governor of England, but soon after Richard's departure Bolingbroke, in defiance of his sentence of banishment, arrives in England and nobles flock to his support. York is faced with a conflict of loyalties, since both Richard and Bolingbroke are his nephews and one is his king and the other has been wronged by that king (II.ii.111–15):

> Both are my kinsmen.
> The one is my sovereign, whom both my oath
> And duty bids defend. The other again,
> Is my kinsman, whom the King hath wronged,
> Whom conscience and my kindred bids to right.

(Incidentally, York is also in the know about Richard's responsibility for Gloucester's murder – York, feeling helpless in the situation in which he finds himself, wishes 'The King had cut my head off with my brother's', II.ii.102.) When he meets

Bolingbroke York first condemns him for 'braving arms against thy sovereign' (II.iii.112) but then yields to him.

On his return from Ireland Richard complacently assumes that because he has a divinely appointed role he will automatically receive divine protection (III.ii.54–7):

> Not all the water in the rough rude sea
> Can wash the balm off from an anointed king.
> The breath of worldly men cannot depose
> The deputy elected by the Lord.

He thus ignores the Bishop of Carlisle's insistence that he must take action by exercising his God-given power as king (III.ii.29–30):

> The means that heaven yields must be embraced
> And not neglected.

But after hearing that his army in Wales has gone over to Bolingbroke, and even before hearing that York and his army have also gone over to Bolingbroke, Richard lapses into defeatism and self-pity (III.ii.151 ff.):

> Our lands, our lives, and all are Bolingbroke's,
> And nothing can we call our own but death
>   ...let us sit upon the ground
> And tell sad stories of the death of kings...

The Bishop of Carlisle once again urges the need to take action (III.ii.178–9):

> My lord, wise men ne'er sit and wail their woes,
> But presently [immediately] prevent the ways to wail.

But when news comes of York's desertion Richard gives way to complete despair. And, though Bolingbroke's demands are limited to the repeal of his banishment and the handing over of his inheritance (III.iii.40–1,112–14), Richard talks right away of surrendering the crown to Bolingbroke (III.iii.145–8):

> What must the King do now? Must he submit?
> The King shall do it. Must he be deposed?
> The King shall be contented. Must he lose
> The name of king? A [In] God's name, let it go.

An appropriate comment on the way in which Richard has allowed his kingdom to go to waste is made by the gardener in York's garden where Richard's queen has been whiling away the time during Richard's absence – this gardener, having heard that Richard is now in Bolingbroke's power, observes (III.iv.55–66):

> O, what pity is it
> That he had not so trimmed and dressed his land
> As we this garden...
> Had he done so, himself had borne the crown,
> Which waste of idle hours hath quite thrown down.

Before Parliament in Westminster Bolingbroke seeks publicly to discover the facts about Gloucester's murder. He begins (IV.i.3–5) by asking Bagot, one of Richard's supporters, to state

> What thou dost know of noble Gloucester's death,
> Who wrought it with the King, and who performed
> The bloody office [work] of his timeless [untimely] end.

(We see here that Bolingbroke has no doubts about Richard's involvement.) Bagot names the Duke of Aumerle (who is York's son) as having been directly responsible for the murder, and this charge is upheld by Lord Fitzwater: Fitzwater heard Aumerle boast of having caused Gloucester's death (IV.i.36–7), and he also heard Mowbray say that Aumerle had sent two of his men to murder Gloucester (IV.i.80–2). At this point York enters to announce that Richard has 'with willing soul' yielded the throne to Bolingbroke (IV.i.108–10), and Bolingbroke, hailed by York as King Henry IV, decides to ascend the throne (IV.i.112–13). The Bishop of Carlisle immediately calls for resistance against the overthrow of 'noble Richard' (IV.i.119), God's 'captain, steward, deputy elect' (IV.i.126) – Carlisle's speech shows a courageous loyalty to his king, but the description of Richard as 'noble' is clearly unacceptable. York then fetches Richard who, after some dithering, presents Bolingbroke with the crown and sceptre, but he has the audacity to compare himself to Christ when betrayed by Judas (IV.i.170–1) and handed over by the Roman governor Pontius Pilate to be crucified (IV.i.240–1) – Pilate by washing his hands (IV.i.239) had sought to cast the blame for Christ's death onto the Jews who were clamouring for that death,[52] but, says Richard to the assembled Parliament, 'water cannot wash away your sin' (IV.i.242). When confronted with a list of his own crimes Richard's only answer is self-pity, and he subsides into self-pity for the rest of the play. God, York tells his wife in the last Act, has 'steeled/The hearts of men' against pitying Richard (V.ii.34–5), and we are surely meant to accept York's verdict on Richard's deposition (V.ii.37–9):

> heaven hath a hand in these events,
> To whose high will we bound our calm contents [we calmly confine our desires].
> To Bolingbroke are we sworn subjects now...[53]

Richard has thus been punished by heaven, as John of Gaunt (in I.ii) believed he should be.

As for Bolingbroke, he is certainly ruthless. Soon after his return to England he sent two of Richard's supporters, Bushy and Green, to be executed on the grounds that they had misled King Richard and had plundered the estates that Bolingbroke should have inherited (III.i.8–27), and in the last scene Bolingbroke as the new king applauds the killing of several leaders of a rebellion against him (V.vi.7–18). But he is shown to be capable of generosity. When he hears that Mowbray (whom he refers to as 'mine enemy', IV.i.88) is dead, he wishes Mowbray well in the hereafter ('Sweet peace conduct his sweet soul...', IV.i.103) – here Bolingbroke is probably bearing in mind that the charge he directed against Mowbray in I.i should, as it now appears, have been directed against Aumerle. Aumerle, who as well as being allegedly responsible for

Gloucester's murder has been involved in the rebellion against Bolingbroke as king, is actually pardoned by Bolingbroke (in V.iii) in response to an appeal made by Aumerle's mother, the Duchess of York, despite opposition from the Duke of York who says that his son does not deserve to be pardoned. (In this scene the Duchess refers to her son as Rutland since he had recently become Earl of Rutland after being demoted from the rank of duke, as the Duchess was told by her husband in V.ii.41–3). And the Bishop of Carlisle, who was also involved in the rebellion against Bolingbroke, is sentenced by Bolingbroke to no more than banishment since Bolingbroke has a high respect for the Bishop (V.vi.28–9):

> For, though mine enemy thou hast ever been,
> High sparks of honour in thee have I seen.

On Bolingbroke's conscience, however, is the murder of Richard (end of V.v) by Sir Pierce of Exton. Exton acted, not on any direct instructions by Bolingbroke, but after hearing Bolingbroke say (presumably in connection with the rebellion in support of Richard): 'Have I no friend will rid me of this living fear?' (V.iv.2). When at the end of the play Exton tells Bolingbroke that he has murdered Richard, Bolingbroke replies (V.vi.39–40):

> though I did wish him dead,
> I hate the murderer...

And he announces his intention to do penance by going on an expedition to the Holy Land (V.vi.49–50):

> I'll make a voyage to the Holy Land,
> To wash this blood off from my guilty hand.

The play shows that, at least in contrast with Richard, Bolingbroke as Richard's successor has much to commend him. The deposition of Richard did, as we know from the *Henry VI* plays, lead to trouble later, but it may be mentioned that the description of Richard as 'guiltless' in *2 Henry VI* IV.i.95, where a Yorkist supporter condemns the 'shameful murder of a guiltless king', can hardly have been regarded by Shakespeare as acceptable – in *Richard II* Shakespeare shows Richard to be anything but 'guiltless'.

A MIDSUMMER NIGHT'S DREAM (c. 1596)

A *Midsummer Night's Dream* is a comedy of errors, and, just as *The Comedy of Errors* was a representation of the confusions that beset human beings in earthly life, so *A Midsummer Night's Dream* is a representation of the confusions that beset true love between a man and a woman ('The course of true love never did run smooth', I.i.134) – with true love shown as finally triumphing, instead of being defeated as in *Romeo and Juliet*.

In the first scene we hear that Lysander and Hermia are in love with each other but that their desire to marry is opposed by Hermia's father, Egeus, who wants Hermia to marry Demetrius and invokes a traditional Athenian law whereby a daughter who fails to obey her father in this matter may be put to death (I.i.41–5). This law is upheld by Theseus, the Duke of Athens, and Lysander protests in vain that Demetrius is an 'inconstant man' (I.i.110 – 'inconstant' in the sense that Proteus was inconstant in *The Two Gentlemen of Verona*) in that he transferred his affections to Hermia after winning the wholly devoted love of Helena (Demetrius 'won her soul', I.i.108). Left alone with Hermia, Lysander asserts that according to all that he has read and heard 'The course of true love never did run smooth', and he cites various examples of obstacles set in the path of true love (I.i.135–42). Hermia agrees that such is the destiny of true lovers (I.i.150–1):

> If then true lovers have been ever [always] crossed,
> It stands as an edict in destiny.

When Lysander asks Hermia to meet him in a wood outside

Athens the following night with a view to marrying where Athenian law does not apply, Hermia swears by Cupid and by Venus (I.i.169,171) that she will do so: we note that here both Cupid and Venus are associated with general attraction between the sexes, as is Cupid for the most part in *Love's Labour's Lost*, rather than with physical desire or lust, as in Sonnet 154 and *Venus and Adonis*. But as a force that causes individuals to fall in love Cupid is himself a source of confusion, as Helena has reason to complain in a soliloquy at the end of the first scene, where she laments that Cupid caused Demetrius to fall in love with Hermia after he had pledged his devotion to Helena (I.i.240–5). In this soliloquy Helena also admits that her love for Demetrius is an example of love's blindness to the faults of the loved one – 'Love looks not with the eyes, but with the mind', a mind which, like that of Cupid, lacks 'judgment' (I.i.234–6). This is a kind of blindness which is meant to win our sympathy, the kind of blindness in love described in Sonnet 113.

A Midsummer Night's Dream is of course notable for the part played by fairies – the title refers to the belief that midsummer night was a time when spirits were especially active, even though the nocturnal events in the play occur during the night preceding May Day (see IV.i.129–30). The fairies in the play are an amalgam of folk lore, literary tradition and Shakespeare's own invention, but there seems to be at least a suggestion that these fairies are symbolic of supernatural forces at work in human life. In *The Comedy of Errors* (II.ii.188–91) the inhabitants of 'fairy land' were described as spirits that torment human beings, but the fairies in *A Midsummer Night's Dream*, though associated with destructive activities, are capable of being inspired by a desire to promote the cause of true love among mortals.

When the fairies make their first appearance – in the wood where Lysander and Hermia are to meet – we hear that Puck is a 'knavish sprite' (II.i.33) who plays ill-natured practical jokes, such as leading 'night wanderers' astray (II.i.39) and causing elderly women to fall when he appears to be a stool which they try to sit on (II.i.51–4). Oberon, king of the fairies, who is amused by Puck's heartless tricks (II.i.44 ff.), is engaged in a quarrel with Titania, his queen, over the possession of a changeling Indian boy, a quarrel which provokes severe disturbances in the physical world (widespread floods and confusion among the seasons) – as Titania says (II.i.115–16):

> this same progeny of evils comes
> From our debate, from our dissension.

In order to 'torment' Titania (II.i.147) Oberon sends Puck to fetch some magic juice which, when squeezed onto the eyes of a person who is asleep, makes that person when waking fall in love with the first living creature seen: Oberon hopes that Titania, after receiving this juice when she is asleep in the wood, will on waking fall in love with some animal there in the wood. But then Oberon becomes aware of Helena's plight when he sees and hears her being rejected by Demetrius (who has come to the wood in pursuit of Hermia and is himself pursued by Helena): Oberon's sympathy is aroused and he instructs Puck to put some of the magic juice on Demetrius's eyes at a time when Helena will be the first person he sees on waking from his sleep. When Puck mistakes Lysander for Demetrius and causes Lysander to fall in love with Helena instead of Hermia, Oberon shows his concern for the cause of true love by complaining to Puck of the result of his mistake – 'Some true love turned, and not a false turned true' (III.ii.91). Oberon himself, by applying the juice to the sleeping Demetrius, is able to achieve the desired aim of making Demetrius fall in love with Helena, and he makes Puck responsible for seeing that the juice is used to restore Lysander's love for Hermia. Oberon also declares his intention of becoming reconciled with Titania. He thus looks forward to a time when 'all things shall be peace' (III.ii.377), and he now regards himself as aligned with the forces of goodness – when Pucks talks of the need for all 'damnèd spirits' to depart before daylight (III.ii.382–7) Oberon insists that 'we are spirits of another sort'[54] (III.ii.388). As for Puck, although he admits to a malicious enjoyment of the confusion he has caused (he is pleased that things should 'befall preposterously' for the lovers, III.ii.121, and that 'jangling' breaks out amongst them, III.ii.352–3), he does finally enter into the spirit of Oberon's goodwill – as he squeezes the juice onto Lysander's eyes he talks happily of supplying the required 'remedy' to Lysander the 'Gentle lover' (III.ii.452), so that 'all shall be well' (end of III.ii – here he echoes Oberon's previous words, 'all things shall be peace'). Meanwhile Oberon has come to 'pity' (IV.i.44) Titania who has fallen in love with Bottom the weaver after an ass's head has been placed on him by Puck: Oberon applies juice to Titania's eyes to replace her love for Bottom as an ass with love for himself. Now he and Titania 'are new in amity' (IV.i.84), and on the following night they will bless Duke Theseus's palace where a wedding between Theseus and Hippolyta is shortly to be celebrated (IV.i.85–7) – this wedding was spoken of in the opening words of the play.

When Theseus discovers that there is now 'gentle concord' amongst the lovers (IV.i.140), he overrules Egeus's right to decide whom Hermia should marry ('Egeus, I will overbear your rule', IV.i.176). 'These couples shall eternally be knit' in marriage, says Theseus, at the same time as Hippolyta and himself (IV.i.177–8). But it is a limitation on Theseus's part that he is unwilling to take into account the operation of supernatural powers in human life. A strong hint that we should give credence to such powers comes out in Demetrius's remark as to how the return of his love for Helena came about (IV.i.161–2):

> I wot [know] not by what power,
> But by some power it is...

Theseus, in conversation with Hippolyta, dismisses the lovers' account of the night's happenings as 'fantasies...More than cool reason ever comprehends' (V.i.5–6). We are meant to be impressed by Hippolyta's reply (V.i.23–7) that the lovers' story

> More witnesseth than fancy's images
> And grows to something of great constancy [that is beyond doubt],
> But howsoever [nonetheless] strange and admirable [to be wondered at].

Theseus also takes too rational a view of love between the sexes. In his speech upholding 'cool reason' he regards both lovers and poets as having the some kind of 'imagination' as madmen (V.i.7–8):

The lunatic, the lover, and the poet
Are of imagination all compact [compounded].[55]

As a lover himself Theseus (who before he met Hippolyta was, according to Oberon, guilty of rape and desertion, though these allegations are stoutly rejected by Titania,[56] II.i.77–81) has no understanding of the kind of madness characteristic of true love in its early phase – the kind of madness that Helena confessed to (blindness and a lack of 'judgment') at the end of the first scene. (Clearly there is satirical irony in Lysander's belief that he is guided by reason when he finds himself in love with Helena instead of Hermia: 'reason says you are the worthier maid' he says to Helena, II.ii.116, and 'I had no judgment when to her [Hermia] I swore', III.ii.134. But of course Lysander's mental confusion here is due to the magic juice.) Another character in the play who dismisses love as being irrational is Bottom the weaver ('reason and love keep little company together nowadays', III.i.129+), and for the entertainment of Theseus and his bride, Bottom and his fellow workmen are preparing to put on a play that is quite unsuited to themselves as actors – a play about the tragic love of Pyramus and Thisbe. (In the story of Pyramus and Thisbe, which Shakespeare derived from Ovid's *Metamorphoses*, Bk. IV, the two lovers, like Lysander and Hermia, have to meet in secret because of parental opposition to their marrying, but Pyramus and Thisbe come to a tragic end, similar to that of Romeo and Juliet.) Bottom and company are absurdly insensitive to the plight of Pyramus and Thisbe – this play is described by Peter Quince, the director, as a 'lamentable comedy' (I.ii.10–11) and by Bottom as a 'merry' play (I.ii.l4–), 'a sweet comedy' (end of IV.ii). It is therefore ironic that Theseus, who ridicules the imagination of lovers and poets, should suggest that this farcical presentation by Bottom and company at least shows some 'imagination' (V.i.210–11) – Theseus seems to have in mind such stage effects as the wall that separates Pyramus and Thisbe being represented by an actor. Theseus's attribution of imagination to these actors is promptly refuted by Hippolyta.

Unlike the love of Pyramus and Thisbe, which ended in death instead of marriage, love in *A Midsummer Night's Dream* ends with the happy anticipation of the marriages of Theseus and Hippolyta and the other two couples, and we are assured that, following the blessings given by the fairies, true love will be the lasting foundation of all three marriages (V.i.396–7):

> So shall all the couples three
> Ever true in loving be.

THE MERCHANT OF VENICE (c. 1596)

The Merchant of Venice, like *Romeo and Juliet*, is concerned with love and hate, but it presents not so much a conflict between love and hate as a contrast between them. In *The Merchant of Venice* love includes friendship as well as love between the sexes, and, whereas in *Romeo and Juliet* there was hate between two families and their supporters, in *The Merchant of Venice* hate is concentrated in one person: Shylock.

In the first scene the prevailing atmosphere is one of love between friends. The Venetian merchant Antonio is in a melancholy mood and the laughter-loving Gratiano speaks as a friend in appealing to Antonio to be light-hearted (I.i.86–101):

> I tell thee what, Antonio –
> I love thee, and 'tis my love that speaks –
> ...fish not with this melancholy bait...

And then Antonio's friend Bassanio expresses his gratitude to Antonio for the love he has shown Bassanio in helping him financially (I.i.130–1):

> To you, Antonio,
> I owe the most, in money and in love.

But, in contrast to these professions of love, in I.iii Shylock, the Jewish moneylender, says of Antonio in an aside (I.iii.37–9):

> I hate him for he is a Christian,
> But more for that in low simplicity [shameful folly]
> He lends out money gratis...

Since Bassanio needs money to compete against rival suitors of Portia in Belmont (I.i.168–76) and all Antonio's wealth is at present locked up in his merchant ships at sea, Antonio is prepared for Bassanio's sake to borrow money from Shylock. Antonio freely admits his contempt for Shylock as a usurer (it must be remembered that usury, condemned by the Church in the Middle Ages, continued to be offensive to Christians in Shakespeare's time), and he makes it clear that any loan from Shylock is to be regarded as a hard business deal (I.iii.127–30):

> If thou wilt lend this money, lend it not
> As to thy friends...
> But lend it rather to thine enemy...

But then to Antonio's surprise Shylock offers to lend him the money without charging interest, for, says Shylock, 'I would be friends with you and have your love' (I.iii.133). Such talk we know to be hypocrisy in view of the hatred Shylock expressed previously in his aside, but Antonio, being kind himself, believes that Shylock's offer is an act of genuine kindness ('there is much kindness in the Jew', I.iii.148), so that he is not deterred from entering into what Shylock calls 'a merry sport' (I.iii.140) by signing an agreement whereby, if the money is not repaid by a certain date, Shylock can cut off a pound of Antonio's flesh. It seems that Shylock is well aware that Antonio may not be able to repay the money by the agreed date – in conversation with Bassanio about the loan Shylock poses as being generous in offering a loan at all since Antonio's ships are exposed to piracy and to 'the peril of waters, winds and rocks' (I.iii.25–).

Shylock's lack of love and kindness is shown in his own home. His servant Launcelot Gobbo complains 'I am famished in his service' (II.ii.93+), yet Shylock thinks that Launcelot has too much to eat – he is 'a huge feeder' (II.v.45): Shylock willingly parts with Launcelot who becomes a servant to Bassanio (II.ii.131–5, II.v.48–50). And Shylock's own daughter, Jessica, says 'Our house is hell' (II.iii.2), and she escapes in order to marry Bassanio's friend Lorenzo, taking with her some money and jewellery. Jessica's departure causes great distress to Shylock, his distress being due not to the loss of his daughter but to the loss of the ducats and jewellery – 'My daughter! O my ducats!...And jewels – two stones, two rich and precious stones' (II.viii.15–20). And later he says (III.i.71+) he would be glad if Jessica were dead, so that he might recover the jewels from her person and the ducats from her coffin ('I would my daughter were dead at my foot and the jewels in her ear! Would she were hearsed at my foot and the ducats in her coffin!').

As regards love between the sexes in the play, the love between Lorenzo and Jessica receives only brief treatment as an example of true love. Lorenzo is in no doubt that Jessica is 'wise, fair and true' (II.vi.56) and she has won his constancy ('And therefore...Shall she be placèd in my constant soul', II.vi.56–7). Much more detailed treatment is given to the love between Bassanio and Portia. As a suitor Bassanio has to face a test devised by Portia's late father. In the second scene of the play (I.ii.23+) Nerissa, Portia's waiting-woman, observes that 'holy men' such as Portia's father 'at their death have good inspirations', and she recalls that Portia is required by her father's will to marry the first suitor to make the right choice between three caskets, one of gold, one of silver, and one of lead: it is to be confidently assumed that the right choice will be made by 'one who you [Portia] shall rightly love'. Wrong choices are made by suitors in II.vii and II.ix – the Prince of Morocco chooses the gold casket, and the Prince of Aragon the silver one. When Bassanio comes to make his choice in III.ii Portia frankly tells him that she loves him ('One half of me is yours, the other half yours', III.ii.16) but that she must abide by the rules and cannot tell him which casket to choose. She does, however, provide a hint in the form of a song that is sung while Bassanio is deliberating – the words of the song warn that 'fancy', here meaning love between the sexes, will die if it is concerned only with what is outwardly attractive to the 'eyes' (III.ii.63–9). Consciously or subconsciously influenced by the song, Bassanio dismisses gold as 'gaudy' and silver as a metal used merely as coinage (III.ii.101 and 103–4), and so chooses the lead casket, which is the correct choice since there is a picture of Portia inside it. The inscriptions on all three caskets were read out by the suitor in the first casket scene (II.vii), and the inscription on the lead casket was one calling for complete dedication – 'Who chooseth me must give and hazard all he hath' (II.vii.10). As soon as Bassanio has made the right choice Portia pledges her own dedication – she tells Bassanio (III.ii.164–6) that her 'gentle spirit'

> Commits itself to yours to be directed
> As from her lord, her govenor, her king.

(Portia thus echoes Katherina's words in the final scene of *The Taming of the Shrew*, V.ii.155–6: 'Such duty as the subject owes the prince,/Even such a woman oweth to her husband.')

Just after Bassanio has chosen the right casket he receives a letter from Antonio saying that all his ships have miscarried (III.ii.315+). It is in the previous scene (III.i) that we first hear of Antonio's loss of ships. After a report that Antonio has lost one ship Shylock is asked what use Antonio's flesh would be to him should Antonio default on the repayment of the loan: his reply is that 'it will feed my revenge' (III.i.44+). He then, because of Antonio's denunciation of him as a usurer, gives vent at some length to self-pity, presenting himself as the persecuted Jew – 'Hath not a Jew eyes? Hath not a Jew hands, organs, dimensions, senses, affections, passions...?' (III.i.44+). We see therefore that all this self-pity is linked to a thirst for revenge and that Shylock's self-pity, like that of Shakespeare's Richard II, goes with an obliviousness of any wrongdoing on his own part. On hearing of the loss of another of Antonio's ships Shylock positively gloats – 'I thank God!...Good news, good news! Ha, ha!' (III.i.88–92). And when it is clear that Antonio will not be able to repay the loan Shylock wastes no time in claiming his pound of flesh. In the Venetian court of justice the Duke fails to persuade Shylock to show 'mercy', to be 'touched with human gentleness and love', to take 'pity' on Antonio (IV.i.20,25,27): Shylock is determined to pursue his case because of 'a lodged hate and a certain loathing I bear Antonio' (IV.i.60–1). (Shylock, who is so full of self-pity, is pitiless to others.) But the law is turned against Shylock by Portia, who arrives disguised as a male lawyer (having been briefed by a real lawyer on the details of the case). Shylock soon abandons his claim for a pound of flesh when told by Portia that he will be put to death if he takes more than an exact pound, and he is then told that he faces a death sentence for conspiring against the life of a Venetian citizen. The death sentence, which is at the Duke's discretion, is immediately waived by the Duke, who tells Shylock (IV.i.363–4):

> That thou shalt see the difference of our spirit,
> I pardon thee thy life before thou ask it.

This pardon refutes Shylock's earlier assertion (III.i.62–) that a Christian desires revenge against a Jew just as much as a Jew does against a Christian, that in fact the Jew has been taught revenge by the Christian ('The villainy you teach me I will execute'). And, though for his offence Shylock is liable to have his whole estate confiscated, he is allowed to keep half of it on condition that on his death all that he possesses passes to his daughter and her husband Lorenzo, and on condition also that he becomes a Christian.

The last scene of the play (V.i) begins with love as associated with moonlight and music. While Portia has been away in Venice Lorenzo and Jessica have been staying in her house in Belmont, and music is now about to be played by Portia's musicians to greet her return in the late evening. Lorenzo says to Jessica (V.i.54–6):

> How sweet the moonlight sleeps upon this bank.
> Here will we sit and let the sounds of music
> Creep in our ears.

Then, looking up at the night sky, Lorenzo goes on (V.i.60–5):

> There's not the smallest orb which thou behold'st
> But in his [its] motion like an angel sings,
> Still quiring [singing with the other orbs] to the young-eyed cherubins.
> Such harmony is in immortal souls,
> But whilst this muddy vesture of decay [the body]
> Doth grossly close it in [smother the harmony] we cannot hear it.[57]

And a few lines later Lorenzo observes (V.i.83–5):

> The man that hath no music in himself,
> Nor is not moved with concord of sweet sounds,
> Is fit for treasons, stratagems and spoils [acts of plunder].[58]

Thus music is seen to represent purity of soul, and it is to music that Lorenzo and Jessica as lovers are especially responsive. The reference to an inability to respond to music as being a sign of villainy seems to point to Shylock in particular – early on in the play he had scornfully dismissed 'the vile squealing' (II.v.29) of the fife (a kind of flute) enjoyed by revellers, and in the trial scene he talked with apparent approval of men who detest 'the bagpipe' (IV.i.49–50).

The play ends light-heartedly. In the casket scene Bassanio, after winning Portia as his wife, learnt that Gratiano (who had accompanied Bassanio to Belmont) had won the love of Portia's waiting-woman Nerissa (III.ii.193–209), and at the end of the trial scene Portia and Nerissa, disguised as lawyer and lawyer's clerk, had insisted that as a reward for the successful verdict against Shylock Bassanio and Gratiano should part with the rings that Portia and Nerissa had given them after the two couples were married in Belmont. In the last scene of the play Portia and Nerissa, now back in Belmont, profess to be shocked at the two men's unfaithfulness in parting with the rings. Portia and Nerissa then produce the rings, saying that they obtained them by sleeping with the lawyer and the lawyer's clerk respectively (V.i.258–62) – whereupon Portia reveals that she and Nerissa were in fact the lawyer and the clerk. Shakespeare thus shows that true love can go hand in hand with non-puritanical jokes.

Finally, there is one aspect of this play that cannot be ignored: its anti-Jewish bias, a bias which (though attempts have been made to argue that Shakespeare presents Shylock sympathetically) Shakespeare seems clearly to have shared with his contemporaries. This bias was mainly on account of the Jewish practice of usury and the fact that a Jew was a non-Christian. In I.iii Shylock complains that Antonio has shown contempt for him as a usurer to the point of calling him a 'cut-throat dog' and also spitting on him (I.iii.106–22). Antonio, far from being ashamed of his behaviour, says (I.iii.125–6):

I am as like to call thee so again,
To spit on thee again, to spurn thee too.

(This from the character in a play of whom it is said 'A kinder gentleman treads not the earth', II.viii.35.) It is true that when Shylock says he will lend Antonio money without charging interest Antonio is prepared to believe that Shylock is capable of kindness, but he seems to assume that kindness is a Christian virtue, not a Jewish one – 'The Hebrew will turn Christian: he grows kind' (I.iii.173). Later in the play Lorenzo refers to Shylock as 'a faithless Jew' (II.iv.37), meaning that because a Jew is not a Christian he cannot be regarded as having a faith, and Launcelot Gobbo tells Jessica she is 'damned' because she is the daughter of Jewish parents (III.v.1–15) – from such damnation she trusts she will be 'saved' because she has been converted to Christianity by Lorenzo (III.v.15+). (Launcelot Gobbo then makes a crude anti-Semitic joke about the price of pork being raised if too many Jews convert to Christianity and so take to eating pork, III.v.22–.) And in the trial scene, though Shylock's life is spared and he is allowed to keep half his estate, he is forced to become a Christian (IV.i.381–2). For the modern liberal-minded student of Shakespeare this anti-Jewish bias must inevitably mar a play which otherwise excels in its vividly presented contrast between love and hate.

The First Part of Henry IV (c. 1596)

Some years after the appearance of the tetralogy that consisted of the *Henry VI* in three Parts and *Richard III* Shakespeare went on to compose a second tetralogy by following up *Richard II* with *Henry IV* in two Parts and then *Henry V*. King Henry IV, having replaced Richard II on the throne, is fully engaged in promoting order, and the main theme in both Parts of *Henry IV* is the struggle of order against disorder. In *1 Henry IV* King Henry has to contend with a rebellion led by three members of the Percy family – the Earl of Northumberland, Northumberland's brother the Earl of Worcester, and Northumberland's son Henry Hotspur, men who had formerly helped to put Henry on the throne. The King is also faced with the problem of the apparently dissolute behaviour of his son, Prince Henry, who by the end of the play, however, has shown himself to be a worthy heir to the throne.

In the opening speech of the play the King refers to his intention (announced at the end of *Richard II* as penance for the murder of Richard) of taking English soldiers to fight against pagans in the Holy Land, but this expedition has to be set aside because of news that an English army sent to crush a Welsh rebellion has been massacred by the Welsh, and also because Hotspur, the 'Young Harry Percy' (I.i.53), after defeating a Scottish army, is refusing to hand over his Scottish prisoners to the King. In the first part of I.iii we hear that Hotspur is refusing to hand over the prisoners until the King ransoms Hotspur's brother-in-law, Mortimer, Earl of March, who led the English army against the Welsh and who, Hotspur believes, was taken prisoner, though the King claims that Mortimer treacherously joined the Welsh and married the daughter of the Welsh leader, Owen Glendower. (It becomes clear from a later scene, III.i, in which Glendower's daughter appears as Mortimer's wife, that the King's information is correct.) Hotspur, in a rage against the King, is easily persuaded to join a rebellion planned by his uncle the Earl of Worcester after being told (I.iii.145–57) that Mortimer was proclaimed heir to the crown by Richard II. Hotspur's father, Northumberland, who previously helped to overthrow Richard, now hypocritically professes to be penitent for having wronged him ('Whose wrongs in us [the wrongs done to him by us] God pardon', I.iii.149). For Hotspur this proposed rebellion is a matter of 'honour', to be upheld whatever the danger (I.iii.195–6):

> Send danger from the east unto the west,
> So honour cross it from the north to south...

Hotspur is genuinely a man of honour who, however, is carried away by blind passion and so is easily manipulated by his less than honourable uncle and father. According to Worcester's plan Hotspur is to join forces with the Scots led by the Earl of Douglas, while Worcester himself arranges a link-up with the Welsh under Glendower. Later an agreement is reached between the rebel leaders and Glendower and Mortimer (III.i.70–9), whereby Wales is to be left to Glendower and England is to be made over to Mortimer, except for the north which is to be allotted to the Percy family. (Mortimer would thus become king, but of a truncated England.)

As regards Prince Henry, the King (who had already in *Richard II* V.iii.7 deplored his son's association with 'unrestrained loose companions') says regretfully that, whereas Hotspur is 'the theme of honour's tongue' (I.i.81), he sees 'riot and dishonour stain the brow/Of my young Harry' (I.i.85–6). The second scene of the play begins with a bantering exchange between the Prince and the disreputable Sir John Falstaff, and there is humorous dramatic irony in Falstaff's description of himself and his companions as 'men of good government', a description based on the absurd argument that, since they carry out robberies by moonlight, they are 'governed' by the moon, presided over by Diana, goddess of chastity (I.ii.28–). Falstaff's contempt for the law comes out more clearly when he expresses the hope that the Prince, when he becomes king, will dispense with 'the rusty curb' of the law (I.ii.60–). Later in this scene the Prince is persuaded by his friend Poins to take part in a robbery with Falstaff and the others, the idea being that after the robbery the Prince and Poins should then appear in disguise and rob the robbers – as Poins says (I.ii.183–): 'The virtue of this jest will be the incomprehensible lies that this same fat rogue will tell us when we meet at supper: how thirty at least he fought with ... and in the reproof [refutation] of this lies the jest.' In II.ii Falstaff and his men carry out their robbery of some travellers, and as the disguised Prince and Poins are about to go into action the Prince talks enthusiastically about the trick they are going to play on Falstaff as being 'laughter for a month and a good jest for ever' (II.ii.92–). Later the Prince shows the same kind of enthusiasm in the tavern in Eastcheap, London, when he says to Poins, just before Falstaff and the others arrive, 'Shall we be merry?' (II.iv.85), to which Poins replies 'As merry as crickets, my lad.' Fun is had by all as Falstaff tells 'the incomprehensible lies' that Poins had predicted and the Prince and Poins are able to expose these lies (about how many men Falstaff had fought with before giving up the stolen money, when actually he was too scared to fight even the two disguised attackers): when his lies are exposed Falstaff shows no offence – he merely pretends he knew who his attackers were all the time. The Prince and Falstaff then play the fool by enacting a mock interview between the Prince and the King (the Prince has been summoned to appear before his father the following morning), in the course of which Falstaff, when denounced by the Prince acting the part of the King, defends himself by claiming that 'to be old and merry' surely cannot be regarded as 'a sin' (II.iv.449 +). This long tavern scene is brought to a close with the Prince saying that the money stolen frown the travellers will be paid back again, 'with advantage [interest]' (II.iv.530–). We see that in these comic scenes Falstaff is presented sympathetically in so far as he is the embodiment of merriment – in this respect he is akin to Gratiano in *The Merchant of Venice* who says (I.i.78–9): 'Let me play the fool./With mirth and laughter let old wrinkles come.' And the Prince himself is presented sympathetically as one who is able to enter into the spirit of merriment. But the Prince does have a sense of moral responsibility. In a soliloquy at the end of I.ii he makes it clear to the audience that he intends to reform. And, when in his actual interview with the King in III.ii the King tells him of the rebellion that is afoot and talks enviously of Hotspur, the Prince promises (III.ii.144–6):

> the time will come
> That I shall make this northern youth exchange
> His glorious deeds for my indignities.

For most of the last two Acts the play is set near Shrewsbury, where the battle is fought between the King and the rebels. A setback for Hotspur, as a fervent believer in the rebel cause, is that his own father, Northumberland, and the Welsh leader Glendower fail to arrive (IV.i): thus we see that Hotspur's faith in the reliability of his associates is unfounded – earlier in the play (II.iii.32–) Hotspur was warned in an anonymous letter that his 'friends' in the plot were 'uncertain', but he was convinced that these friends were 'true and constant'. Hotspur hears from a royal messenger (Sir Walter Blunt) that if the rebels submit their grievances to the King he will do his best to settle these grievances and the rebel leaders and their supporters will be pardoned (IV.iii.41–51). Hotspur sends Worcester to discuss this offer with the King, but Worcester is determined to suppress what he himself privately admits to be a 'liberal and kind offer' (V.ii.2): on his return he tells Hotspur that the King intends to fight (V.ii.31). (We may assume that Worcester has in fact no justifiable grievances but merely wants control of territory. We also note that Hotspur is commander of the rebel troops in the field but that he is really used as a front to Worcester's unscrupulous purposes.)

The Prince acquits himself admirably at Shrewsbury. Before the battle starts he suggests that to save lives the battle should be decided by single combat between himself and Hotspur (V.i.96–100), but the King refuses this offer ('considerations infinite/Do make against it', V.i.102–3). In the actual battle the Prince comes to the aid of his father when he is under attack from the Scottish leader Douglas, whereupon the King pronounces in gratitude 'Thou hast redeemed thy lost opinion' (V.iv.48). The Prince then comes face to face with Hotspur and delivers a fatal wound. In contrast to the Prince Falstaff, not surprisingly, disgraces himself. The Prince, after promising to serve the King, acted irresponsibly in one respect in that he obtained for Falstaff a command of foot soldiers ('a charge of foot', III.iii.185). Having been given the power to pressgang recruits, Falstaff took bribes from those able to buy their way out and so ended up with a collection of riff-raff (IV.ii.9 +). On the battlefield Falstaff's concern is to keep out of danger (for him staying alive is more important than getting killed for the sake of 'honour', V.i.125 + , V.iii.50 +), and when attacked by Douglas he immediately shams death. But then, seeing Hotspur dead on the ground, he lifts the dead Hotspur onto his back and claims that he, not the Prince, killed Hotspur. The Prince shows his modesty by not denying Falstaff's claim (V.iv.156–7):

For my part, if a lie may do thee grace,
I'll gild it with the happiest terms I have.

In the course of the play the Prince, of whom his father formerly despaired as standing in shameful contrast to Hotspur, has emerged as no less honourable than Hotspur, while at the same time possessing a fuller, more balanced, personality.

By the end of V.iv the battle has been won by the King's forces, and in the last scene (V.v) Worcester is led off to be executed, though at the Prince's request Douglas, deemed to be an honourable fighter, is pardoned. In the final speech of the play the King talks of the action that needs to be taken against other rebel leaders: Northumberland, one Scroop (Archbishop of York, who was also brought into the rebellion – see I.iii.264–71 and the brief scene IV.iv), and Glendower and Mortimer in Wales. The King is confident that political order will be fully established after another victory such as the one at Shrewsbury (V.v.41–2):

Rebellion in this land shall lose his [its] sway,
Meeting the check of such another day.

The reference in this final speech to the work still to be done points forward to the second Part of *Henry IV*.

THE MERRY WIVES OF WINDSOR (c. 1597)

The Merry Wives of Windsor, written, according to tradition, to meet Queen Elizabeth's request for a play about Falstaff in love, is a farce in which Falstaff attempts to seduce two wives in Windsor, Mistress Ford and Mistress Page. In this play Falstaff and his associates are transferred from the London setting to which they belong in both Parts of *Henry IV*, and Mistress Quickly, hostess of the tavern in Eastcheap in the two *Henry IV* plays, is transformed into the servant of Doctor Caius in Windsor. *The Merry Wives* shows Falstaff as being the victim of lust rather than being in love, but the play is concerned not only with Falstaff but also with three suitors of the young Anne Page, and the theme of the play as a whole is true love in contrast with Falstaff's lust and with human failings connected with marriage.

Ford and Page are two well-to-do Windsor gentlemen, and in I.iii Falstaff announces to his attendants Nym and Pistol 'I do mean to make love to Ford's wife', who, he claims, has given him 'the leer of invitation' (I.iii.37+), and he also claims that similar encouragement has been given him by Page's wife (I.iii.54+). For Falstaff a further source of interest is that each wife has a free use of her husband's purse (I.iii.50–,61+). Falstaff has accordingly written a love letter to each of these ladies, and he instructs Pistol and Nym to deliver his letters. When both Pistol and Nym refuse to do so Falstaff, who needs to reduce his expenses, dismisses them from his service: in revenge the two men vow to inform the two husbands of Falstaff's intentions. In II.i the two wives, who are close friends, discover that Falstaff has sent identical love letters. (In each letter Falstaff describes the lady as 'merry' like himself – according to what is said later, in IV.ii.91, it seems that it was the ladies' merriness that Falstaff misinterpreted as amorous feeling towards him). Mistress Ford, referring to Falstaff's 'love' as 'lust', says (II.i.60–): 'I think the best way were to entertain him with hope, till the wicked fire of lust have melted him in his own grease.' The ladies themselves are faithful wives. Mistress Ford says of any proposed plot against Falstaff 'I will consent to act any villainy against him that may not sully the chariness of [our strict regard for] our honesty' (II.i.86–8), though unfortunately her husband is given to 'jealousy' (II.i.89), whereas Mistress Page can say of her husband 'he's as far from jealousy as I am from giving him cause' (II.i.91–2). After Pistol and Nym have informed the two husbands of Falstaff's designs Ford is in fact so jealous (i.e. suspicious) that in order to put his wife to the test he actually encourages Falstaff to try to seduce her – in II.ii he appears in disguise before Falstaff as a man called 'Brook' who says that he himself wants to seduce Mistress Ford but would like Falstaff to prepare the way! In a soliloquy at the end of II.i Ford contemptuously describes Page as 'a secure fool' (i.e. a fool because of his complete confidence in his wife, II.i.207+), and similarly at the end of II.ii he says (II.ii.255+): 'Page is an ass, a secure ass – he will trust his wife, he will not be jealous.'

As regards the suitors of Page's daughter Anne, the first to be introduced to us appears in the first scene of the play – young Slender, 'cousin' (I.i.6) of Shallow, Justice of the Peace ('cousin' means kinsman, and we hear later, in III.iv.38–41, that Shallow is Slender's uncle). Anne Page is recommended to Slender as a wife purely for the sake of her money (she has been left £700 by her grandfather, quite apart from any provision by her father). A second suitor is introduced in I.iv: Dr Caius, an egoistic Frenchman who is determined to have Anne as his wife ('I will myself have Anne Page', I.iv.107–8) and will tolerate no opposition – when he hears that Slender is supported as a suitor by a Welsh parson, Hugh Evans, he immediately decides to challenge the parson to a duel (this challenge is later, in III.i, defused). The third suitor is Fenton, who has been rejected by Anne's father and admits that he had at first wooed Anne because of her father's wealth (III.iv.13–14). But he has now come to experience true love (III.iv.15–18):

> Yet, wooing thee, I found thee of more value
> Than stamps in gold [gold coins] or sums in sealèd bags,
> And 'tis the very riches of thyself
> That now I aim at.

(Fenton has thus undergone the same moral conversion as Petruchio in *The Taming of the Shrew*, whose motive for marriage changed from money to love. Incidentally, Fenton's true love is partly indicated by his speaking in verse in a play where most of the dialogue is in prose.) And in this scene (III.iv) in which Fenton first appears with Anne it is clear that Fenton is Anne's own choice as a husband, though her father supports Slender and her mother favours Caius (that her mother favours Caius is emphasised in a soliloquy at the end of IV.iv).

Falstaff receives an invitation to visit Mistress Ford on two occasions, on both of which he is subjected to indignities when her jealous husband is sighted as being on his way to enter the house. On the first of these occasions (III.iii) Falstaff is hidden in a laundry basket containing dirty clothes and is later (as we hear in III.v) tipped into the River Thames, and on the second occasion (IV.ii) he is escorted out of the house disguised as an old woman known to be a fortune-teller but regarded by Ford as a witch, with the result that Falstaff receives a beating from Ford. The two wives have worked together on these occasions, and Mistress Page is of the opinion that Falstaff deserves all he gets for assuming that because they are merry wives they are therefore adulterous – 'Wives may be merry and yet honest too' (IV.ii.91). The wives agree that the time has come to tell their husbands how they have treated Falstaff, and after they have done so Ford apologises for his jealousy and swears that henceforth he will trust his wife completely – for him now her 'honour' is 'As firm as faith' (IV.iv.8–10). The husbands are taken fully into the confidence of the wives in their plan for a third trick to be played on Falstaff – he is to be persuaded to meet the two women at midnight in Windsor Park, where he is to appear disguised as Herne the Hunter, a local ghost, and where, just after meeting the wives, he will be set upon by Anne Page and various children, all disguised as fairies (malicious ones), who will torment Falstaff by pinching him.

Other operations are planned (IV.vi.19–47) to proceed under cover of the trick against Falstaff – Anne's father has arranged for Anne to be carried off by Slender and be married to him, and her mother has arranged for the same to be done by

Caius, but Anne, though she has led her father and mother to believe that she will fall in with each of their plans, has in fact arranged to steal away with Fenton. After the tormenting of Falstaff, which is accompanied by a song sung by the 'fairies' that condemns 'lust' (V.v.92–3), all is revealed to him, and he at last seems to have learnt his lesson (V.v.339–40): 'This is enough to be the decay of lust and late-walking through [throughout] the realm.' And the play ends on a note of happy reconciliation as regards Anne and Fenton. When Fenton announces that he and Anne are now married ('now so sure [firmly united] that nothing can dissolve us', V.v.211), Anne's father and mother accept the situation, and they both express warm feeling towards Fenton – 'Fenton, heaven give thee joy!', 'Master Fenton,/Heaven give you many, many merry days!' (V.v.223, 226–7).

THE SECOND PART OF HENRY IV (c. 1598)

In the second Part of *Henry IV*, as in the first, the main theme is the struggle of order against disorder, but, whereas the disorder in the first Part was primarily political, in this second Part there is much more emphasis on moral disorder, or moral corruption. The main political rebel leader to be dealt with is Scroop, the Archbishop of York (who appeared only in a brief scene, IV.iv, in *1 Henry IV*) – as regards the other two rebel leaders still at large at the beginning of *2 Henry IV*, the Earl of Northumberland puts up no active resistance, and the Welsh leader Glendower fades out of the picture with the report of his death in III.i.102–3. In this play moral corruption is found on the King's side: the leaders of the army sent to defeat the Archbishop succeed by employing treacherous tactics, in contrast to the Archbishop himself, who is an honourable man (and not the dupe of dishonourable rebels as Hotspur was in *1 Henry IV*). And, whereas moral disorder as portrayed in Falstaff in *1 Henry IV* was at least partly redeemed by his merriment, in *2 Henry IV* the dominant impression we are given of him is his moral depravity. At the end of the play the ascent to the throne of the reformed Prince Henry as King Henry V points the way forward to the triumph of order – though as regards the reform of the Prince there is an inconsistency with *1 Henry IV* in that in *2 Henry IV* the Prince's reform and his reconciliation with his dying father occur without any acknowledgement of the reform and reconciliation that had already occurred by the end of *1 Henry IV*.

2 Henry IV begins with an 'Induction' in which Rumour personified tells us that false reports have been received by the Earl of Northumberland in his castle about his son Hotspur having been victorious against the King's forces in the battle at Shrewsbury: we also hear that the sickness given in *1 Henry IV* as Northumberland's reason for failing to join the rebels at Shrewsbury was feigned – he was (and still is) 'crafty-sick' (Induction, line 37). In the first scene of the play Northumberland receives news of what actually happened at Shrewsbury and learns that Hotspur is dead. There is satirical irony in the report that 'noble Worcester' (I.i.125) was taken prisoner (we know from *1 Henry IV* that Worcester was the evil mastermind behind the rebellion in that play), and there is satirical irony too when Northumberland puts on an act of being so enraged by Hotspur's death that he finds his sickness overcome by a renewed vitality (I.i.137–52). His rage takes the form of a passionate desire to ally himself with the destructive forces in the world, and the theme of the play is underlined when he proclaims (I.i.154): 'Let order die!' On being told that an army has now been mustered against the King by the 'gentle' (I.i.189) Archbishop of York, a man generally regarded as 'sincere and holy in his thoughts' (I.i.202), Northumberland immediately talks of organising support for the Archbishop. But in I.iii, where the Archbishop himself is discussing the situation, doubts are cast on Northumberland's reliability, and the decision is made to fight without counting on his support. Satire occurs once again when in II.iii Northumberland tells his wife and his daughter-in law (Hotspur's widow) that he cannot risk the loss of his 'honour' by staying away from the fighting ('my honour is at pawn', II.iii.7), and such posturing provokes a long outburst from Lady Percy (Hotspur's widow) in praise of Hotpur's true 'honour'. At the end of this scene Northumberland decides to retire to Scotland rather than join forces with the Archbishop, and he thus remains the dishonourable rebel that he was in *1 Henry IV*.

Falstaff appears in the second scene of the play and is immediately associated with 'diseases' (I.ii.5) – 'diseases' abound in Falstaff according to a doctor who has examined his urine. In this scene Falstaff encounters the Lord Chief Justice, who becomes important in the play as the representative of law and order. Falstaff evades the issue of his having ignored a summons to appear before the Lord Chief Justice for questioning about previous misconduct, but the Lord Chief Justice does not pursue this matter since he has heard that Falstaff is to depart with the troops to be led by Prince John, Prince Henry's younger brother, against the Archbishop of York. In II.iv the prostitute Doll Tearsheet arrives at the tavern in Eastcheap to minister to Falstaff's needs, and she is identified as a principal source of Falstaff's 'diseases' ('you help to make the diseases, Doll – we catch of you', II.iv.46–). In IV.ii of *1 Henry IV* Falstaff described how he abused his power to pressgang soldiers, and in III.ii of *2 Henry IV* we see him doing this, on this occasion selecting recruits from men provided by two country Justices of the Peace, Shallow and Silence. (Shallow appears in *The Merry Wives of Windsor* in different circumstances.) In contrast to the Lord Chief Justice Shallow and Silence are absurdly inadequate administrators of the law. Shallow and Falstaff had known one another in their earlier years, before Falstaff had acquired his knighthood. Now Shallow ingratiates himself with 'Sir John' and laughs heartily at Falstaff's heartless jokes about the men presented to him ('Ha, ha, ha! Most excellent, i' faith!', III.ii.107). Shallow is momentarily surprised when Falstaff does not select the two fittest men (the reason being that these men have paid bribes to be passed over), but Shallow shows little concern and is effusive in his good wishes when Falstaff leaves ('Sir John, the Lord bless you! God prosper your affairs!', III.ii.283+).

The King does not appear in the play until III.i, where by now he is a sick man. In soliloquy he laments the lack of sleep caused by kingly responsibilities ('Uneasy lies the head that wears a crown', III.i.31), and he also laments the state of the country – he says to two of his noblemen (III.i.38–40):

> you perceive the body of our kingdom,
> How foul it is, what rank diseases grow,
> And with what danger, near the heart of it.

It is in Yorkshire that the rebels are encountered by Prince John in command of the royal troops and assisted by the Earl of Westmoreland. When Westmoreland demands to know why the Archbishop, a man of God, is disturbing the peace, the Archbishop in answer begins by referring (like the King in III.i) to the diseased state of the country ('we are all diseased', IV.i.54), and then says that his aim is to have a number of grievances attended to in order to establish true peace ('to establish here a peace indeed', IV.i.86). The Archbishop accepts an invitation to submit a list of these grievances (we are not told in the play precisely what they are), and in the next scene (IV.ii) Prince John promises that the grievances will be redressed if the Archbishop disbands his troops 'As we will ours' (IV.ii.60–2). The Archbishop agrees, and the leaders on both sides drink one another's health, with Westmoreland saying to the Archbishop (IV.ii.75–6) 'my love to ye/Shall show itself more openly hereafter'. The royal troops in fact are not disbanded, and as soon as the disbanding of the rebel troops has been completed the Archbishop and two other rebel leaders are arrested for high treason, for which they will be executed. Then, with shameless hypocrisy, Prince John proclaims (IV.ii.121): 'God, and not we, hath safely fought today.' (When the King said that corruption – 'rank diseases' – grew 'near the heart' of his kingdom, his words were truer than he knew.)

Back in the palace at Westminster the King is complaining that Prince Henry is a wastrel, indulging in 'headstrong riot' (IV.iv.62 – it is noticeable that the play here takes no account of the reform of the Prince in *I Henry IV*), when news arrives of the defeat of the rebels in Yorkshire (the King is not told how this was achieved) and also of the defeat of Northumberland in Scotland. At this point the King suddenly has a relapse and is carried into another chamber where, left alone with the Prince, he falls asleep. Believing that the King has stopped breathing, the Prince removes the crown from the King's pillow, whereupon the King wakes and bitterly denounces the Prince for wishing him dead – but the Prince's denial of such a wish is so obviously sincere that father and son become reconciled. Knowing that death is approaching, the King first expresses regret for the 'indirect crooked ways' by which he obtained the crown from Richard II (IV.v.184–6) – he may be less than fair to himself here: earlier in the play (III.i.72–4) he said he was forced by 'necessity' to take the crown, and this view seems to be nearer the truth according to the situation as presented in *Richard II*. The King then gives words of advice to the Prince as his heir. He says he had hoped to allay discontent by leading an expedition to the Holy Land (IV.v.210–13 – his previously expressed wishes, in III.i.107–8 and IV.iv.1–4, to go to the Holy Land did not, however, suggest a purely political motive, nor does his reference to the Holy Land in his last speech in the play, IV.v.237–41), and his advice to the Prince now is 'to busy giddy [restless] minds/With foreign quarrels' (IV.v.214–15) – this certainly sounds cynical, but it may not have been regarded as such by Shakespeare, since the claim to the French throne in *Henry V* is perhaps to be taken as the putting into practice of Henry IV's advice. Of King Henry IV as portrayed by Shakespeare it must at least be said that he was a king who was seriously concerned with the promotion of order.

In the last Act of the play Prince Henry has become King Henry V. He encounters the Lord Chief Justice who, according to a brief reference in I.ii.50+, had on a past occasion committed the Prince to prison after the Prince had struck the Lord Chief Justice in a dispute concerning one of Falstaff's companions (Bardolph). The Prince, now King, far from showing vindictiveness, praises the Lord Chief Justice for having fearlessly dispensed justice on that occasion (V.ii.102–17): this praise is an important indication of the new king's respect for what the Lord Chief Justice calls 'The majesty and power of law and justice' (V.ii.78). In this last Act two scenes are devoted to a visit paid by Falstaff, after the crushing of rebellion, to Shallow's house in Gloucestershire. A contrast is perhaps intended between justice as administered by the Lord Chief Justice and Shallow's blithe lack of impartiality in the administration of justice – Shallow's servant Davy has a friend who is involved in a local dispute and, though Shallow knows this man to be 'an arrant knave', he promises at Davy's request to decide in favour of Davy's friend (V.i.34+). When Falstaff receives news that his old companion is now King of England he is overjoyed and promises to obtain high office for Shallow (V.iii.122–37): 'Master Robert Shallow, choose what office thou wilt in the land – 'tis thine ... the laws of England are at my commandment. Blessed are they that have been my friends, and woe to my Lord Chief Justice!' What Falstaff says here has already been shown to be wrong by the new king's encounter with the Lord Chief Justice in the previous scene (V.ii), and in V.iv, the scene immediately following Falstaff's confident assertion, two of his 'friends', Mistress Quickly (hostess of the Eastcheap tavern) and Doll Tearsheet, are arrested for being involved in a brawl in which a man was killed. When Falstaff arrives in London, in the final scene of the play, he is told by the King himself (V.v.64–71) that henceforth he must not come within ten miles of the King's person, though financial provision will be made to keep him out of poverty ('That lack of means enforce you not to evils'), and with good behaviour this financial provision will be increased. Thus under the new king law and order are to be fully upheld.

MUCH ADO ABOUT NOTHING (c. 1598)

Whereas the conflict between love and hate is the theme of *Romeo and Juliet* and the contrast (rather than conflict) between love and hate is the theme of *The Merchant of Venice*, the theme of *Much Ado about Nothing* is the contrast between those working for the promotion of love and those working for its destruction. The title of the play must be regarded as ironically flippant since, though the 'ado' or fuss may be about 'nothing' in so far as it is about an accusation of guilt which is in fact groundless, the effect of this false accusation reaches a tragic climax in Act IV of the play, where we become keenly aware of the destructive power of evil – evil which by the end of the play is happily overcome.

The play is set in Messina, Sicily, at a time when Sicily was part of the Spanish kingdom of Aragon, and Don Pedro, Prince of Aragon, is a guest of Leonato, Governor of Messina. Accompanying Don Pedro are two young Italians (one from Florence and the other from Padua) who have distinguished themselves in Don Pedro's army – Claudio (on whom 'Don Pedro hath bestowed much honour', I.i.9–) and Benedick (a man 'stuffed with all honourable virtues', I.i.46+), and in the opening scene we hear how these two men differ in regard to love. Benedick, having previously visited Messina, has a relationship with Beatrice, Leonato's niece, which involves not love but a witty exchange of insults ('a skirmish of wit', I.i.53): it appears that Benedick loves women no more than Beatrice loves men – of women Benedick says 'I love none' (I.i.108), to which Beatrice replies 'I had rather hear my dog bark at a crow than a man swear he loves me' (I.i.111–12). Claudio, on the other hand, who has also visited Messina before, now finds himself in love with Hero, Leonato's daughter – 'That I love her, I feel' he tells Benedick and Don Pedro (I.i.197). Accordingly Don Pedro offers to help Claudio (I.i.281–9) by impersonating Claudio in a masked dance which is to take place that evening and wooing Hero on Claudio's behalf: if her response is favourable Don Pedro will then arrange for her father, Leonato, to consent to a marriage between them.

Sharply contrasted with the helpful Don Pedro is his brother Don John (Don John is actually Don Pedro's half-brother, since we hear later that Don John is a bastard – IV.i.188, V.i.185–). Don John hates Don Pedro ('I had rather be a canker in a hedge than a rose in his grace', I.iii.21+), and he bluntly describes himself as 'a plain-dealing villain' (I.iii.21+). Richard III (or the Duke of Gloucester as he then was) also frankly revealed himself to be 'a villain' (*Richard III* I.i.30), but, whereas Richard was a villainous seeker of political power, Don John, like Aaron in *Titus Andronicus*, is a villain dedicated to malice for its own sake. Don John is quick to receive news of Claudio's desire to marry Hero since one of Don John's followers, Borachio, overheard Don Pedro's conversation with Claudio, and Don John's immediate interest in such news is: 'Will it serve for any model [ground plan] to build mischief on?' (I.iii.41–). Don John receives this news in time to poison Claudio's mind during the masked dance by telling him that Don Pedro, far from wooing Hero on Claudio's behalf, seeks Hero for himself. After listening to Don John Claudio is convinced that Hero is lost to him ('Farewell, therefore, Hero!', II.i.162) – until Don Pedro informs him that all is well and the way clear for him to marry Hero.

Don Pedro, having assisted Claudio, now wants to bring Benedick and Beatrice together ('I will in the interim undertake one of Hercules' labours, which is to bring Signior Benedick and the lady Beatrice into a mountain of affection, the one with the other', II.i.326+). He enlists the help of Leonato, Claudio and Hero to set about making Benedick fall in love with Beatrice and Beatrice fall in love with Benedick. This plot (presented in terms of light comedy) is completely successful. When Benedick is sitting in an arbour in Leonato's orchard Don Pedro, Claudio and Leonato, knowing that Benedick can hear them, talk of Beatrice being passionately in love with Benedick, and after they have gone Benedick says to himself (II.iii.200+): 'This can be no trick [there is of course comic dramatic irony here]...They say the lady is fair – 'tis a truth...I will be horribly in love with her.' And later, again in Leonato's orchard, Hero, after arranging for Beatrice to be drawn into the arbour, talks to one of her waiting-gentlewomen, Ursula, about Bendick's love for Beatrice, love which for Benedick's own sake Beatrice should not be told about because she would scorn it and mock it. Beatrice's reaction is (III.i.109–11): 'Contempt, farewell! And maiden pride, adieu!...Benedick, love on. I will requite thee.'

Meanwhile Borachio (Don John's follower who overheard Don Pedro and Claudio) has suggested (in II.ii) a plan to undermine the impending marriage between Claudio and Hero. Borachio has close relations with Margaret, Hero's other waiting-gentlewoman, and the plan is that on the night before the wedding Claudio and Don Pedro should be brought to hear Borachio talking to Margaret at Hero's bedroom window and addressing Margaret as Hero to make it seem that Borachio is Hero's lover – that Hero is 'a contaminated stale' (a whore, II.ii.23). When Don John tells Claudio and Don Pedro that Hero is 'disloyal' (III.ii.92) and invites them to be witnesses that night to the conversation at Hero's bedroom window, Claudio is already prepared to find that Don John's accusation is true and he says that if it proves to be so he will go to the church and shame Hero in front of the congregation (III.ii.110–12). We hear in III.iii that Borachio's evil plan has been carried out successfully, and in IV.i, in front of those gathered in the church for the marriage ceremony, Claudio rejects Hero, saying to her father (IV.i.30–1):

There, Leonato, take her back again.
Give not this rotten orange to your friend.

Claudio's behaviour shows that the evil proceeding from Don John has evoked an evil response in Claudio himself, and there is also an evil response on the part of Leonato. After being told about the talk at the bedroom window Leonato hopes that Hero, who has swooned after being denounced by Claudio, will die (IV.i.115–16):

Death is the fairest cover for her shame
That may be wished for.

Unlike Leonato, Friar Francis, who was attempting to perform the marriage ceremony, has faith in Hero's innocence, and, like Friar Lawrence in *Romeo and Juliet*, he seeks to promote the cause of love. He proposes that it should be given out that Hero (who has actually recovered from her fainting fit) is dead, in the hope that Claudio, who along with Don Pedro and Don John left the church immediately after Hero fainted, may be moved to remorse – in the hope that (IV.i.223–5):

> When he shall hear she died upon his words,
> The idea of her life shall sweetly creep
> Into his study of imagination...

In the last Act the effects of evil are gradually overcome. Leonato soon comes to believe in his daughter's innocence ('My soul doth tell me Hero is belied', V.i.42), and he turns against Claudio to the point of challenging him to a trial by combat (V.i.63–6):

> Thou hast so wronged mine innocent child and me
> That I... Do challenge thee to trial of a man.

Claudio is also challenged to a duel by Leonato's brother Antonio, and then by Benedick – Benedick was urged on (in IV.i) to make this challenge by Beatrice, who, like the Friar, has never doubted Hero's innocence. At this point, however, Hero's innocence its clearly established by a confession made by Borachio, caught by the local 'watch' (the policemen of Shakespeare's day): Borachio is now genuinely repentant and accepts death as his rightful punishment ('I desire nothing but the reward of a villain', V.i.229–30). Borachio's confession is enough to restore Claudio's love for Hero (V.i.237–8):

> Sweet Hero, now thy image doth appear
> In the rare semblance that I loved it first.

Claudio agrees to Leonato's earnest request that he should marry a niece who is 'Almost the copy of my child that's dead' (V.i.275), and just before the marriage ceremony Claudio discovers that his new bride is none other than Hero, a Hero who, she says, is no longer 'defiled' by slander (V.iv.63):

> One Hero died defiled, but I do live.

In this final scene we hear that Benedick and Beatrice are about to marry and that Don John, who attempted to escape, has been captured.

Hovering over the defeat of evil in the play may be a Shakespearean hint of divine aid. The farcical characters in the play, Dogberry the 'master constable' and his men of the watch, though simpletons, were able to bring Borachio to justice, these men of the watch having overheard Borachio telling Conrade, another follower of Don John, about how the deception of Claudio and Don Pedro was carried out (III.iii). Dogberry is very talkative and is constantly misusing words, as when he says of Borachio's act of deception 'Thou wilt be condemned into everlasting redemption for this' (IV.ii.52–3). This last remark at least shows an insistent awareness, albeit a muddled one, of justice as administered by God. And 'God' is a word repeatedly used by Dogberry, even though his invocation of God may be absurdly inappropriate – as when he begins his interrogation of Borachio and Conrade by asking 'Masters, do you serve God?' (IV.ii.15). In his last speech in the play Dogberry says to Leonato (V.i.305+): 'God keep your worship... God restore you to health.' Such words may suggest that God has already helped to restore Leonato – and Claudio – to health. Borachio in his speech of repentance says to Don Pedro and Claudio about Dogberry and his men (V.i.217+): 'What your wisdoms could not discover these shallow fools have brought to light.' These 'shallow fools' may have been the instruments of some power greater than themselves.

HENRY V (1599)

*H*enry V completes the tetralogy in which *Richard II* was followed by the two *Henry IV* plays, and the theme of this last of the four plays is England achieving 'honour' (an important word in this play as in *1 Henry IV*) under the leadership of an ideal king. In this play England achieves honour by going to war against France in pursuit of a claim to the French throne. This claim was in fact a disputable claim, made by Henry V's great-grandfather Edward III and renounced by Edward over fifty years before its resumption by Henry, and Henry's invasion of France in pursuit of such a claim may well seem to us today to be nothing short of a war of aggression. For Shakespeare, however, there were no doubts on this score: he follows Holinshed in seeing the claim to the French throne as wholly justifiable, and the play presents Henry's French campaign as a gloriously patriotic venture blessed by God.

In a conversation between the Archbishop of Canterbury and the Bishop of Ely in the first scene tribute is paid to Henry's qualities as a king: he is 'a true lover of the holy Church' (I.i.23), and he is eloquent in talking about religion, state affairs and war, and combines mastery of theory with practical skills (I.i.38–52). The play then moves quickly on to the question of Henry's claim to the French throne, 'Derived from Edward, his great-grandfather' (I.i.89). This claim has been investigated by the Archbishop of Canterbury, who in the second scene delivers a long speech (the substance of which Shakespeare derives from Holinshed) about the French Salic Law, a law banning the inheritance of the crown by females. It becomes apparent that Henry's claim depends on descent from a female,[59] and the Archbishop argues that the Salic Law should not be regarded as a bar to Henry's claim since in the history of the French monarchy there have been claims to the throne (which the Archbishop specifies) that have in fact been based on a descent from a female. The Archbishop has no hesitation in urging Henry to send his loyal subjects to France, 'With blood and sword and fire to win your right' (I.ii.131). When Henry expresses fear of leaving the way open to attack by the Scots he is told both by his uncle the Duke of Exeter and by the Archbishop that arranging for some troops to stay at home to protect England from the Scots while others fight in France should present no problem to a well-ordered society – Exeter and the Archbishop give a full description of the well-ordered society (I.ii.180–233) which it is assumed that England now possesses.

Accordingly preparations for France go ahead. The Chorus at the beginning of Act II speaks of Englishmen as being inspired by 'honour's thought' to follow Henry, 'the mirror of all Christian kings' (Chorus, lines 3 and 6). What honour impels England to perform is, however, almost undermined by traitors (Chorus, 18–19):

> What mightst thou [England] do that honour would thee do
> Were all thy children kind and natural!

At Southampton, just before embarking for France, Henry publicly exposes three English noblemen who have accepted bribes from France to murder him, and he regards the fact that this treachery was discovered as being an indication that the expedition to France carries God's blessing (II.ii.184–7):

> We doubt not of a fair and lucky war,
> Since God so graciously hath brought to light
> This dangerous treason lurking in our way
> To hinder our beginnings.

Act III takes us to France, with Henry cheering his men on to occupy the town of Harfleur (III.i.17–34):

> On, on, you noblest English,
> ... and upon this charge
> Cry 'God for Harry, England and Saint George!'

We find that in the English army there are three captains who are keen supporters of Henry even though they come from outside England itself – Fluellen comes from Wales, Macmorris from Ireland, and Jamy from Scotland. Fluellen drives men forward into the attack (III.ii.19–20), Macmorris takes fierce pride in his work as a military engineer (III.ii.81 +), and Jamy wishes to do 'gud service' even if that involves death (III.ii.107 +) – Jamy's presence in the English army shows that not all Scots are the enemies of England, as they had been referred to as being in the second scene (I.ii.144–54). On the other hand, the English army contains some dishonourable Englishmen, as represented by the associates of Falstaff in the *Henry IV* plays (in *Henry V*, II.iii, Falstaff himself is reported as having died). In II.i.1–3 we heard that Nym had become a corporal, Bardolph a lieutenant, and Pistol an 'ancient' (infantry officer of the lowest rank), and now in France we hear that Nym and Bardolph are thieves ('sworn brothers in filching', III.ii.53–) and that Pistol puts on a false show of being a fighter ('he hath a killing tongue and a quiet sword', III.ii.26+, and he lies about being personally involved in military exploits, III.vi.65+). Henry as a military commander, though he exhorts his men to 'imitate the action of the tiger' in battle (III.i.6), is well aware that the atrocities of 'impious war' may be committed by conquering soldiers in their treatment of enemy civilians (III.iii.11–27), and when Harfleur surrenders he orders mercy to be shown to all the French citizens ('Use mercy to them all', III.iii.54). He also insists that as English soldiers march through French villages there must be no looting ('nothing taken but paid for', III.vi.110–) – Bardolph is likely to be executed for robbing a French church (III.vi.38–9, 93+).

Act IV begins with the night before the Battle of Agincourt, a time of stress for the English since they are heavily outnumbered by the army now assembled by the French. The opening Chorus describes Henry moving round amongst his men, raising their dejected spirits (Chorus, 35–42):

> Upon his royal face there is no note
> How dread an army hath enrounded him...
> But freshly looks and overbears attaint [overcomes infected morale]
> With cheerful semblance and sweet majesty,
> That every wretch, pining and pale before,
> Beholding him, plucks comfort from his looks.

And in the first scene of this Act Henry, concealing his royal identity under a borrowed cloak, listens to the fears and grievances of common soldiers. Then, in a long soliloquy (IV.i.226–80), he expresses his consciousness of the responsibilities weighing upon a king. (This soliloquy is an elaboration of the soliloquy on the same theme delivered by his dying father in *2 Henry IV* III.i.4–31.) Speaking to his noblemen just before the battle, Henry seeks to offer solace for the English inferiority in numbers by arguing that in this situation the greater is the honour to be won ('The fewer men, the greater share of honour', IV.iii.22), and he adds 'if it be a sin to covet honour I am the most offending soul alive' (IV.iii.28–9). As it happens, the battle swings in England's favour as the ranks of the over-confident French are broken (IV.v), but at this point we find Shakespeare being inexcusably indulgent towards a brutal decision by Henry. Having presented Henry as a merciful commander at Harfleur, Shakespeare now condones the order he gives, as the French prepare to return to the attack, that 'every soldier kill his prisoners' (IV.vi.37). (It seems that mercy should be shown to enemy civilians, but not to enemy prisoners of war.) In the scene that immediately follows (IV.vii) one of Henry's captains, Gower, talks of Henry's decision as having been taken in retaliation for the French killing of non-combatant boys left in the English camp, but in the previous scene Henry's order was given without any indication that at that time he knew of the French atrocity, and even if we are meant to take Gower's explanation as being correct it must jar on modern ears to hear his words of high praise (IV.vii.10–): 'the King most worthily hath caused every soldier to cut his prisoner's throat. O, 'tis a gallant king!' The battle ends with a resounding victory for the English, a victory Henry wholeheartedly attributes to God: when he tells Fluellen 'God fought for us' (IV.viii.118), his sincerity contrasts with the hypocrisy of the similar words used by the treacherous Prince John in *2 Henry IV* (IV.ii.121 – 'God, and not we, hath safely fought today'). In the early hours of the morning, before the battle had begun, Henry had prayed to God to overlook his father's taking of the crown from Richard II (IV.i.288–90):

> Not today, O Lord,
> O, not today, think not upon the fault
> My father made in compassing the crown.

In view of the victory at Agincourt it would seem that God responded favourably to Henry's prayer. As for the dishonourable former associates of Falstaff, both Bardolph and Nym have been hanged for looting (IV.iv.63 +), and after the battle Pistol, having mocked Fluellen as a Welshman, is forced by Fluellen's use of a cudgel to eat a leek: there is dramatic irony in Pistol's lament that Fluellen has stripped him of his 'honour' (V.i.78–9).

The play ends with the complete acceptance by the French of peace on England's terms. Though earlier in the play the French Dauphin had expressed contempt for Henry (I.ii.249–58, II.iv.26–9,130–1), in the last scene, despite the French defeat, the King and Queen of France both greet Henry as 'brother England' (V.ii.10,12), and the Queen hopes that the meeting between the kings of the two countries 'Shall change all griefs [grievances] and quarrels into love' (V.ii.20). And the Duke of Burgundy speaks at length of the blessings of Peace, 'Dear nurse of arts, plenties, and joyful births' (V.ii.35). Much of this last scene is given over to Henry's wooing of Katherine, daughter of the French King, and, though this wooing clearly has a political motivation since such a marriage would be in keeping with Henry's desire to become King of France, his expression of love for Katherine has a genuine ring ('By mine honour, in true English, I love thee, Kate', V.ii.215 +) – Shakespeare shows that true love can go hand in hand with a political motive, just as he showed with Petruchio in *The Taming of the Shrew* and with Fenton in *The Merry Wives of Windsor* that true love could grow out of a money motive. Following Henry's wooing of Katherine the French King gives his formal consent to all Henry's demands, including a declaration that Henry is to be the heir to the French throne. The French King hopes that from henceforth there will be 'Christian-like accord' (V.ii.344) between England and France, and the Queen hopes that the marriage between Henry and Katherine may represent a lasting marriage between the two nations (V.ii.350–9). And in so far as these two nations are regarded as Christian it is significant that during his wooing of Katherine Henry reveals a vision of a combined Anglo-French nation giving a lead to Christian Europe in confronting the Turkish Muslims in Constantinople (Shakespeare seems to be referring here to the capture of Constantinople by the Turks in 1453, which occurred after Henry's lifetime) – Henry says to Katherine (V.ii.209–): 'Shall not thou and I, between Saint Denis and Saint George, find a boy, half-French, half-English, that shall go to Constantinople and take the Turk by the beard?'

The final Chorus of the play, after saying that this play has sought to present the great achievement of Henry, 'This star of England', has to point out that, though Henry's infant son was crowned Henry VI, King of France and England, English misrule led to the collapse of Henry's achievement, as previously shown on the stage in Shakespeare's *Henry VI* plays.

JULIUS CAESAR (c. 1599)

Julius Caesar is a dramatic presentation of the assassination of Julius Caesar and is the first of Shakespeare's plays to derive its material from Plutarch's *Lives* (written in Greek at the end of the 1st or the beginning of the 2nd century AD and translated into English, from a French translation, by Sir Thomas North, 1579). This play is based on material from the Lives of Julius Caesar, Mark Antony and Brutus. While drawing on Plutarch in considerable detail, Shakespeare is more forceful than Plutarch in condemning the assassination of Caesar as an evil act. We know from Shakespeare's English history plays that he regarded the murder of a legitimate king (such as Henry VI and Richard II) as a crime, even if that king had serious defects, and in *Julius Caesar*, though Caesar is not a king who has inherited a crown, in the Rome of his day he has become an established ruler, and he is also a ruler whom Shakespeare sees as a man of integrity. (There are incidental references to Julius Caesar in Shakespeare's *Henry VI* plays. In *1 Henry VI* I.i.55–6 Caesar is referred to as 'glorious' – though less so than Henry V – and in *2 Henry VI* IV.i.136–7 and in *3 Henry VI* V.v.53–5 the murder of Caesar is referred to as a dastardly crime.[60]) The main theme of *Julius Caesar*, therefore, is the evil overthrow of an established ruler. Brutus, who becomes the official leader of the conspirators, is seen as honourable but misguided, like Hotspur in *1 Henry IV*, but Brutus differs from Hotspur in being involved in a mental conflict between good and evil. Whereas most of Shakespeare's previous characters were either good or bad, Brutus is the first notable example of a Shakespearean character where there is a conflict between good and evil within the one character (the earliest example is Tarquin in *The Rape of Lucrece*, lines 185–247).

In the opening scenes we hear much of the claim that Caesar is a potential tyrant, but gradually it becomes apparent that this claim is not justified. In the first scene citizens who have taken to the streets to greet Caesar on his return to Rome after triumphing over his rival Pompey are sternly condemned by two Roman officials, the tribunes Flavius and Marullus: according to Flavius, Caesar's intention is to 'keep us all in servile fearfulness' (I.i.76). A similar view is put forward by Cassius in the second scene, who sets about persuading Brutus to join a conspiracy against Caesar. Brutus's initial response is to assert that, if what he is required to do is for the general good, he will let honour be set alongside danger of death and will be indifferent to any personal considerations (I.ii.85–7):

> If it be aught toward general good,
> Set honour in one eye and death i' the other,
> And I will look on both indifferently.

(Here we may recall Hotspur's words in *1 Henry IV* I.iii.195–6, when he is drawn into a rebellion against the King:

> Send danger from the east unto the west,
> So honour cross it from the north to south...)

Cassius insists that what he is advocating is indeed a matter of 'honour' (I.ii.92) since it concerns the need to curb Caesar's power: 'I was born free as Caesar, so were you' says Cassius to Brutus (I.ii.97), yet now Caesar (I.ii.135–6)

>   doth bestride the narrow world
> Like a Colossus...

Cassius's attitude may well be in tune with modern egalitarianism, but Shakespeare (who in *Henry V*, the play that probably immediately preceded *Julius Caesar*, venerates 'obedience' in a society headed by a king – see *Henry V* I.ii.183ff.) would expect his audience to accept the comment made by Caesar himself in the second of his brief appearances in this second scene – Caesar says of Cassius (I.ii.208–10):

> Such men as he be never at heart's ease
> Whiles they behold a greater than themselves,
> And therefore are they very dangerous.

(And Caesar's remark that Cassius does not like music – 'he hears no music', I.ii.204 – recalls Lorenzo's observation in *The Merchant of Venice* V.i.83–5 that the man who is not moved by music 'Is fit for treasons, stratagems and spoils'.) In this same scene Brutus is given a contemptuous report by Casca (I.ii.220ff.) of how Caesar, some minutes previously, refused a king's crown offered him three times by his supporter Mark Antony before a crowd of citizens in the market place: after refusing the crown Caesar collapsed, foaming at the mouth – Caesar, as Brutus points out, suffers from 'the falling sickness' (epilepsy, I.ii.255–). Though Casca is contemptuous of Caesar, his report gives an impression of Caesar that is very different from the tyrannical Colossus depicted by Cassius. And, though Casca says Caesar really wanted the crown ('he would fain have had it', I.ii.230+) but refused it only because the crowd loudly protested against him having it, it could be that the Roman Senate is more concerned than Caesar about his having the crown – an indication of the Senate's intention in this matter comes from Casca himself when he is talking to Cassius in the next scene (I.iii.85–6):

> they say the senators tomorrow
> Mean to establish Caesar as a king.

In this next scene we hear of fearsome supernatural occurrences witnessed in the streets of Rome, occurrences which Cassius tells Casca are a 'warning/Unto some monstrous state' (I.iii.70–1), meaning that they are a warning, as he gives Casca clearly to understand, of what will happen if Caesar remains in power. But Cicero, the Roman philosopher and statesman, who appears at the beginning of this scene, says of the supernatural occurrences (I.iii.34–5):

> men may construe things after their fashion [in their own way],
> Clean from the purpose of the things themselves.

And by the end of the play there can be little doubt that these supernatural occurrences are to be regarded as a warning, not of the consequences of Caesar's political power, but of the consequences of his murder.

Meanwhile Cassius, in his campaign to win Brutus over to the conspirators, has resorted (I.ii.314–19) to throwing through Brutus's windows letters which purport to come from various citizens and which strongly hint that Brutus should stand up to Caesar's 'ambition'. And, having recruited Casca as a conspirator, Cassius fully agrees with Casca (I.iii.157–62) that Brutus is needed as the official leader of the conspirators since 'he sits high in all the people's hearts' and so will give a gloss of 'virtue' and 'worthiness' to the conspiracy. II.i shows Brutus succumbing to the forces of evil. In soliloquy (II.i.10–34) he reflects, rightly, that

> The abuse of greatness is when it disjoins
> Remorse [conscience] from power.

And he admits that as yet he has not known Caesar to be guilty of such 'abuse':

> to speak truth of Caesar,
> I have not known when his affections [desires] swayed
> More than his reason.

Yet he seeks to justify his acceptance at the beginning of the soliloquy that Caesar must be put to death ('It must be by his death') by arguing that his death is necessary to prevent the mere possibility of his being corrupted by power:

> So Caesar may.
> Then, lest he may, prevent.

Brutus, ever since Cassius roused him against Caesar, has been in a state of mental agitation, sensing that he is being drawn into evil (II.i.61–5):

> Since Cassius first did whet [incite] me against Caesar
> I have not slept.
> Between the acting of a dreadful thing
> And the first motion, all the interim is
> Like a phantasma or a hideous dream.

And on the arrival of the conspirators at his home at dawn Brutus is at first repelled by conspiracy's 'dangerous brow', by its 'monstrous visage' which needs to be concealed by false 'smiles and affability' (II.i.77–85). But when Cassius presents the conspirators to him in his orchard Brutus succumbs completely and shakes hands with them one by one (II.i.113). After the conspirators have left, Brutus's wife, Portia, says 'You have some sick offence [illness] within your mind' (II.i.268), and, when at the end of the scene Brutus persuades Caius Legarius, a Roman in ill health, to join the conspiracy, there is dramatic irony in Brutus's description of the conspiracy as 'A piece of work that will make sick men whole [restore sick men to health]' (II.i.327).

On the morning of the conspirators' dawn visit to Brutus Caesar is confronted by various bad omens, and, after at first refusing to be deterred by these omens, he gives way to his wife, Calphurnia, who begs him to stay at home. Among the bad omens is a dream that Calphurnia has had of Romans bathing their hands in blood running from Caesar's statue (II.ii.76–9). Caesar is, however, finally persuaded to go to the Senate House by the conspirator Decius Brutus (another Brutus): Decius interprets Calphurnia's dream as meaning that Caesar will be the source of a great Roman revival (II.ii.83–90), and he also points out, professedly out of 'dear dear love' for Caesar, that Caesar would be mocked as a coward if he allowed himself to be frightened by his wife's dreams (II.ii.96–104). The other conspirators then arrive to escort Caesar to the Senate House in order to murder him – the dramatic irony of Caesar's thanks to them for their 'pains and courtesy' (II.ii.115) and his offering of wine to his 'Good friends' before they leave (II.ii.125–6) arouses strong sympathy in us for Caesar. On Caesar's arrival at the Senate House Decius Brutus asks him to accept a petition from Trebonius, a petition which must be intended to mislead Caesar since Trebonius is a conspirator, and Artemidorus, a well-wisher who has gained knowledge of the conspiracy, tries to give Caesar a written warning: when Artemidorus pleads with Caesar to read his petition first because it is of concern to Caesar himself, Caesar again wins our sympathy by answering 'What touches us ourself shall be last served' (III.i.8) – thus missing what might have been a chance to save his life.[61] And when, according to the conspirators' prearranged plan, Metellus Cimber, in order to distract Caesar's attention, asks him to revoke the banishment of his brother, Publius Cimber, Caesar wins our respect as a man who makes firm (and by implication carefully considered) decisions (III.i.60–73):

> But I am constant as the northern star...
> Let me a little show it, even in this,
> That I was constant Cimber should be banished,
> And constant do remain to keep him so.

The conspirators thereupon stab Caesar to death, and immediately there follows, in words of resounding hollowness, the proclamation 'Liberty! Freedom! Tyranny is dead!' (III.i.78).

The true description of the consequences of Caesar's murder is in fact given by Antony (III.i.264 ff.):

> Domestic fury and fierce civil strife
> Shall cumber all the parts of Italy...

But it is Antony himself who initiates this civil strife. After hypocritically praising the conspirators as 'The choice and master spirits of this age' (III.i.164) and welcoming them as friends (III.i.185–90), Antony gains Brutus's permission to speak at Caesar's funeral after Brutus himself has spoken, and in his funeral oration he completely outshines Brutus – his modesty in saying 'I am no orator as Brutus is' (III.ii.217) is clearly false. He whips up the citizens into a destructive fury against the conspirators – 'Seek! Burn! Fire! Kill! Slay! Let not a traitor live!' shout the citizens (III.ii.204–5) – and Brutus and Cassius are driven out of Rome. In the process a poet, Cinna, is torn to pieces because he happens to have the same name as one of the conspirators (III.iii). In IV.i Antony has been joined by Octavius Caesar (Julius's grandnephew), and Rome is under the control of three men – Antony, Octavius and Lepidus. In this scene the three of them are busy putting marks against the names of people, including members of their own families, who are to be executed, and Antony, having told the people at Caesar's funeral that Caesar had bequeathed money and land to the public (III.ii.241–52), now cynically proposes to cut down these legacies (IV.i.8–9).

At this point in the play Shakespeare shows that unpredictable changes occur in the flow of good and evil in human beings (a brief earlier example was the sudden repentance of the villain Borachio in *Much Ado about Nothing*). In Act IV of *Julius Caesar*, while there is strong movement towards evil in Rome under Julius Caesar's political heirs, there is, surprisingly, a movement towards goodness in the two former leading conspirators. Brutus and Cassius are in command of armies in Greece, and IV.iii begins with a quarrel between them, due largely to Brutus's nervous strain after hearing of Portia's suicide, brought on by the triumph of Antony and Octavius in Rome and by Brutus's long absence from home (IV.iii.141–54). But after the quarrel Brutus and Cassius become united in a true spirit of love – over a bowl of wine Brutus says 'In this I bury all unkindness, Cassius', and Cassius replies 'I cannot drink too much of Brutus's love' (IV.iii.157,160). Before going into battle against the forces of Antony and Octavius at Philippi Brutus and Cassius, well aware that they may be defeated, bid each other 'For ever and for ever farewell' (V.i.116,119). When the battle turns against them they put an end to their own lives, and as they die they both feel that they deserve to die as a punishment for murdering Caesar. Cassius's last words are (V.iii.45–6):

> Caesar, thou art revenged,
> Even with the sword that killed thee.

Brutus, before the battle, was visited by Caesar's ghost, which described itself as Brutus's 'evil spirit' (IV.iii.280), thereby suggesting that Caesar's murder was a crime that should weigh on Brutus's conscience, and in the final scene Brutus expresses his gladness that in taking his own life he may be able to set Caesar's ghost at rest (V.v.50–1):

> Caesar, now be still.
> I killed not thee with half so good a will.

As the battle was drawing to an end Antony was impressed by the devotion shown by one of Brutus's friends, Lucilius, who allowed himself to be taken prisoner and claimed that he was Brutus in order to give the real Brutus the chance to escape – Antony says of Lucilius (V.iv.28–9): 'I had rather have/Such men my friends than enemies.' In the final scene, when the battle is over and Antony and Octavius learn of Brutus's death, Octavius expresses his wish to take into his own service ('entertain') all those who fought for Brutus ('All that served Brutus, I will entertain them', V.v.60). It seems, therefore, that the glowing tribute paid by Antony at this point to the dead Brutus is intended to win over Brutus's supporters. Whereas at Caesar's funeral Antony had mocked Brutus's reputation as 'an honourable man' (III.ii.81–99), he now acclaims Brutus as an honourable man indeed (V.v.68–72):

> This was the noblest Roman of them all.
> All the conspirators save only he
> Did that they did in envy of great Caesar.
> He only in general honest thought
> And common good to all made one of then.

Octavius duly promises that Brutus shall be given an

honourable burial, and then, in the last line of the play, speaks triumphantly of 'the glories of this happy day' (happy, that is, for the victors).

In this last line there is surely dramatic irony, partly because the battle as it has just been presented to us has been the reverse of glorious and happy (since our sympathy has been aroused for Brutus and Cassius), but also because this line might appear to suggest that the play as a whole has a happy ending. Earlier on Brutus, just before he made the decision to engage the enemy at Philippi, received reports from Rome of the putting to death of a large number of Roman senators (following the talk about death sentences in IV.i) – one hundred according to one report, seventy according to another, Cicero being one of them (IV.iii.171–6). The play as a whole, therefore, shows that for Rome the final outcome of the death of Julius Caesar has been tragic: though Caesar's supporters have triumphed over his murderers, the result has been not glory or happiness but a bloodbath.

As You Like It (c. 1600)

As You Like It, as the title suggests, is a light-hearted play (in the Epilogue the invitation goes out 'to like as much of this play as please you'), and as a comedy it has its fair share of improbable incidents, derived largely from Thomas Lodge's pastoral novel *Rosalynde* (1590). But the main theme is serious enough: the prime value of love in all human relationships. The word 'love' occurs repeatedly in the play.

We hear in the first scene how Orlando, the youngest of the three sons of Sir Rowland de Boys, has been maltreated by his brother Oliver: according to their dead father's will Oliver as the eldest son should have provided for Orlando's education, yet in fact Orlando has had to endure a life of 'servitude' (I.i.22–). Orlando has offered himself as a challenger to Charles, a wrestler at the Duke's court (the Duke is named in the second scene as Frederick), and when Charles comes, out of 'love' for Oliver, to warn him that Orlando may suffer serious injury

(I.i.109+), Oliver says (quite untruthfully, as we soon discover) that Orlando is a villain who deserves to be punished (I.i.122+). In a soliloquy at the end of the scene Oliver says 'I hope I shall see the end of him, for my soul, yet I know not why, hates nothing more than he.' (Shakespeare of course had already had much to say about hate as well as love in *Romeo and Juliet* and *The Merchant of Venice*.) The next sentence of the soliloquy shows that Oliver does have a reason for hating Orlando – Orlando is 'of all sorts enchantingly beloved', with the result, says Oliver, 'that I am altogether misprised [despised]'.

In this first scene Charles's gossip about affairs at court reveals a parallel estrangement between two other brothers (I.i.89+), though here it is the younger brother who is at fault: Duke Frederick is a usurper who has ejected his elder brother – the rightful duke is unnamed in the dialogue of the play but is referred to in later stage directions as Duke Senior. Duke Senior, like Orlando, is beloved of others – 'three or four loving lords have put themselves into voluntary exile with him' and so have had their estates confiscated (I.i.89+). We also hear that, though Duke Senior has been banished, his daughter Rosalind has stayed on at court because she and Duke Frederick's daughter are devoted to each other – 'never two ladies loved as they do' (I.i.103). We are at first led to believe that Duke Frederick, though a usurper, is a loving man – according to Charles, Rosalind 'is no less beloved of her uncle than his own daughter' (I.i.103–), and in the second scene Touchstone, the court jester, talks of a courtier whom Frederick 'loves' (I.ii.74). But we soon find that this impression of Duke Frederick as a loving man is false: Rosalind, because people pity her as the daughter of her banished father, becomes the object of Duke Frederick's 'malice' (I.ii.256–62), and he orders her to leave (I.iii), despite protests from his daughter Celia (I.iii.68–72). Celia, true to her love for Rosalind, secretly decides to accompany her into exile, and it is agreed that for security's sake Rosalind will be dressed as a man and be called 'Ganymede', while Celia will adopt the name 'Aliena'.

Orlando as a challenger to Charles the wrestler is, miraculously, the victor and, when he tells Rosalind at court (shortly before she is ordered to leave) that he is the son of Sir Rowland de Boys, Rosalind says 'My father loved Sir Rowland as his soul' (I.ii.214). Orlando instantly finds himself in love with Rosalind – he has been 'overthrown', not by Charles, but by Rosalind ('O poor Orlando, thou art overthrown!', I.ii.238), and early in the next scene (I.iii) it becomes clear that Rosalind is in love with Orlando. Orlando on his return home (II.iii) is warned by the elderly servant Adam that Oliver, having heard of Orlando's victory over Charles, plans to murder him, and now that Orlando has to leave home for his own safety Adam, despite his years ('almost fourscore', II.iii.71), insists on going with him. Orlando and Adam make their way to the Forest of Arden (the French Ardennes in Lodge's novel), where Adam collapses from exhaustion. It is in the Forest of Arden that Duke Senior and his lords are living in exile, and when Orlando comes upon them he begs for food for Adam 'Who after me hath many a weary step/Limped in pure love' (II.vii.130–1). Duke Senior is only too willing to help and is delighted to learn that Orlando is the son of Sir Rowland – 'I am the duke/That loved your father' says Duke Senior (II.vii.195–6), thus confirming what Orlando was told by Rosalind (I.ii.214). In contrast to the loving Duke Senior, Duke Frederick, after discovering that his daughter has left with Rosalind, vents his wrath on Orlando's brother Oliver. Because Celia's lady attendant thought that Celia and Rosalind might be found in the company of Orlando whom Rosalind so admired (II.ii), Duke Frederick goes to Oliver's house demanding to know of Orlando's whereabouts. There is satirical dramatic irony when Duke Frederick suspects Oliver of trying to shield Orlando and orders Oliver to find him: Oliver protests 'I never loved my brother in my life', only to be told by the Duke, hardly a loving brother himself, 'More villain thou' (III.i.14–15).

In II.iv Rosalind and Celia have found their way into the Forest of Arden shortly before Orlando and Adam arrive there, and in the forest Rosalind and Celia overhear a young shepherd, Silvius, talking to an old shepherd, Corin, about his ardent love for a shepherdess, Phebe. Here we are meant to accept sympathetically love's association with ridiculous behaviour (just as we were meant to be sympathetic towards love's association with 'folly' in *The Two Gentlemen of Verona* II.i.65+ and its association with 'madmen' in *A Midsummer Night's Dream* V.i.4–8). Says Silvius (II.iv.25–33 – though a shepherd he speaks in blank verse!):

> But if thy love were ever like to mine –
> As sure I think did never man love so –
> How many actions most ridiculous
> Hast thou been drawn to by thy fantasy?...
> If thou rememberest not the slightest folly
> That ever love did make thee run into,
> Thou hast not loved.

And listening to these words Rosalind recognises her own love for Orlando (II.iv.39+):

> Alas, poor shepherd, searching of [probing] thy wound,
> I have by hard adventure found my own.

Orlando himself displays the ridiculous behaviour of a lover by hanging on trees in the forest love poems addressed to Rosalind (III.ii), and when Rosalind, disguised as 'Ganymede', encounters Orlando she tells him (III.ii.372–) that 'Love is merely a madness', a form of 'lunacy' that is widely prevalent, and she playfully undertakes, still concealing her true identity under the guise of Ganymede, to cure him of this madness by allowing him to woo her, pretending that she (as Ganymede) is Rosalind (!). In this role of therapist Rosalind teases Orlando by making fun of love – when he says he would die for love, she tells him 'men have died from time to time, and worms have eaten them, but not for love' (IV.i.97–). But after Orlando's departure she talks to Celia of her deep love for him ('I cannot be out of sight of Orlando', IV.i.195–).

Notable as a character who makes fun of love is Touchstone, the court jester, who accompanies Celia and Rosalind into exile, but he makes fun of love because he himself lacks it. He professes to support Silvius's remarks about the folly of love by giving a farcical account (II.iv.39+) of his love of a girl called Jane Smile: his account is a mocking caricature (he says, for instance, that he kissed the udders of a cow milked by Jane's pretty hands), in which not only a lover's foolish behaviour but love itself is ridiculed. As a courtier Touchstone displays shallow sophistication – when he tells Corin the shepherd 'if thou never wast at court thou never sawest good manners' (III.ii.35+) and pronounces Corin to be a 'Most shallow man' (III.ii.57+), it is clearly Touchstone himself who is the shallow man. (It is interesting to note that, though courtiers figure prominently in Shakespeare's plays, in *As You Like It* he shows respect for the merits of simple country folk, as we see in Corin's reply to Touchstone: 'Sir, I am a true labourer. I earn that I eat, get that I wear, owe no man hate...') Touchstone concluded his mocking account of the wooing of Jane Smile with the words 'We that are true lovers run into strange capers' (II.iv.52–), but a true lover he certainly is not. In the Forest of Arden he finds a simple-minded country girl called Audrey whom he arranges to marry (III.iii.34+) – but he would welcome a flawed marriage ceremony (performed by a priest under a bush rather than in church) as 'a good excuse for me hereafter to leave my wife' (III.ii.80–1). To promote his own selfish intentions Touchstone drives away Audrey's honest-to-goodness country suitor, William (V.i).

Another character who is foreign to the spirit of love is Jaques, one of Duke Senior's courtiers, but a man who is completely out of sorts with life and his fellow human beings – he is described by Duke Senior (II.vii.5) as being 'compact of jars' (full of discord). Though he has accompanied the Duke into exile he certainly differs in temperament from the Duke's 'loving lords' (referred to by Charles the wrestler in I.i.89+): when he is told that the Duke has been looking for him all day, he replies 'And I have been all this day to avoid him' (II.v.33–). He is introduced as 'the melancholy Jaques' (II.i.26,41), melancholy being an attribute he takes a pride in acknowledging ('I can suck melancholy out of a song as a weasel sucks eggs', II.v.10+). Duke Senior observes that Jaques likes to 'moralise' (II.i.44), which as far as Jaques is concerned means that he likes to find fault with people and complain about the misery of life.

According to a report in II.i he displays pity for a wounded stag and denounces human beings for killing deer in their 'native dwelling-place' (II.i.60–3), yet in a later scene (IV.ii) he applauds a man who has killed a deer by calling for him to be crowned with the deer's horns. There is one occasion in the play when Jaques is reported as being 'merry' (II.vii.4) – but he is so only because he has heard Touchstone railing against Fortune (II.vii.16) and noting that with the passage of time 'we rot and rot' (II.vii.27). After this encounter with Touchstone Jaques fancies the role of jester, who by general acceptance was allowed to make caustic remarks about everybody – Jaques would like to have the jester's freedom 'To blow on whom I please' (II.vii.49). But when he claims that in this way he could perform the function of moralist, Duke Senior, though usually indulgent towards Jaques ('I love to cope [come upon] him in these sullen fits', II.i.67), now says bluntly (II.vii.64–6) that Jaques would do

> Most mischievous foul sin in chiding sin,
> For thou thyself hast been a libertine,
> As sensual as the brutish sting itself.

Thus we learn that Jaques in his time has been aroused by lust, not love. His contempt for love comes out in an encounter with Orlando: after Orlando has declined his invitation to rail against the misery of human life, Jaques tells Orlando 'The worst fault you have is to be in love' (III.ii.265). And in a discourse on melancholy delivered to Rosalind (as Ganymede) he speaks of a lover as experiencing a melancholy that consists of several forms of melancholy merged into one (IV.i.9+). What may seem surprising is Jaques's insistence that Touchstone should be properly married to Audrey in a church rather than under a bush (III.iii.71+), but we may take it that he finds perverse amusement in the prospect of the sophisticated Touchstone being bound in wedlock to an ignorant country girl – 'O knowledge ill-inhabited, worse than Jove in a thatched house' is Jaques's earlier comment in this scene (III.iii.6+).

From IV.iii onwards the play moves rapidly to a happy conclusion. Oliver, ordered by Duke Frederick to find Orlando, has been rescued from a lioness in the forest by Orlando himself, who was moved by 'kindness, nobler ever than revenge' (IV.iii.127), and Oliver, the beneficiary of 'my brother's love' (IV.iii.143), has undergone a 'conversion' (IV.iii.135). And with amazing suddenness Oliver and Celia fall in love with each other (V.ii.25+). In the last scene (V.iv) Hymen, the god of marriage, descends from heaven to join four couples in marriage 'If truth holds true contents' (V.iv.124) – i.e. if they are truly committed to one another. The four couples are: Orlando and Rosalind (who has revealed her true identity to Orlando and to her father, Duke Senior); Oliver and Celia; Silvius and Phebe (who had become attracted to 'Ganymede' until Rosalind revealed that she was a woman); and Touchstone and Audrey. But there is serious doubt about the last couple – Touchstone says to Duke Senior 'I press in here, sir, amongst the rest of the country copulatives [couples], to swear and to forswear, according as marriage binds and blood [lust] breaks' (V.iv.51+), and as regards the forswearing of the marriage oath Touchstone no doubt has himself in mind. We then hear of a second conversion: Duke Frederick, on his way with soldiers to seize Duke Senior, was converted by 'an old religious man' (V.iv.154–6), and the dukedom is to be restored to Duke Senior. News of Duke Frederick's conversion inspires yet another conversion: Jaques has a sudden desire to join the 'convertites' among whom Duke Frederick is now living (V.iv.178–9). And with Jaques's change of heart comes a respect for love: addressing Orlando, Oliver and Silvius in turn, he indicates that they deserve the happiness that love should bring (V.iv.182–4), but he tells Touchstone that by the end of two months there will be 'wrangling' between him and Audrey – 'thy loving voyage/Is but for two months victualled' (V.iv.185–6). Thus the happy ending to the play is marred only by Touchstone's unregeneracy.

HAMLET (c. 1600)

The theme of *Hamlet* is the subjection of a kingdom – the kingdom of Denmark – to the insidious power of evil, evil which brings about the deaths of a number of Denmark's leading figures but which is finally brought to a halt with the help, it is strongly hinted, of divine intervention. Like England in *Richard III* and *Richard II*, Denmark suffers under an evil king, but what is notable about *Hamlet* is that it shows the destructive effects of evil on the individual mind, the mind, in particular, of the central character, Prince Hamlet. (To a lesser extent the power of evil to undermine an individual mind was shown in Brutus in *Julius Caesar*.) *Hamlet* has been generally recognised as being a complex play, and that complexity depends partly, I think, on its use of dramatic irony – dramatic irony is often used in Shakespeare's plays, but in *Hamlet* especially we need to be careful to notice where we should not take the words of certain characters at their face value.

Hamlet opens with the dramatic appearance of a ghost, which seems to be that of the late king, Prince Hamlet's father, also named Hamlet. In the course of the first scene we find that this apparition is not of the same kind as the ghosts of Richard III's victims that appeared in Richard's sleep before his death on the battlefield, or the ghost of Julius Caesar that presented itself to Brutus before the battle at Philippi. Unlike those ghosts, the ghost in *Hamlet* is an evil ghost. This ghost, witnessed by Prince Hamlet's friend Horatio along with two soldiers on night duty, behaves like an evil spirit: with the approach of daylight, heralded by the crowing of a cockerel, 'it started like a guilty thing/Upon a fearful summons' (I.i.148–9). Such behaviour contrasts with the character of the person in whose likeness the ghost appears – Hamlet senior was in fact 'a goodly king' (I.ii.186). Having been told about the ghost, Hamlet on the following night, in the company of Horatio and the soldier Marcellus, sees it with his own eyes. His first reaction is to feel the need for protection against something evil ('Angels and ministers of grace defend us!', I.iv.39), but then, though uncertain as to whether this apparition comes from 'heaven' or from 'hell' (I.iv.41), he decides to speak to it. When the ghost beckons to him he follows it, despite Horatio's warning that it may 'draw you into madness' (I.iv.74). After Hamlet has gone off with the ghost, Marcellus and Horatio comment on the situation in a way which almost sums up the theme of the play. Marcellus perceives that evil is at work in Denmark – 'Something is rotten in the state of Denmark' (I.iv.90). But Horatio is confident that this evil will not go unheeded by Heaven – 'Heaven will direct it' (I.iv.91).

Young Hamlet, even before hearing about the ghost, was in a deeply disturbed state of mind because his mother, within a month of his father's death, had married Claudius, his father's brother, such a marriage being regarded at that time as incestuous (I.ii.157). In I.v the Ghost tells Hamlet that he is the ghost of Hamlet's father who was murdered by Claudius: it is Hamlet's duty, the Ghost insists, to seek 'revenge' for this murder (I.v.7,25). It is almost certain that Shakespeare expects his audience to realise that this ghost is a devil, or the Devil, appearing in the guise of Hamlet's father – as Hamlet himself, later in the play, accepts as possible (II.ii.594–9):

> The spirit that I have seen
> May be a devil,[62] and the Devil[62] hath power
> To assume a pleasing shape, yea, and perhaps,
> Out of my weakness and my melancholy,...
> Abuses [deceives] me to damn me.[63]

Seen in this light the Ghost in what he has to say to Hamlet is a confidence trickster and a hypocrite. He claims, as the ghost of Hamlet's father, to be very conscious of his sins on earth, for which he is now doing penance in Purgatory[64] (till his crimes are 'purged away', I.v.13), and he affects to be disgusted (as Hamlet already is) by Claudius's 'incestuous' marriage (I.v.42). Before leaving he asks Hamlet not to taint his mind ('Taint not thy mind...', I.v.85) by seeking revenge against his mother, whom he should leave to be punished by 'heaven' (I.v.85–6) – yet the Ghost has himself been tainting Hamlet's mind by inciting him to take revenge against Claudius instead of leaving Claudius to be punished by heaven too. (Compare John of Gaunt who, in *Richard II* I.ii.40, says of Richard's responsibility for the murder of Gaunt's brother: 'Let heaven revenge'.) After the Ghost's departure it is clear that Hamlet has fallen completely under its spell – he proclaims that what the Ghost has commanded will take precedence in his brain over everything else (I.v.102–4):

> And thy commandment all alone shall live
> Within the book and volume of my brain,
> Unmixed with baser matter.

We should therefore see the dramatic irony in Hamlet's confident assertion to Horatio that 'It is an honest ghost' (I.v.138), and there is dramatic irony also in Hamlet's pity for the Ghost as a 'perturbèd spirit' (I.v.182) when it is Hamlet himself who has been made even more 'perturbed' by the Ghost than he already was.

When Claudius as Denmark's new king first appears in the play (I.ii) he may seem to be sincere in talking to his courtiers about bearing 'our hearts in grief' for 'our dear brother's death' (I.ii.1–3), but this expression of grief is revealed (retrospectively) to be hypocritical in so far as we are to believe what the Ghost says in I.v about Claudius as being the murderer of his brother (later in the play Claudius's guilt is established beyond doubt). That Polonius, the King's senior assistant ('assistant' is how he describes himself in II.ii.165), is a hypocrite is soon revealed by his own behaviour. When his son Laertes is leaving for France Polonius regales him with a list of moral 'precepts' (I.iii.58–80), putting the greatest emphasis on the need for personal integrity (I.iii.78–80):

> This above all – to thine own self be true,
> And it must follow, as the night the day,
> Thou canst not then be false to any man.

But then, after Laertes has gone, Polonius sends his servant Reynaldo to spy on Laertes – Reynaldo is to get into conversation with other Danes in Paris who are acquainted with Laertes, and he is then to attribute various faults to Laertes, such as gambling and visiting brothels, to see whether the other Danes confirm these faults (II.i.6–68). In so far as Claudius is a murderer there is dramatic irony in Polonius's profession of loyalty to him (II.ii.44–5 – after we have heard the Ghost's charges against Claudius):

> I hold my duty, as I hold my soul,
> Both to my God and to my gracious king.

And there is certainly dramatic irony in Claudius's praise of Polonius as 'a man faithful and honourable' (II.ii.129).

Just before Hamlet sees the Ghost he makes a remark about what may happen to 'particular men' to the effect that it takes only a small quantity of evil (a 'dram of eale') to undermine 'the noble substance' of an individual's character (I.iv.23–38). Though this remark was omitted in the First Quarto and the First Folio editions of *Hamlet*, it is probably intended by Shakespeare to indicate how Hamlet himself is infected by evil. This evil began with Hamlet's excessive reaction against the marriage of his mother to Claudius – because of this marriage he regards the whole human world as being possessed by evil (by 'things rank and gross in nature', I.ii.136) and all women as being corrupt ('Frailty, thy name is woman', I.ii.146). And, though this was Hamlet's attitude before the Ghost's visit, that visit can only have had the effect of intensifying it. The outcome of this attitude is Hamlet's cruel rejection of Polonius's daughter Ophelia, to whom he had previously declared his love ('never doubt I love' he said to her in a poem, II.ii.120–). He now tells her that he is a sinner like all men ('We are arrant knaves, all', III.i.130–), and he also tells her to get to a nunnery rather than marry and 'be a breeder of sinners' (III.i.120+) – or, if she does marry, she should marry a fool, since wise men know that women (and he clearly implies that Ophelia would be no exception) are unfaithful to their husbands ('wise men know well enough what monsters you make of them', III.i.140–). Ophelia, who unlike her father represents genuine goodness, calls upon divine powers to restore Hamlet to a state of mental health ('O, help him, you sweet heavens', 'O heavenly powers, restore him', III.i.134, 141): her immediate reaction is to be appalled not so much by his cruelty to her as by the tragic change in his character – 'O, what a noble mind is here o'erthrown!' (III.i.150). Yet Hamlet's mind is not completely 'o'erthrown', since he is able to see that his friend Horatio (a student friend, I.ii.177), far from being an arrant knave (all men are knaves, he told Ophelia), does in fact possess the balanced mind that he, Hamlet, now lacks (III.ii.66–72):

> blest are those
> Whose blood [passion] and judgment are so well commingled
> That they are not a pipe for Fortune's finger
> To sound what stop she please. Give me that man
> That is not passion's slave, and I will wear him
> In my heart's core, ay, in my heart of heart,
> As I do thee.

It is also a sign of health that in this middle part of the play Hamlet has been able to recognise that the Ghost may have been the Devil in 'a pleasing shape' (II.ii.595–6 – in the lines I quoted earlier). When, however, he proves to his own satisfaction that Claudius is indeed a murderer (Claudius betrays his guilt when, in III.ii, Hamlet stages in his presence a play re-enacting the murder as described by the Ghost), misgivings about the Ghost vanish – 'I'll take the ghost's word for a thousand pound' says Hamlet (III.ii.280–1), now quite blind to the Ghost as being a promoter of evil.

There follows a proliferation of evil in the play. Hamlet, impatient to perform the act of revenge required of him, kills Polonius by mistake (III.iv) – Polonius, hiding behind a tapestry to overhear a conversation between Hamlet and his mother, cries out for help when Hamlet seems to be threatening his mother with violence, and Hamlet thinks the cry comes from Claudius. When he discovers his mistake Hamlet believes that in the killing of Polonius he has been employed by 'heaven' as an instrument of punishment (III.iv.173–5), but in fact this killing has evil consequences. Ophelia, as a result both of being rejected by Hamlet and of the killing of her father by Hamlet, lapses into madness – her song about an unmarried girl losing her virginity (IV.v.46–64) reflects the hurt Hamlet inflicted on her since in her madness she acts out his sexual insinuations (amongst his insults he questioned her 'honesty', i.e. chastity, III.i.103–15), and her song about the death of an old man with a beard 'as white as snow' (IV.v.186–95) clearly refers to the death of Polonius. And soon afterwards it is reported that Ophelia in her madness has fallen into a brook and drowned (IV.vii.165–85). Another consequence of the killing of Polonius is that Claudius is able to persuade Laertes to enter into a plot to kill Hamlet. Claudius, after seeing the play staged by Hamlet, was briefly repentant ('O, my offence is rank, it smells to heaven...A brother's murder', III.iii.36–8), but his repentance was indeed brief since we soon find him arranging for Hamlet to be shipped off to England and be put to death there (IV.iii.44–65). Laertes, back from France, at first assumes that Claudius was responsible for Polonius's death and, at the head of an angry mob, he threatens to overthrow Claudius (there is dramatic irony in Claudius's assumption that as king he is automatically protected by God – 'There's such divinity doth hedge a king...', IV.v.120–2: compare Richard II's similar false assumption, *Richard II* III.ii.54–7), but Claudius is able to turn this situation to his advantage by giving full encouragement to Laertes's desire for 'revenge' and convincingly declaring his own innocence in the matter (IV.v.132–49,199–214). In IV.vii Claudius tells Laertes that it was Hamlet who killed Polonius and Claudius is about to say what action was taken against Hamlet when letters arrive from Hamlet himself: herein Hamlet announces his return to Denmark. (In the previous scene, IV.vi, Laertes received a letter telling him how Hamlet escaped transportation to England by boarding a pirate ship.) Laertes, therefore, readily cooperates in a plan for the killing of Hamlet: a fencing contest between Hamlet and Laertes is to be arranged, and in this contest Laertes's foil will be tipped with poison and there will be a goblet of poisoned wine for Hamlet to drink from (IV.vii.140–62). (There is a parallel between the Ghost and Claudius as inciters to revenge – both exploit a son's love for his father. Compare the Ghost's 'If thou didst ever thy dear father love...', I.v.23, with Claudius's 'Laertes, was your father dear to you?', IV.vii.107.)

In the last Act of the play there are indications of a return to mental health in Hamlet. Whereas earlier he had lost his mirth ('I have of late... lost all my mirth', II.ii.290+), he now, though in the macabre setting of a graveyard where Ophelia is about to be buried, recalls with enthusiasm the 'merriment' of Yorick, the court jester of earlier days, whose skull he addresses – he speaks of Yorick's 'flashes of merriment that were wont to set the table on a roar' (V.i.176+). Hamlet's love for Ophelia now returns, albeit in over-passionate form – when he sees Laertes leap into Ophelia's grave to embrace his dead sister, Hamlet, not to be outdone in the expression of love for Ophelia, also leaps into her grave, proclaiming as he emerges from it (V.i.263–5):

> I loved Ophelia. Forty thousand brothers
> Could not with all their quantity of love
> Make up my sum.

There is also a proper appreciation of divine involvement in human affairs: whereas previously Hamlet had falsely imagined that his killing of Polonius was instigated by 'heaven' (III.iv.173–5), he now justifiably perceives divine involvement in his escape from transportation – he says, in relation to that escape, 'There's a divinity that shapes our ends' (V.ii.10), and here this view is heartily endorsed ('That is most certain', V.ii.11) by Horatio, the representative of sanity throughout the play. And, whereas on two previous occasions Hamlet had contemplated committing suicide (at the beginning of his first soliloquy in the play, I.ii.131–2, and in the famous 'To be, or not to be' soliloquy, III.i.56ff.), he is now prepared to accept death as Providence shall decide (V.ii.210+):

> There's a special providence in the fall of a sparrow. If it [death] be now, 'tis not to come. If it be not to come, it will be now. If it be not now, yet it will come. The readiness is all.

In the last scene (V.ii) evil takes a heavy toll, but is finally halted. During the fencing contest the Queen (who at least as a mother has shown genuine devotion to Hamlet) dies after drinking the poisoned wine meant for Hamlet. Hamlet himself dies, as intended, after being wounded by Laertes's poisoned foil, but Laertes also dies, since he too was wounded by the poisoned foil which after a scuffle was picked up by Hamlet, not Laertes. But Laertes before he dies is moved to reveal the King's part in the plot against Hamlet, so that Hamlet immediately stabs the King to death. In his last words Laertes says (V.ii.321) 'Exchange forgiveness with me, noble Hamlet', and Hamlet's expressed wish that Laertes should be absolved by heaven of his own guilt in plotting Hamlet's death ('Heaven make thee free of it', V.ii.324) is probably to be taken as suggesting that Laertes, as an essentially good character, will pass to heaven, as probably will Hamlet himself, as suggested by the words spoken by Horatio immediately after Hamlet's death: 'flights of angels sing thee to thy rest' (V.ii.352). As regards punishment, we hear that Rosencrantz and Guildenstern, two former friends of Hamlet who became the servile instruments of Claudius and who carried the instructions to England for Hamlet to be put to death there, were themselves put to death: Hamlet tells Horatio (V.ii.12–53) that before he escaped back to Denmark he discovered the King's instructions and was able to substitute instructions for Rosencrantz and Guildenstern to be put to death because he happened to have with him the King's signet needed to give royal authority for these instructions – 'even in that was heaven ordinant' says Hamlet (V.ii.48), and we are probably to take it that heaven was in fact 'ordinant' (i.e. directing the course of events) in this punishment of Rosencrantz and Guildenstern. (There was dramatic irony when at the beginning of III.iii Rosencrantz and Guildenstern spoke reverentially of Claudius as a responsible holder of kingly power – Rosencrantz referred to him as 'That spirit upon whose weal [well-being] depends and rests/The lives of many', III.iii.14–15.) Just before Hamlet dies the arrival is announced of Fortinbras, nephew of the King of Norway, and Hamlet in his dying words strongly recommends that Fortinbras should be elected as King of Denmark (Denmark's monarchy being elective). Hearing briefly of Denmark's tale of woe, Fortinbras says 'with sorrow I embrace my fortune (V.ii.380), and in view of Hamlet's recommendation Fortinbras's 'fortune' will almost certainly involve his becoming Denmark's new ruler. Thus order in

Denmark will be restored, so fulfilling Horatio's earlier prophecy that, though there was something rotten in the state of Denmark, 'Heaven will direct it' (I.iv.91).

THE PHOENIX AND TURTLE (1601)

In 1601 there was published a poem by Robert Chester entitled *Love's Martyr*, and to this poem were appended poems by various poets on the 'subject' of 'the Phoenix and Turtle'. One of these poems, a poem of 67 lines, was attributed to Shakespeare, and though it had no separate title it is usually given the title *The Phoenix and Turtle*.

The poem takes the form of a lament on the death of a turtle dove and his queen, the phoenix. Their marriage is presented as a supreme example of 'constancy' in love (line 22), of both 'beauty' and 'truth' (i.e. constancy, line 53). We have here a clear link with Shakespeare's Sonnets, which also stress the need for constancy in love and for physical beauty to be accompanied by constancy. And in this poem we are told that the phoenix and the turtle were completely united in love (lines 25–6):

> So they loved as love in twain
> Had the essence but in one.

Here we have an echo of Sonnet 36 where the Poet says of himself and his Friend 'our undivided loves are one', and similarly in *A Midsummer Night's Dream* (II.ii.47–8) Lysander says to Hermia 'my heart unto yours is knit/So that but one heart we can make of it'.[65]

Where this poem differs from what is said about love by Shakespeare in other works is in its praise of 'married chastity' (line 61), by which is meant sexual abstention within marriage, since the poem praises the married pair for not begetting children (the fact that they left 'no posterity' was not due to 'infirmity', the physical inability to have children – lines 59–60). The opposite view of marriage is presented in *Romeo and Juliet* where Juliet in her soliloquy at the beginning of III.ii longs for physical love within marriage, following chastity before marriage. And as regards marriage and children, in a number of the Sonnets (1–4, 6, 7, 12, 13) the Poet appeals to his young friend, who possesses physical beauty, to beget children so that this beauty may be passed on to another generation. Similarly in *Twelfth Night*, probably written soon after *The Phoenix and Turtle*, Viola says (I.v.225–7) to the beautiful Olivia, who at beginning of the play is in a state of mourning and has renounced the company of men:

> Lady, you are the cruell'st she alive
> If you will lead these graces to the grave
> And leave the world no copy.

The phoenix and the turtle, on the other hand, are praised for having 'no posterity' even though they do possess 'beauty'. But perhaps the Phoenix and Turtle poem should be taken, not as advocating sexual abstention in all marriages, but as paying tribute in its own special way to spiritual love as the highest kind of love.

TWELFTH NIGHT, OR WHAT YOU WILL (c. 1601)

What You Will, the second part of the title of this play, like *As You Like It*, suggests a light-hearted play, as also does the first part of the title, *Twelfth Night*, seemingly an indication that the play is appropriate for performance in the festive season (in the play itself there is no reference to Twelfth Night). And, like *As You Like It*, *Twelfth Night* is a light-hearted play with a serious theme concerning love. In *Twelfth Night* the main theme is true love contrasted with false conceptions of love and of marriage (to which, for Shakespeare, love between the sexes is linked).

In the opening speech Orsino, Duke of Illyria, is indulging in love as sentiment, and sentiment that is subject to sudden changes of mood:

> If music be the food of love, play on...
>   Enough, no more.
> 'Tis not so sweet now as it was before.

The brief first scene ends with the Duke wandering off to indulge his 'love-thoughts' in the setting of 'sweet beds of flowers' (I.i.40–1). We are informed in the first and second scenes that the Duke's love thoughts are centred on the Countess Olivia (I.i.19, I.ii.34), and, though his sentimentalism as a lover touches on the absurd, he is, we hear, a man to be respected – 'A noble duke, in nature as in name [rank]' (I.ii.25).

In the second scene we are introduced to Viola, a young woman brought ashore on the Illyrian coast after the ship in which she was travelling was wrecked at sea, and in I.iv Viola, disguised as a young man called 'Cesario', has obtained employment by being taken into the Duke's service. In II.iv the Duke talks to Cesario about love, and, though he claims to be representative of all true lovers ('such as I am all true lovers are', II.iv.16), he makes remarks which lack the perception of a true lover. He praises women's love as being superior to men's love, but does so by making a shallow generalisation about the love of all men (II.iv.32–4):

> Our fancies are more giddy and unfirm,
> More longing, wavering, sooner lost and worn [worn out],
> Than women's are.

This remark is then contradicted by his assertion that no woman's love can be compared with his love for Olivia (II.iv.92–102):

> There is no woman's sides
> Can bide the beating of so strong a passion
> As love doth give my heart...
>   Make no compare
> Between that love a woman can bear me
> And that I owe [have for] Olivia.

In I.iv the Duke assigned to Cesario the task of going to Olivia 'to act my woes' (I.iv.25), and the Duke's melodramatic view of his sufferings as a lover is reflected in a song the Duke has heard sung by Feste, Olivia's clown, who is brought to the Duke to sing this song again. The song ('Come away, come away, death') is about a lover who dies of a broken heart because he has been rejected: 'I am slain by a fair cruel maid' (II.iv.53). After the song has been sung the Duke actually refers to Olivia as 'sovereign cruelty' (II.iv.79) – even though her only offence, as Viola tries to point out (II.iv.86–91), is that she cannot return the Duke's love. In an 'aside' at the end of I.iv Viola revealed that she herself had fallen in love with the Duke, and now in II.iv a contrast emerges between the Duke's sentimental-melodramatic love and Viola's true love. Viola expresses her secret love for the Duke by appearing to talk about the love experienced by a sister (II.iv.109–14):

> She never told her love,
> But let concealment, like a worm i' th' bud,
> Feed on her damask [pink rose] cheek...
> She sat like Patience on a monument [Patience personified, probably as a statue on a tombstone],
> Smiling at grief. Was not this love indeed?

Here the verse does indeed have the ring of true love, and, though Viola has to suffer by keeping her love secret, there is no sentimental melodrama: instead of being 'slain' she conceals her grief by smiling. There is subtle irony in the lines that immediately follow (II.iv.115–17) – Viola, having expressed her own love as a woman, pretends as the male Cesario to echo the Duke's earlier tribute to women's love as being superior to men's, but her words are at heart not a facile generalisation about men and women but a plea for unobtrusive sincerity and dedication in love, and she may be secretly protesting against what she feels to be an excess of outward display in the Duke's love for Olivia:

> We men may say more, swear more, but indeed
> Our shows are more than will [real strength of feeling], for still we prove
> Much in our vows, but little in our love.

Viola, besides providing the central example of true love in the play, becomes the means by which true love is aroused in Olivia. At the beginning of the play we hear that out of love for her dead brother Olivia has entered into a state of mourning for seven years (I.i.26–32) and has abjured the company of men (I.ii.39–41). Viola as Cesario, visiting Olivia on the Duke's behalf, dutifully acts out the Duke's love by describing it in extravagant terms, with due emphasis on the woeful aspects (I.v.239–40): the Duke loves Olivia

> With adorations, fertile tears,
> With groans that thunder love, with sighs of fire.

Olivia remains unmoved, saying of the Duke (I.v.242–6): 'I suppose him virtuous, know him noble...yet I cannot love him.' But she invites Cesario to say how he would persist in the expression of his love if he were the Duke, and Viola, obviously inspired by her own love for the Duke, proclaims that she would (I.v.252–8)

> Make me a willow cabin at your gate...
> Halloo your name to the reverberate hills,
> And make the babbling gossip of the air
> Cry out 'Olivia!'

Olivia, who has clearly forgotten all about being in mourning for her dead brother, is now attracted to Cesario, saying in soliloquy after he has gone (I.v.280–2):

> Methinks I feel this youth's perfections
> With an invisible and subtle stealth
> To creep in at mine eyes.

She accordingly sends him a ring as a love token (II.ii), and when he comes again she frankly declares her love (III.i.147–9):

> By maidhood, honour, truth, and everything,
> I love thee so, that, maugre [despite] all thy pride,
> Nor wit nor reason can my passion hide.

This shows the feeling of true love, the snag of course being that she does not know that Cesario is female, a problem that, Viola has told herself, can be resolved only by time ('O Time, thou must untangle this, not I', II.ii.38). Though the Duke in I.i praised Olivia for going into prolonged mourning out of love for her dead brother, we are probably meant to take the view that the mourning Olivia imposed on herself was excessive and that it is therefore a healthy sign that her interest in Cesario has roused her out of her mourning. That Olivia should not cut herself off from youthful love seems to be the point of the song which Feste the clown sings in II.iii.38–51 about his 'mistress', if we may take this as referring to his mistress Olivia: 'O mistress mine... your true love's coming...What is love? 'Tis not hereafter... In delay there lies no plenty...'

At the beginning of Act II true love of another kind is briefly introduced. Viola's twin brother Sebastian, who was travelling with her in the ship that was wrecked and who was last seen clinging to a mast in the sea by the ship's captain (I.ii.11–14), has been rescued by another captain, Antonio, and Sebastian and Antonio arrive together on the Illyrian coast (though neither Sebastian nor Viola knows of the other's safe arrival). Sebastian has become the object of Antonio's 'love' (i.e. devotion, II.i.7–, 31), even to the point of the word 'adore' being used ('I do adore thee so' says Antonio in soliloquy, II.i.42). We know from the Sonnets that Shakespeare attaches high value to love between men (not physical homosexual love), and Antonio's love for Sebastian bears comparison with Viola's love for the Duke in that it shows a selfless devotion to the loved one: though Antonio has enemies in Illyria (II.i.40 – we hear later, III.iii.26–7, that he took part in a sea-fight against the Duke's ships), he insists on staying in Illyria so that he may be at hand if Sebastian needs his help.

In contrast to true love, and apart from the kind of contrast indicated by the Duke's deficiencies as a lover, there are two situations in the play, both presented as farce, where courtship is involved but where true love is blatantly absent.

The first of these situations involves an attempt to foist a husband onto Olivia. Early on in the play we hear that Olivia's uncle, Sir Toby Belch, has brought 'a foolish knight', Sir Andrew Aguecheek, to be Olivia's wooer (I.iii.12+). Sir Andrew has little inclination to go through with the wooing ('Faith, I'll home tomorrow', I.iii.98+), but Sir Toby urges him to persevere ('there's life in't, man', I.iii.104). In II.iii we discover Sir Toby's motive in promoting this marriage. Sir Toby wants to ensure that Sir Andrew does not run out of money, presumably because Sir Andrew is Sir Toby's drinking companion (see I.iii.33–4) and money is needed to pay for their drinking bouts: 'Thou hadst need send for more money' says Sir Toby (II.iii.171–2), and Sir Andrew replies 'If I cannot recover [win] your niece, I am a foul way out.' When Sir Andrew says that he'll stay no longer because he has observed that Olivia seems more attracted to Cesario than to him, Sir Toby, with assistance from Olivia's servant Fabian, pushes Sir Andrew into challenging Cesario to a duel in the hope that Sir Andrew will outshine Cesario sufficiently to win Olivia's favour (III.ii).

The other piece of farce concerns Olivia's steward, Malvolio, who is unpopular in her household because of his self-importance, described by Olivia herself as 'self-love' (I.v.84+) – this term 'self-love' points to an attitude of mind that lies at the opposite extreme from Viola's selfless love. Olivia's waiting gentlewoman Maria perceives that Malvolio's conceit leads him to believe 'that all that look on him love him' (II.iii.144–), and it is because of this belief that he becomes the victim of a practical joke that Maria plays upon him (II.v). She leaves a letter for him to pick up which, composed by herself but written in Olivia's style of handwriting, purports to be a love letter from Olivia inviting Malvolio to show that he returns her love by wearing cross-gartered yellow stockings and smiling perpetually. Malvolio readily believes that Olivia is in love with him, and when (in III.iv) he appears before her in the way required in the letter (he also persists in quoting phrases from the letter which to Olivia are unintelligible), he is treated as a madman and locked in a dark room (III.iv.126+, IV.ii).

In the last two Acts the play's complications are resolved. Olivia's love for Cesario ends in a marriage – in a marriage with Sebastian whom she mistakes for Cesario but who was only too willing to be married to her: when Olivia arrives with a priest to perform the marriage ceremony Sebastian promises that he, 'having sworn truth [fidelity], ever will be true' (IV.iii.33), and the two of them are joined in 'A contract of eternal bond of love' (V.i.150). (This coming of Sebastian into Olivia's life is perhaps to be taken as the fulfilment of Feste's prophecy in his 'O mistress mine' song – 'your true love's coming', II.iii.39.) Viola, when confronted by Sir Andrew in a duel, was suddenly rescued by Antonio who mistook her for Sebastian (III.iv.296–301), and in the last scene Viola's identity as a woman is revealed when she and Sebastian come face to face in the presence of the Duke and Olivia. The Duke now recognises Viola's love for him and he offers her his hand in marriage (V.i.312–13):

> Here is my hand. You shall from this time be
> Your master's mistress [wife].

And in his final speech he speaks of the close relationship that will result from Olivia's marriage to Sebastian being followed by his own marriage to Sebastian's twin sister (V.i.369–70):

> A solemn combination shall be made
> Of our dear souls.

As for Malvolio, he is released from the dark room, but when the trick played on him is explained he storms off, vowing 'I'll be revenged on the whole pack of you' (V.i.364). But in connection with this trick another marriage is announced. When the trick was being played Sir Toby was so delighted with Maria for thinking of it that he exclaimed 'I could marry this wench for this device' (II.v.162), and now in the last scene we hear that in 'recompense' for that trick he has indeed married her (V.i.351). This marriage has hardly arisen out of true love, as have the other marriages, but on the other hand it does not seem to be motivated by the desire for money.

The play thus ends with three marriages, but the play as a whole is rounded off with a song from Feste about 'the wind and the rain' – these words are repeated in the second line of each of the five four-line stanzas. In the third stanza the 'I' in the song says that, when the time came to 'wive', 'By swaggering could I never thrive', and the fourth stanza refers to 'toss-pots' (drunkards) going to bed with 'drunken heads'. A possible interpretation of the song's relevance to the play is that among those left in the wind and the rain of life (as against those able to enjoy the sunshine of happiness) are swaggerers like Malvolio and drunkards: there are two references in the play to Sir Toby being drunk (I.v.109, V.i.186–), and the fourth stanza in Feste's song is perhaps a warning that Sir Toby's marriage will not bring happiness if he does not mend his drunken ways.

TROILUS AND CRESSIDA (c. 1602)

It could be said that in *Troilus and Cressida* there is a combination of the theme of *The Two Gentlemen of Verona* (the need for 'constancy' in love) with the theme of *King John* (the need for integrity in a nation's leaders). *Troilus and Cressida* is a dramatic presentation of Troilus's love for Cressida and her betrayal of him (here the woman is the betrayer, whereas in *The Two Gentlemen of Verona* the betrayer was a male), but the play is also very much concerned with the ethics of the Trojan War, fought by the Greeks against the Trojans (according to Homer's *Iliad*) because Paris, son of Priam, King of Troy, had abducted Helen, wife of the Greek king Menelaus. In Shakespeare's play there is a lack of integrity amongst the leaders on both sides which takes the form of false justifications of the war (whereas in *King John* the lack of integrity largely took the form of broken pledges) – the war is unjustifiable since the Trojans are fighting in defence of an abduction and the Greeks are fighting to recover Helen who is in fact faithless to her Greek husband and has no desire to be returned to him. Here we have a notable contrast with *Henry V* where Shakespeare sees the war against France as being wholly justified. The theme of *Troilus and Cressida*, therefore, is the need for integrity both in love (which should involve 'constancy', 'faith', 'truth') and in war (where true 'honour' should be involved).

The first scene is set in Troy with Troilus, a son of the Trojan king, declaring himself to be madly in love with Cressida ('I am mad/In Cressid's love'. I.i.50–1) and waiting for Cressida's uncle, Pandarus, to bring him and Cressida together. And in the second scene we see Pandarus trying to arouse Cressida's interest in Troilus by praising him in glowing terms ('Brave Troilus, the prince of chivalry!...O admirable youth!...O admirable man!', I.ii.221 ff.). But the play soon moves on to the wider issue of the war between the Greeks and the Trojans. In I.iii the Greek leaders Agamemnon, Nestor and Ulysses discuss the situation at some length, and we are at first led to believe that the war calls forth fine human qualities. Agamemnon, the commander-in-chief, regrets that Troy, after being besieged by the Greeks for seven years, is still not defeated, but he argues (I.iii.17–30) that by standing up to the challenge of misfortune the Greeks have shown themselves to be 'rich in virtue'. And Ulysses speaks of the 'wisdom' (I.iii.198) and the calm deliberation ('still and mental parts', I.iii.200) displayed by himself and his fellow leaders in their conduct of the war. But Ulysses deplores the disloyalty of the Greek warrior Achilles who listens to the 'scurril [scurrilous] jests' (I.iii.148) made by Patroclus about the Greek leaders, and similarly Nestor deplores the misconduct of Ajax in listening to the 'slanders' fabricated by Thersites (I.iii.193). (It is in connection with this indiscipline that Ulysses makes his well-known remarks – I.iii.83–124 – about harmony in a human society depending upon 'degree', upon obedience being shown to one's superiors according to one's place in a social hierarchy.) At this point the Trojan Aeneas enters the Greek camp – there has been a truce in the fighting for some time (I.iii.262) – to announce an offer from Hector, King Priam's warrior son, to face a Greek warrior in single combat: Shakespeare makes Aeneas speak like a medieval knight[66] in saying (I.iii.265–79) that a Greek should be inspired to meet Hector's challenge by a desire to fight in honour of his beloved 'mistress' and to show himself to be 'true in love'. We begin to doubt the integrity of the Greek leaders when they resort to a shabby trick in their choice of an opponent to Hector: though Achilles would be the obvious choice, he is to be punished for his insolence by having the choice put to lottery, a lottery to be rigged in favour of Ajax, thereby arousing jealousy in Achilles against Ajax – as the Greek leader Nestor observes with satisfaction, 'Two curs shall tame each other' (I.iii.390).

As the play proceeds it becomes increasingly clear that the war is unjustifiable. On the Trojan side this is frankly admitted by Hector in the discussion that takes place in the Trojan camp in II.ii. This discussion arises out of a Greek demand that Helen should be surrendered (II.ii.3–7). Hector's immediate response is 'Let Helen go' (II.ii.17), and he goes on to state (II.ii.174–86) that marriage is an institution to be respected and the 'moral laws/Of nature and of nations' require that Helen should be returned to her husband. That, says Hector, is his opinion 'in way of truth' (i.e. in accordance with what is morally right, II.ii.189), but then he suddenly changes tack and says (II.ii.189–93) that, after all, the Trojans should 'keep Helen still' – in order to preserve their 'dignities'. And in this discussion Troilus, whose obsession with Cressida in the first scene of the play caused him to feel utterly detached from the war ('Fools on both sides!', I.i.89), now shows a manifestly false sense of honour by claiming that Helen must be retained in order to uphold the 'honour' of King Priam of Troy (II.ii.26–8): Helen 'is a theme of honour and renown' (II.ii.199). On the Greek side Thersites is of the opinion that Greek lives should not be lost in an attempt to recover a faithless woman (II.iii.66 +): 'All the argument is a whore and a cuckold, a good quarrel [he says with bitter sarcasm] to... bleed to death upon.' Foul-mouthed though Thersites may be, his description of Helen as 'a whore' is at least partly confirmed in the one scene in the play where Helen makes a personal appearance – III.i. Here Pandarus speaks enthusiastically to Helen and Paris of 'fair desires', wishing that Helen may have 'fair thoughts' as associated with her 'fair pillow' (III.i.44–), and Helen enters into the spirit of this bawdy innuendo by welcoming Pandarus's 'fair words' (III.i.45). Helen and Paris then greatly enjoy a love song sung by Pandarus (III.i.108–19) which describes Cupid as arousing physical desire: Cupid's arrow 'tickles still the sore... ha, ha, ha!'

When Pandarus at last brings Troilus and Cressida together

Troilus passionately declares his belief in true love, love that is to be identified with 'constancy' (III.ii.157), with 'integrity and truth' (III.ii.161), and Cressida declares herself to be bound by true love for Troilus ('If I be false, or swerve a hair from truth...', III.ii.180–92). Pandarus, having, as we have seen, shown in the previous scene (III.i) a delight in the lechery between Helen and Paris, now, after paying lip service to constancy in love ('If ever you prove false to one another...', III.ii.200–), steers Troilus and Cressida towards 'a chamber and a bed' (III.ii.205–). The following morning is reminiscent of *Romeo and Juliet*, with Troilus about to leave as he hears the sound of the lark at daybreak (IV.ii.10– – compare *Romeo and Juliet* III.v.6–11), the important difference being that there has been no marriage ceremony between Troilus and Cressida, as there had been between Romeo and Juliet. Pandarus greets Cressida with the question 'How go maidenheads?' (IV.ii.25–) and makes mocking jests about lost virginity. But then comes the news that Cressida must join her father Calchas who, convinced that the Trojans would be defeated, went over to the Greeks (III.iii.4–6) and then was able to persuade Agamemnon to agree to the releasing of a Trojan prisoner on condition that in return the Trojans would allow Cressida to leave Troy (III.iii.18–32). Before departing with the Greek Diomedes who has been sent to fetch her, Cressida promises to be 'true' to Troilus (IV.iv.68 – just as she pledged herself to 'truth' in III.ii), and they give each other a love token. But Troilus soon finds her promise to be short-lived. He accompanies Hector when Hector presents himself to the Greeks to fight in single combat, and there, amongst the Greeks, Troilus has the mortification of seeing Cressida hand over his love token (a sleeve) to Diomedes (V.ii.65): Troilus vows to kill Diomedes in battle (V.ii.167–74).

As regards the war, Thersites's view that the Greeks should not fight for the sake of a woman who is 'a whore' receives endorsement from other Greeks. When Diomedes arrives in Troy to fetch Cressida Paris asks him for his opinion as to who deserves to have Helen – himself (Paris) or Menelaus? Diomedes replies that she is 'a whore' who brings dishonour to both men

(IV.i.56–68), and he deplores the loss of life on both sides because of her (IV.i.71–4):

> For every drop in her bawdy veins
> A Grecian's life has sunk; for every scruple [minute amount]
> Of her contaminated carrion weight
> A Troyan [Trojan] hath been slain.

And in IV.v even Ulysses and Menelaus himself show contempt for Helen – Ulysses describes the Paris-Helen affair as the 'theme of all our scorns' (IV.v.30), and Menelaus says much the same when told by Hector (on the occasion of Hector's visit to the Greek camp to fight Ajax) that Helen wished to send no personal greetings to Menelaus – Menelaus replies (IV.v.181): 'Name her not now, sir. She's a deadly theme.' In this scene, IV.v, what does credit to both sides is the temporary friendship that occurs when Hector breaks off the fight with Ajax because of their family connection (IV.v.119–38) – Ajax's mother was a Trojan, sister of Hector's father: Hector and Ajax are therefore cousins (in I.ii.13 Ajax was said to be Hector's 'nephew', but there 'nephew' means cousin). This display of generous feeling by Hector wins a warm response from the Greek leaders – Agamemnon says that with 'faith and troth' and 'most divine integrity' the Greeks welcome him (IV.v.168–71), and Nestor embraces him as a 'worthy warrior' (IV.v.199–200). Shakespeare must be suggesting here, therefore, that Greeks and Trojans have good reason to be friends rather than enemies. Achilles too has a personal relationship with a Trojan – he is in love with one of King Priam's daughters (III.iii.193–4, V.i.35–42). But then both sides return to the battlefield, and Achilles treacherously kills Hector when he is unarmed (V.viii).

After the death of Hector the Greeks are confident of victory (V.ix.9–10), though before Hector's death they had many casualties (V.v.6–15). In the last scene Troilus, though he has been defeated in combat by Diomedes (V.v.1–5) and though the Trojans face 'sure destructions' (V.x.9), is determined to fight on to seek 'revenge' against the Greeks (V.x.31). In a brief encounter with Pandarus Troilus bitterly denounces him (V.x.33–4) for his shameful role as 'broker' between himself and Cressida, a role that deserves to 'live aye with thy name' (the word 'pander' has in fact lived on as meaning procurer or pimp – Pandarus had himself referred to this possibility in III.ii.200–), and the play ends with a self-pitying soliloquy by Pandarus admitting that he is to be classed amongst 'traders in the flesh' (V.x.45).

Hector is the hero of the play in so far as he is associated with love in terms of medieval chivalry (I.iii.265–79) and puts family ties above the antagonism of war, but he showed a lack of integrity as a leader in supporting the continuation of the war after he himself had argued that the retention of Helen was morally wrong. And Troilus, though he pleads for integrity in love, showed the same lack of integrity as Hector in claiming that the retention of Helen was a matter of 'honour'. It is tragically ironic that Troilus should be betrayed by a woman who proves to be as faithless as Helen in fact was. (Cressida is dismissed by Ulysses as 'sluttish', IV.v.62, and Thersites, who had described Helen as 'a whore' in II.iii.66+, applies the same word to Cressida in V.iv – in his opening speech and in V.iv.20+.)

ALL'S WELL THAT ENDS WELL (c. 1603)

The theme of *All's Well That Ends Well* is the need for 'honour' (a word frequently used in the play) in love as well as in war – this is a theme that has some similarity to that of *Troilus and Cressida*, which was possibly written shortly before *All's Well*. An extremely brief summary of the plot of *All's Well* might suggest that Bertram, the young Count of Rousillon, is the victim of Helena, who forces him into a marriage with her and then, after he has escaped, tricks him into returning to her. In fact, however, Helena is presented as performing a divine mission to bring true love to Bertram, whose main concern hitherto has been to seek distinction in war.

The play opens in Rousillon (in the south of France, bordering on Spain) where Bertram, the young Count, is on the point of leaving for Paris at the command of the King of France who, having been a close friend of Bertram's late father, wants Bertram to be his ward. Helena, since the death of her father who was a distinguished physician, has lived as a dependant in the Rousillon palace, and in a soliloquy she reveals her secret love for Bertram, lamenting that in rank 'he is so above me' (I.i.81). However, in her soliloquy at the end of the first scene she feels she is being urged on by some mysterious power (I.i.206–7):

> What power is it which mounts my love so high,
> That makes me see and cannot feed mine eye?

And at the end of this soliloquy we hear that she has in mind a 'project' which may help her to achieve what she aspires to. Bertram's mother, the widowed Countess, greatly admires Helena (I.i.40–) and, when told by her steward about Helena's love for Bertram (the steward had overheard Helena speaking aloud about it), the Countess asks Helena to confess her love, 'As heaven shall work in me for thine avail' (I.iii.175). Following Helena's confession of her love the Countess gives full support to Helena's wish to go to Paris and use one of her father's special remedies to cure the King of a disease that afflicts him – this is the 'project' Helena had in mind in her soliloquy at the end of I.i ('The King's disease' was mentioned in I.i.214), and she freely admits that her wish to go to Paris is connected with Bertram's presence there (I.iii.223–6). In this first Act of the play cynical comments are made about chastity and marriage, comments which are of significance in relation to Bertram's conduct later in the play. Parolles, just before leaving for Paris as Bertram's companion, expresses the opinion that virginity should be disposed of as quickly as possible – 'Away with't' (I.i.140). And the resident clown at the Rousillon palace argues that adultery is inevitable since human nature is governed by 'flesh and blood' (I.iii.40+). He recites lines of verse which suggest that the adulterer is like a cuckoo (traditionally associated with cuckoldry) that 'sings by kind' (i.e. according to the promptings of its nature, I.iii.60), and more lines of verse from the Clown (I.iii.66–75) suggest that Helen of

Troy's infidelity (strongly condemned by Shakespeare in *Troilus and Cressida*) is typical of the behaviour of nine women out of ten.

In Paris Helena makes her offer of medical assistance to the King, asking him to put his trust in heaven (II.i.153): 'Of heaven, not me, make an experiment.' (Whereas in I.i.202–3 Helena wanted to encourage herself to take positive action by emphasising the human will –

> Our remedies oft in ourselves do lie
> Which we ascribe to heaven –

she now gives full recognition to the power of heaven, II.i.150–1:

> But most it is presumption in us when
> The help of heaven we count the act of men.)

The King is impressed by Helena's words ('Methinks in thee some blessed spirit doth speak', II.i.174) and accepts the terms proposed by Helena that if the remedy fails she will face death, but if she succeeds she will be empowered by the King to choose the man she wants as husband. We soon hear of the King's recovery, which is acclaimed by the elderly French lord Lafeu as miraculous: Lafeu pours scorn on those who say that 'miracles are past' (II.iii.1 – in her first meeting with the King Helena expressed her faith in miracles as described in 'holy writ', II.i.137–40), and he sees in the King's recovery the 'Very hand of heaven' (II.iii.30). When Helena chooses Bertram as a husband Bertram complains that she is of lower social rank than he is, but the King insists that honour does not depend on social rank (II.iii.133–5):

> Honours thrive
> When rather from our acts we them derive
> Than our foregoers.

Bertram is thus obliged to accept Helena as his wife, but after the marriage ceremony he tells Parolles that he will never 'bed' Helena (II.iii.263,266). On being required by Bertram to return home to Rousillon Helena's response is 'I am your most obedient servant' (II.v.71): her hint that Bertram might kiss her before they part (II.v.84) is ignored. Once home Helena receives a letter from Bertram saying that she will never be able to call him husband unless she can get possession of the ring he wears permanently on his finger and can give birth to a child fathered by him (III.ii.58–). The letter is delivered by two soldiers who tell the Countess that Bertram has gone to fight for the Duke of Florence. Soon after arriving in Paris Bertram had wanted to obtain 'honour' in battle (II.i.30–3) by joining some French volunteers who were going to fight for Florence against Siena (the Sienese are referred to as 'Senoys', I.ii.1), but the King had refused to let him go because he was too young (II.i.27–8): now, after being married to Helena, he has been determined to have his own way in this matter. The Countess asks the two soldiers who have delivered the letter to Helena to tell Bertram 'that his sword can never win/The honour that he loses' (III.ii.92–3 – i.e. as a soldier he cannot win the honour he loses by deserting Helena), and later the Countess says of Bertram and Helena to her steward (III.iv.26–9):

> He cannot thrive
> Unless her prayers, whom heaven delights to hear
> And loves to grant, reprieve him from the wrath
> Of greatest justice.

And the Countess refers to Helena's 'pure love' (III.iv.38).

Bertram succeeds in winning military honour – we hear (III.v.4ff.) that he 'has done most honourable service' by capturing the Sienese commander-in-chief and killing the brother of the Sienese Duke. This information comes from talk between a Florentine widow and her daughter and a friend, but then it emerges from this talk that Parolles and Bertram under Parolles's influence are attempting to seduce Florentine virgins (III.v.10ff). Helen arrives in Florence in the guise of a holy pilgrim who is on her way to a saint's shrine, and she learns from the Florentine widow (who is to provide her with lodging) that the widow's daughter, Diana, is a victim of Bertram's 'unlawful' attentions (III.v.64–9). The widow, after Helena has revealed that she is Bertram's wife, agrees to a plot whereby Diana will appear to be willing to be seduced if Bertram gives her the ring from his finger and then, at the appointed time for the 'encounter', Helena will pass herself off as Diana (III.vii.30–4). And in IV.ii this plan is put into operation: Diana arranges with Bertram that the encounter will take place after midnight – in 'pitchy' darkness, as we hear later (IV.iv.24) – and without any exchange of words.

Parolles's evil influence over Bertram is brought to an end by the exposure of Parolles as a coward and a traitor. Two French 'lords' (two brothers, III.vi.98, Dumain by name as revealed later, IV.iii.163 +, 262–4), who know Parolles to be a vicious person, invite Bertram (III.vi.15–28) to join them in observing Parolles when taken prisoner by Florentine soldiers pretending to be enemy soldiers: Parolles is taken prisoner in this way in IV.i, and under interrogration in IV.iii he betrays military secrets, slanders the Dumain brothers (the two captains who have organised this deception of Parolles), and denounces Bertram himself. Helena, 'supposed dead' (IV.iv.11) after it has been given out that she died after reaching the saint's shrine that was her destination as a pilgrim (IV.iii.45 +), persuades the widow and Diana to go with her to the King of France – Helena says of Diana 'heaven...hath fated her to be my motive [promoter]/And helper to a husband' (IV.iv.18–21). Bertram had told Diana that he would marry her if his wife died (IV.ii.71–2), and in the Rousillon palace, where the King is visiting the Countess and where Bertram has arrived back from the war, Diana reminds Bertram (who believes Helena to be dead) of his promise to marry her and confronts him with the ring he gave her (a ring that has been a valued heirloom in Bertram's family). Bertram tries to dismiss Diana as 'a common gamester [slut] to the camp' (V.iii.186), but has to admit to giving her the ring. There is confusion also about another ring, a ring which Bertram is seen to be wearing but which the King earlier gave Helena and which Bertram supposes he was given by Diana (see IV.ii.61–3) – it was actually given him by Helena posing as Diana. All this confusion recedes with the appearance of Helena as if from the grave (rather like the appearance of

Hero at the end of *Much Ado about Nothing*). Helena reads out the letter Bertram sent her and then indicates that his conditions for accepting her as his wife have now been fulfilled – she has obtained the ring that was on his finger and she is with child by him. At this point Bertram undergoes a moral transformation and he assures the King (V.iii.309–10) that, following a clear explanation from Helena of what has happened,

> I'll love her dearly, ever, ever dearly.

Earlier Helena was confident that the outcome would be 'All's well that ends well' (IV.iv.35, V.i.25), and the play ends with the King saying to characters in the play 'All yet seems well' (V.iii.326) and to members of the audience 'All is well ended' (Epilogue, line 2).

OTHELLO (c. 1603)

The theme of *Othello* is the power of evil as a destructive psychological force. We have seen that, whereas in the earlier historical plays evil was presented primarily as a force promoting disorder and destruction in society, in Brutus in *Julius Caesar* and in Prince Hamlet Shakespeare was becoming concerned with evil as a force working for the undermining of individual minds. In *Othello* Iago, motivated by malicious 'hate' and finally exposed as a 'hellish villain', causes distress to various people, but is above all tireless in his determination to destroy Othello's love for Desdemona – in this play good and evil are closely associated with love and hate, as in *Romeo and Juliet* and *The Merchant of Venice*.

In the first scene Iago, 'ancient' (second lieutenant) to Othello, a Moor who commands the Venetian army, is in conversation with Roderigo, a foolish but well-to-do young Venetian, and Roderigo is complaining that, after giving Iago money to promote a marriage between himself and Desdemona, daughter of Brabantio, a senator, he has just heard that Desdemona is now married to Othello. Iago deflects Roderigo's attention from having received no return for his money by assuring Roderigo that he, Iago, would certainly do nothing to assist Othello in such a marriage since he holds Othello in 'hate' (I.i.7,155) for having passed him over for promotion to lieutenant in favour of Cassio, a man (according to Iago) of little military experience. But as the play proceeds we soon find that Iago is motivated by a 'hate' which takes the form of irrational malice rather than a justifiable resentment of unfair treatment by Othello. It emerges that Desdemona has married Othello without telling her father (seemingly because of his objection to her marrying a Moor – in I.ii.70 he refers insultingly to Othello's 'sooty bosom'), and Iago immediately attempts to discredit Othello by informing Brabantio that his daughter has been seduced by 'an old black ram'[67] (I.i.89), by 'the Devil' (I.i.92). Brabantio takes the latter description of Othello almost literally when in the second scene he accuses Othello of having employed sorcery against Desdemona (I.ii.63): 'Damned as thou art, thou hast enchanted her [cast an evil spell over her].' And in the third scene Brabantio, before the Duke of Venice and the Senate, charges Othello with employing the 'practices of cunning hell' (I.iii.102) – this last phrase and Iago's previous reference to Othello as 'the Devil' are the first examples of a recurrent form of dramatic irony in the play where evil attributed to characters other than Iago really applies to Iago himself. After hearing Othello's account of his wooing of Desdemona – his account of (I.iii.125-6)

How I did thrive in this fair lady's love,
And she in mine –

and after hearing what Desdemona herself has to say, the Duke sees no reason for taking action against Othello and goes ahead with his decision to send Othello to Cyprus (a Venetian colony at that time) to take charge of the defence of the island against the Turks.

Thus by the end of the first Act Iago has failed to strike at Othello through Brabantio. All he has achieved, or helped to achieve, is Brabantio's disowning of Desdemona (I.iii.189-98).

Iago contents himself with persuading Roderigo to continue to part with money in the hope that Iago can prepare the way for him to have an adulterous relationship with Desdemona – we see here that Iago delights in portraying Desdemona as a nymphomaniac whose lust will soon drive her away from Othello in search of another man (I.iii.360–): 'When she is sated with his body she will find the error of her choice.' This scene ends with one of several soliloquies in the play which reveal the inner workings of Iago's mind. We find that his mind is so twisted that he is the victim of self-deception – he suspects that Othello has been having an affair with his own wife (I.iii.381–4), that

> 'twixt my sheets
> He has done my office [performed the function belonging to me].

Iago is then excited by the inspiration that comes to him as to how to hurt Othello and also bring about the dismissal of Cassio from his post – he will deceive Othello into believing that Desdemona is having an affair with Cassio (I.iii.386–90). And he reflects with satisfaction that Othello can be easily deceived because of his trusting nature (I.iii.393–6):

> The Moor is of a free [generous] and open nature[68]
> That thinks men honest that but seem to be so,
> And will be as tenderly led by the nose
> As asses are.

In the last two lines of this soliloquy Iago clearly associates himself with the forces of evil – 'Hell and night', he says, must help to bring his plan to life (I.iii.397–8).

Since Othello has been sent from Venice to Cyprus the play is set there from the second Act onwards. When Othello is reunited Desdemona (who, having been disowned by her father, is allowed to join Othello in Cyprus), he is overwhelmed by joy – 'O my soul's joy!...I cannot speak enough of this content' (II.i.182–94) – and these words evoke in Iago's mind the image of a well-tuned musical instrument which he longs to make discordant (II.i.197–8):

> O, you are well tuned now,
> But I'll set down the pegs that make this music...

Meanwhile in the rest of II.i Iago persuades Roderigo to assist him in a plot against Cassio by telling him that Cassio has become the object of Desdemona's lustful desires and so is an obstacle to Roderigo's own desires in that direction. (Iago, who earlier had the absurd suspicion that Othello had been having an affair with his own wife, in his soliloquy at the end of II.i has the equally absurd suspicion that Cassio too may be doing this – 'I fear Cassio with my nightcap [wife] too', II.i.301.) In II.iii, after Iago has plied Cassio with wine and Roderigo has involved him in a drunken brawl, Iago succeeds in bringing about Othello's dismissal of Cassio as lieutenant. In this way Iago has brought about Cassio's dismissal before leading Othello to believe that there is a sexual relationship between Cassio and Desdemona, but since such a belief is to be a means of tormenting Othello Iago moves straight on to this objective. Immediately after Cassio's dismissal Iago, in order that Cassio may eventually be seen in Desdemona's company by Othello, poses as Cassio's friend and suggests that he should apply to Desdemona for help in securing his reinstatement. In connection with this tactic by Iago Shakespeare reinforces the point that good-natured people, not suspecting evil in others, are unfortunately taken in by hypocrites like Iago (who, as we have seen, is himself paranoiac in his suspicion of others). We heard earlier (I.iii.393–4) that Othello, being 'of a free and open nature', believes men like Iago to be 'honest' (Othello actually refers to Iago's honesty in I.iii.284, 294 and II.iii.169, 239), and now Cassio and Desdemona have the same belief about Iago – 'Good night, honest Iago' says Cassio (II.iii.324), who in the scene immediately following describes him as 'kind and honest' (III.i.40), and later Desdemona says of Iago 'O, that's an honest fellow' (III.iii.5).

In III.iii comes the turning point of the play, since in this scene Othello, subjected by Iago to a relentless barrage of innuendoes and lies, succumbs completely to the power of evil. As Othello and Iago come upon Cassio leaving Desdemona after being in conversation with her (in which she promised to help him to be reinstated), Iago says 'Ha! I like not that' and talks of Cassio as stealing away 'so guilty-like' (III.iii.35,40). He arouses Othello's 'jealousy' (suspicion) by pretending to warn him against it ('O beware, my lord, of jealousy./It is the green-eyed monster...', III.iii.169 ff.), and he encourages the idea that Desdemona is a deceiver by recalling 'She did deceive her father, marrying you' (III.iii.210). Othello's limp acceptance of this last point ('And so she did') contrasts sadly with his vigorous rejection in I.iii of Brabantio's warning that Desdemona, having deceived her father, might deceive him: Othello at that time declared that he would stake his life on Desdemona being faithful to him ('My life upon her faith!', I.iii.294). And we may well assume that when Othello says he is much indebted to Iago for the trouble he is taking there is a tragic pun in the word 'bound' – 'I am bound to thee for ever' (III.iii.217) also suggests that Othello has become enslaved to evil (as Brabantio believed Desdemona to be in saying that she was 'bound' in 'chains of magic [black magic]', I.ii.65). On hearing Iago's description (purely fictitious) of Cassio having on one occasion been dreaming that, as indicated by his spoken words and bodily movements, he was sexually embracing Desdemona, Othello cries out 'I'll tear her all to pieces' (III.iii.435). And the scene reaches its climax when Iago says he has seen Cassio wiping his beard with a handkerchief which Iago knows to have been a love token given by Othello to Desdemona. (Actually Iago acquired this handkerchief after Desdemona had dropped it unknowingly – III.iii.315–19 – and he planned to leave it in Cassio's lodging place – III.iii.325–6 – though he has not yet had time to do this.) Othello is consumed with a desire for vengeance and wants hate to be enthroned in his heart in place of love (III.iii.451–3):

> Arise, black vengeance, from the hollow hell.
> Yield up, O love, thy crown and hearted throne
> To tyrannous hate!

And Desdemona is a 'devil' whom he will find some means of putting to death (III.iii.480–2). He now believes that it is Iago, not Desdemona, who is devoted to him: after Iago has solemnly (but hypocritically) dedicated himself to Othello's service (III.iii.466–73) Othello replies 'I greet thy love' (III.iii.473), and the scene ends with Othello's promotion of Iago to lieutenant ('Now art thou my lieutenant', III.iii.482). In this scene Othello has continued to refer to Iago's honesty (III.iii.122, 246), and he continues do so in the last Act (V.i.31, V.ii.151, 157), but his trust in Iago can no longer be excused as coming from an unsuspecting 'free and open nature' (I.iii.393) since now his trust in Iago has replaced his trust in Desdemona, thus showing how completely he has fallen under Iago's evil spell.

In IV.i Iago baits Othello to the point where he collapses in a fit, calling Desdemona 'devil' once again (IV.i.45–) – we notice that Iago's tormenting of Othello still goes on despite his promotion to lieutenant, whereas in the first scene he claimed that his 'hate' for Othello was due to having been passed over for promotion. By now Iago has put the handkerchief in Cassio's chamber, and Cassio has found it and given it to his mistress, Bianca, to make a copy of it. (Bianca is a prostitute – see IV.i.94–5 – who nevertheless is genuinely in love with Cassio: she sadly misses him when he is away, III.iv.174–7.) Othello in the company of Iago happens to see Bianca returning the handkerchief to Cassio because she suspects it was given him by some other woman, and Iago of course assures Othello that this other woman was Desdemona. Strangely at this point love for Desdemona suddenly asserts itself sufficiently for Othello to praise her ('A fine woman, a fair woman, a sweet woman!...', IV.i.175ff.), though for Othello the pity is that she has declined into corruption ('the pity of it, Iago', IV.i.192). Iago's power over Othello seems for the moment to be slipping, but Iago is soon able to ensure that any feeling of love or pity in Othello gives way to destructive rage ('I will chop her into messes', IV.i.196). Othello is then joined by Lodovico who has just arrived from Venice with instructions from the Senate, and Othello, while looking over these instructions, overhears

Desdemona saying in conversation with Lodovico that she wishes the breach between Othello and Cassio could be healed, 'for the love I bear to Cassio' (IV.i.227). Desdemona here means merely that she regards Cassio as a friend, but Othello, in Lodovico's presence, suddenly strikes her and calls her 'devil' three times (IV.i.238, 240). And in the next scene, scorning Desdemona's protestations that she is a 'true and loyal wife' (IV.ii.35) who as 'a Christian'[69] has faithfully preserved her body for her husband alone (IV.ii.83–5), Othello calls her a 'whore' (IV.ii.73, 87, 90).

Despite Othello's cruel insults Desdemona's love for him remains indestructible – this love is the shining light of the play. Iago's wife Emilia (who by nature is quite different from Iago) has become Desdemona's lady companion, and Desdemona, speaking of Othello, tells Emilia (IV.iii.18–20):

> My love doth so approve him
> That even his stubbornness, his checks, his frowns
> ... have grace and favour in them.

Desdemona then sings a traditional song, the willow song, about a girl who has been deserted by the man she loves, and here Desdemona finds herself inserting words of her own – 'Let nobody blame him, his scorn I approve' (IV.iii.50), words which clearly reflect what she said to Emilia about her love for Othello ('My love doth so approve him') – and she finishes the song by making the false lover say to the girl (IV.iii.55) 'If I court more women, you'll couch with more men.' This introduction of promiscuity into the song comes from the inner recesses of Desdemona's mind and shows the deep hurt inflicted upon her by Othello's accusations, just as similar accusations made by Hamlet against Ophelia prompted her (in her madness) to sing a song about an unmarried girl losing her virginity (*Hamlet* IV.v.46–64). But when Emilia says that wives who are maltreated by their husbands are entitled to take 'revenge' (IV.iii.91), Desdemona replies (IV.iii.102–3) in terms of what may be taken as the Christian doctrine of returning good for evil:

>   God me such uses [habits] send
> Not to pick bad from bad, but by bad mend.

(Desdemona's Christian attitude thus contrasts with Iago's desire for revenge against Othello, I.iii.360+, and with Othello's desire for revenge against Desdemona herself, III.iii.463.)

At the beginning of the last scene (V.ii) the sleeping figure of Desdemona in the bedchamber arouses love rather than hate in Othello (he kisses her), but at the same time he takes an absurdly egocentric view that by executing 'justice' (V.ii.17) upon one he loves he shows saintly self-sacrifice (V.ii.21–2):

>   This sorrow's heavenly,
> It strikes where it doth love.

He thereupon smothers Desdemona to death, her last words (V.ii.128) still being words of love ('Commend me to my kind lord [husband]. O, farewell!'). But when the facts about the handkerchief come to light – Iago stabs Emilia to death for telling Othello that she had found it and given it to Iago – Othello at last comes to see the forces of good and evil in their true colours. He now sees Desdemona as being 'heavenly' (V.ii.281), himself as deserving to be punished in hell (V.ii.280–3), and Iago as being 'a devil' or 'demi-devil' (V.ii.290,304). In his state of shock Othello consoles his ego by protesting that he is an 'honourable murderer' (V.ii.297, meaning presumably that at the time he had believed the murder to be morally justified) and by describing himself (falsely, we are surely meant to realise) as 'one that loved not wisely but too well', as 'one not easily jealous' (V.ii.347–8). But as penance he stabs himself, and he dies kissing the dead Desdemona. Cassio, who in V.i. survived a murder attempt resulting from Othello's 'request' to Iago in III.iii.476–7, is made Governor of Cyprus, and Iago, now publicly identified as 'this hellish villain', will be appropriately punished (V.ii.370–2).

MEASURE FOR MEASURE (c. 1604)

The theme of *Measure for Measure* is the need for justice as administered by a ruler of personal integrity. The word 'justice' frequently occurs in the play, and the theme of justice is indicated by the play's title, as becomes clear when the words of the title are used in the last scene (V.i.409). (The phrase 'measure for measure' actually derives from Gospel texts – 'with what measure ye mete it shall be measured to you again', *Matthew* 7:2, along with similar words to be found in *Mark* 4:24 and *Luke* 6:38.) The need for justice appeared previously as an important theme in *Titus Andronicus, Richard II* and *2 Henry IV* (justice in that play being personified by the Lord Chief Justice), while *King John* and *Troilus and Cressida* pointed to the need for integrity in leaders. *Measure for Measure* is especially concerned with justice in relation to sexual morality, and with integrity in a ruler as regards sexual matters.

The Duke of Vienna announces to his elderly counsellor Escalus, who is fully conversant with the administration of 'common justice' (I.i.12) in the city, that he has chosen Lord Angelo to be his deputy during a period when he himself is to be away from Vienna. The Duke says he has given careful consideration to his choice of Angelo as deputy ('we have with special soul/Elected him our absence to supply', I.i.18–19), and Escalus thinks that Angelo is an excellent choice for a position requiring 'such ample grace and honour' (I.i.24): Escalus himself is appointed to act as Angelo's assistant. In I.iii, in conversation with a friar (Friar Thomas), the Duke explains his reason for being officially absent from Vienna: he admits that, though there have been strict laws in the city, for fourteen years there has been a failure to enforce them, so that 'liberty plucks justice by the nose' (I.iii.29), and, since it would be tyranny on his part suddenly to enforce these laws after such a long period of laxity, he has given Angelo the task of bringing this laxity to an end. The Duke then asks to be allowed to don the habit of the Friar's order so that in disguise he may see how Angelo wields his authority ('behold his sway', I.iii.43) and in particular see whether Angelo, as a man of strict moral principles ('precise', I.iii.50), remains true to these moral principles when occupying a position of 'power' (I.iii.53–4). (Despite the suggestion here that the Duke has doubts as to whether Angelo will be able to live up to his strict moral principles, I assume we are meant to take it that the Duke would not have handed over power to Angelo if he had not been sincere in his praise of Angelo in the opening scene.)

Angelo's first action is to have young Claudio arrested because (I.ii.138–49), though he was bound by 'a true contract' to be married to Juliet, she became pregnant before the 'contract' was solemnised by a marriage ceremony (there was a delay in obtaining Juliet's dowry). With Claudio Angelo is ruthless: ignoring Escalus's appeal to proceed with restraint (II.i.4–16), Angelo orders Escalus to have Claudio executed the following morning (III.i.33–4). In contrast to his action against Claudio Angelo shows little interest when Elbow, a muddle-headed constable who misuses words (like Dogberry in *Much Ado about Nothing*), tries to enforce the 'law' against prostitution by arresting a brothel tapster (Pompey) and a man (Froth) who frequents the same brothel: Angelo leaves Escalus to deal with the matter (II.i.129–31), and Escalus lets the two men off with a warning. As regards Claudio, Angelo is visited by Claudio's sister Isabella, who appeals to Angelo to show 'mercy' as God through Christ does to sinful human beings (II.ii.75–9 – this appeal is similar to that made by Portia to Shylock in *The Merchant of Venice* IV.i.179–92):

> How would you be
> If He [God], which is the top of judgment, should
> But judge you as you are? O, think on that,
> And mercy then will breathe within your lips,
> Like man new made [man redeemed by Christ].

Angelo merely tells Isabella to come again the following day, but after her departure he reveals in a soliloquy that he is 'tempted' (II.ii.163) with desire for her. He is appalled by his own depravity, realising that he utterly fails to live up to his name 'Angelo' ('Let's write "good angel" on the Devil's horn', II.iv.16), but when Isabella comes again his sense of shame does not deter him from trying to force her to commit the very act for which he had condemned her brother to death (II.iv.52–5):

> Which had you rather – that the most just law
> Now took your brother's life, or, to redeem him,
> Give up your body to such sweet uncleanness
> As she that he hath stained?

Such blackmail of course presents Isabella, who is preparing to become a nun, with an intolerable dilemma, which in the next scene drives her to the point where, when Claudio pleads with her to save his life, she condemns him for requiring her to debase herself and shows a complete lack of compassion for him (III.i.137–48):

> O you beast!
> ... I'll pray a thousand prayers for thy death,
> No word to save thee.

What Claudio and Isabella say to each other is overheard by the Duke who, disguised as a friar, visits the prison where Claudio is held. He thus learns of Angelo's corruption, and the main theme of the play is stressed in the Duke's soliloquy at the end of III.ii which asserts that the individual who carries the divinely appointed responsibility of administering justice should be both strict and 'holy' (III.ii.243–4):

> He who the sword of heaven will bear
> Should be as holy as severe.

In speaking to Claudio at the beginning of III.i the Duke (as friar) gave him guidance in facing death ('Be absolute for death' – reconcile yourself fully to the acceptance of death – III.i.5), but after overhearing what had happened he speaks to Isabella of a plan to rescue Claudio. The Duke has heard that Angelo was contracted to marry a lady called Mariana (as Claudio was contracted to marry Juliet) but had abandoned her because her dowry was lost when her brother was drowned at sea (III.i.205– ff.). (If we are right in assuming that in the opening scene the Duke was sincere in his praise of Angelo, it must be that the Duke has come to hear about Angelo's treatment of Mariana some time after the appointment of Angelo as his deputy.) The Duke proposes that Isabella should arrange to visit Angelo during the coming night and that Mariana should be invited to take Isabella's place (this device is similar to that employed by Helena in *All's Well That Ends Well*, when she substituted herself for Diana in a nocturnal encounter with Bertram): as regards this plan, the Duke in his soliloquy at the end of III.ii feels he is justified in resorting to deception in order to counter Angelo's evil doing – 'Craft against vice I must apply' (III.ii.259). The Duke's plan goes ahead, but the next morning he discovers that Angelo has treacherously repeated his order for Claudio to be executed. Fortunately it so happens ("'tis an accident that heaven provides' says the Duke, IV.iii.73) that on that very morning a prisoner of about the same age as Claudio and similar to him in appearance dies of a fever, and the Provost (prison superintendent), who is in the Duke's confidence, sends this prisoner's severed head to Angelo, reporting that the head is Claudio's.

During his inspection of Vienna the Duke (in III.ii) sees the law being enforced by Elbow, who arrests Pompey for ignoring the warning given him after his previous arrest, and the Duke also sees Mistress Overdone, in whose brothel Pompey was employed, being taken to prison under the supervision of Escalus. During this scene the Duke is accosted by Lucio, one of Mistress Overdone's patrons (as indicated in I.ii.45–6), who, not knowing that he is actually talking to the Duke, insolently slanders him by saying that the Duke condoned brothels because he himself frequented them ('he knew the service', III.ii.112–): the Duke then hears Mistress Overdone tell Escalus that Lucio had a child by Kate Keepdown, a child that Overdone herself has been taking care of (III.ii.185+).

In IV.iv Angelo and Escalus receive letters from the Duke instructing them to prepare for his return to Vienna by meeting him at the city gates, after proclaiming an hour beforehand that any petitions for the 'redress of injustice' should be presented to the Duke on his arrival (IV.iv.9–). The Duke himself arranges for such petitions to be presented by Isabella and Mariana (IV.v and vi), with instructions as to what is to be said in their petitions (IV.vi).

On his official arrival in Vienna the Duke, with heavy irony, offers thanks to Angelo as well as Escalus for good work done in the administration of justice – 'we hear/Such goodness of your justice' (V.i.5–6). When Isabella calls for justice against Angelo and gives full details of his shameful conduct (as instructed by the Duke, she says she yielded to Angelo, V.i.101), the Duke pretends to dismiss her accusations as villainous, saying of Angelo that 'his integrity/Stands without blemish' (V.i.107–8). And when Mariana claims Angelo as her husband because she is 'affianced' to him and he has recently had sexual relations with her (V.i.225–8), the Duke pretends to agree with Angelo that both Isabella and Mariana must be inspired by the Devil (according to Angelo they are 'But instruments of some more mightier member/That sets them on', V.i.235–6). The Duke then departs and returns disguised again as a friar, saying that as 'a looker-on here in Vienna' he has seen 'corruption boil and bubble' (V.i.315–16), whereupon his hood is pulled off by the abusive Lucio, thus revealing the identity of the 'friar' to all concerned. The Duke has so far deliberately concealed the fact that Claudio is still alive, and he tells Angelo that, as one who sentenced Claudio to death for violating chastity but then sought to violate chastity himself and also broke his promise to save Claudio's life, he too deserves to be sentenced to death – 'An Angelo for Claudio, death for death...measure still for measure'[70] (V.i.407–9). Both Mariana and Isabella plead for Angelo's life – Isabella thus shows the charity she utterly failed to show when she denounced Claudio in III.i.137–48. Angelo, however, now 'penitent', accepts that he deserves death, not mercy (V.i.473–5). At this point the Duke produces the living Claudio, thus freeing Angelo from the sentence of death, and the play ends with the Duke instructing Angelo to accept Mariana as his wife, Claudio to marry Juliet, and Lucio to marry Kate Keepdown (despite Lucio's protest that she is a whore). And on his own account the Duke asks Isabella to become his wife.

TIMON OF ATHENS (c. 1605)

The theme of *Timon of Athens* is the tragic change in one man from love to hate. There is a parallel here with *Othello*, but, whereas the change in Othello was from love to hate of a woman, in Timon the change is from a love of his fellow human beings to a total hatred of human life. And, whereas the change in Othello was brought about by an evil individual (Iago), the change in Timon is brought about by his being betrayed by his friends – people who are friends only so long as Timon is wealthy.

In the first scene, in Timon's house, his praises are sung by a poet, a painter, a jeweller and a merchant – we hear of his amazing generosity ('Magic of bounty', I.i.6), he is 'A most incomparable man' (I.i.10), and (I.i.58–61):

> His large fortune,
> Upon his good and gracious nature hanging,
> Subdues and properties [wins over] to his love and tendance [care]
> All sorts of hearts.

As soon as Timon appears in the play we see him gladly offering financial help: since Ventidius has been imprisoned for debt Timon will pay it off (I.i.97–106), and since the father of the girl one of Timon's servants wants to marry cannot afford a dowry for his daughter Timon will provide it (I.ii.114–49). Contrasted with Timon in the first two scenes is the malevolent Apemantus (ill-disposed towards everyone – like Jaques in *As You Like It*, only more so). He is a portent of what Timon himself is to become in the second half of the play. There is 'hate' in Apemantus's heart (I.i.231–2), which extends even to himself (there are few things he loves better 'Than to abhor himself', (I.i.62–3). As one of the lords attending Timon's feast observes, Apemantus is 'opposite to humanity', unlike Timon who 'outgoes [surpasses]/The very heart of kindness' (I.i.275–7).

Timon extols the value of friendship as a form of mutual help (I.ii. 103–):

> We are born to do benefits, and what better or properer can we call our own than the riches of our friends? O, what a precious comfort 'tis to have so many, like brothers, commanding one another's fortunes.

But Apemantus will trust nobody (I.ii.62–7):

> Grant I may never prove so fond [foolish]
> To trust man on his oath or bond...
> Or my friends, if I should need 'em.

For him friendship is worthless – 'Friendship's full of dregs' (I.ii.236). Timon enjoys entertaining his friends, and after there has been the dancing of ladies with the male guests Timon thanks the ladies for their contribution to the entertainment – 'You have added worth unto't and lustre' (I.ii.143). But for Apemantus such dancing is 'vanity' and the ladies are 'mad women' (I.ii.126–7). Timon has a love of life, Apemantus is anti-life.

Before the end of Act I Flavius, Timon's steward, reveals to us that Timon now has 'an empty coffer' (I.ii.190) and that his continued acts of generosity have driven him into debt. In Act II he is dogged by bills from his creditors. Previously Timon had not given Flavius the chance to tell him of the situation, but now that he knows the full facts he is confident that he can rely on his friends to help him (II.ii.185): 'I am wealthy in my friends'. Timon clearly has been foolish in his generosity, but we are surely meant to accept his own judgement of himself (II.ii.175): 'Unwisely, not ignobly, have I given.' And, though he may be foolish in putting such reliance on his friends, it is to his credit that, being generous himself, he assumes that others will be so – as Flavius says of his 'bounty', 'Being free [unstinting] itself, it thinks all others so' (II.ii.233–4). Apemantus would not be foolish in this way because he trusts no one, but for Shakespeare it is characteristic of good-natured people that they are unsuspecting of others – in this respect Timon ranks with

Hamlet ('Most generous and free from all contriving', *Hamlet* IV.vii.135) and with Othello before he was corrupted by Iago ('The Moor is of a free and open nature/That thinks men honest that but seem to be so', *Othello* I.iii.393–4). Unfortunately Timon's faith in his friends is nowhere justified. Act III shows them finding excuses for not coming to his rescue, and Timon's bitter disillusionment results in a total transformation of his personality. He invites the friends to a final 'feast' consisting only of hot water in covered dishes. After the dishes have been uncovered he throws the water into the faces of the friends and announces that henceforth he will be motivated by hate (III.vi.104–5):

> Burn, house! Sink, Athens! Henceforth hated be
> Of [by] Timon man and all humanity!

Unknown to Timon, however, the treachery of his friends is at least offset by the devotion of his servants, even though they now find themselves without employment. 'Yet do our hearts wear Timon's livery' says one of them (IV.ii.17), and Flavius the steward regards Timon as a noble victim (IV.ii.37–8):

> Poor honest lord, brought low by his own heart,
> Undone by goodness.

In IV.i Timon, leaving the walls of Athens behind him, delivers a long soliloquy in which he rejects human life in all its aspects, though Shakespeare makes us feel the force of the traditional values which Timon is rejecting, values such as 'peace, justice, truth... Degrees, observances, customs and laws' (IV.i.16–19). Timon wants only destruction: 'Let confusion live' (IV.i.21 – these words recall the purely destructive attitude of the rebel Northumberland in *2 Henry IV* I.i.154: 'Let order die!'). Timon takes up residence in a cave near the seashore, and it is not long before Apemantus appears on the scene, interested to observe the change in Timon (IV.iii.197–8):

I was directed hither. Men report
Thou dost affect [adopt] my manners...

This remark indicates that Timon has now become identifiable with Apemantus, instead of being his opposite as he was at the beginning of the play – though Apemantus insists disparagingly that Timon's newly adopted manners proceed merely from a 'change of fortune' (IV.iii.201–3). Timon and Apemantus hurl insults at each other for some time and, since Timon has discovered gold (while looking for roots to eat – IV.iii.23–6), Apemantus says before leaving that he will broadcast Timon's discovery so that he will be 'thronged' with unwanted visitors (IV.iii.391–2). Quick to hear of Timon's gold are some bandits who are surprised to find that Timon, knowing them to be thieves, is only too keen to give them gold and actually incites them to go about their evil business ('Rob one another... Cut throats... Break open shops', IV.iii.443–5) – the effect of this incitement is to make one of the bandits ashamed (IV.iii.449–50): 'He has almost charmed me from my profession by persuading me to it.' Among the unwanted visitors are the poet and the painter who were Timon's guests in I.i and who now propose to 'tender our loves' to Timon (V.i.10+) in order to benefit from his gold. Having heard what these two hypocrites were saying to each other outside his cave, Timon, with savage sarcasm, addresses them repeatedly as 'honest men' (V.i.69–78), and finally drives them away with blows. Standing out in contrast to these hypocrites is Flavius the steward who also has found his way to Timon's cave. Flavius is distressed by the baseness to which Timon has been reduced, deaf to the principle that man should 'love his enemies' (IV.iii.466 – the reference here is surely to Christian doctrine,[71] even though historically the play is set in the 5th century BC), but for Flavius Timon is his 'dearest master' and he wishes to 'serve him with my life' (IV.iii.471). Timon is prepared to accept Flavius as the 'One honest man' in all mankind (IV.iii.496–501), and a momentary doubt about Flavius's motives is dispelled by Flavius's fervent declaration 'That which I show, heaven knows, is merely love' (IV.iii.515).

But Timon refuses to let Flavius stay and sends him away with gold and with the instruction that he should 'Hate all, curse all, show charity to none' (IV.iii.527).

An important character in the later part of the play is Alcibiades, the army general who appeared as one of Timon's guests near the end of I.i. In III.v Alcibiades pleads on behalf of a friend who has been condemned to death by the Athenian Senate for having killed a man in a fight – in which, as Alcibiades points out, his friend was defending his reputation against gross slander (III.v.18–20) – but the Senate is adamant, and because Alcibiades persists in protesting against its decision he is banished. (Historically, of course, the Senate was a Roman governing body, not an Athenian one.) In his soliloquy at the end of III.v Alcibiades expresses his determination to return with his army to defeat the corrupt Senate (he condemns the Senators for their practice of usury, III.v.99–100, 107–10 – usury is condemned in this play as it was in *The Merchant of Venice*). In exile Alcibiades encounters Timon outside his cave. Timon proudly presents himself as a misanthropist ('I am Misanthropos and hate mankind', IV.iii.52), and when he hears that Alcibiades intends to make a military attack on Athens he gives Alcibiades gold for this purpose but curses not only the Athenians but Alcibiades himself (IV.iii.103–4, 126–8):

> The gods confound them all in thy conquest,
> And thee after, when thou hast conquered!
>
> There's gold to pay thy soldiers.
> Make large confusion, and, thy fury spent,
> Confounded be thyself!

In the last scene the Athenian Senators submit to the conquering Alcibiades who announces his intention of bringing 'justice' and 'peace' to the city (V.iv.61, 83 – 'justice' and 'peace' were two of the social values rejected by Timon in IV.i.16). Just before the end of the play Alcibiades receives a report of Timon's death: Alcibiades pays tribute to Timon by speaking of the faults of his latter days as 'faults forgiven' (V.iv.79) and of the Timon that is to be remembered as being 'noble Timon' (V.iv.80).

We see, therefore, that in the second half of the play Timon's negative withdrawal into hatred is contrasted with Flavius's persistent love and Alcibiades's positive action to counter injustice.

KING LEAR (c. 1605)

It is generally agreed that *King Lear* is broader in scope than any of the other Shakespeare plays. Its broad theme may be briefly defined as the conflict between good and evil in the human world and the relation of human life to higher powers. Good is associated in particular with true love, loyalty, and pity for the oppressed, evil with hypocrisy, lust, self-interest, cruelty, and social discord. The play is notable for the expression of differing attitudes amongst its characters towards the 'gods', astrology, and 'Nature', but the play as a whole shows that with divine help the tragically destructive power of evil can be overcome.

Lear, an elderly king of Ancient Britain (according to Holinshed and other sources), announces his intention, because of his age, to shed his responsibilities as a ruler and divide the kingdom among his three daughters (the two elder daughters are married and the youngest has two suitors) 'that future strife may be prevented now' (I.i.43–4) – the play shows later that dividing the kingdom is in fact a cause of strife. Lear goes on to say that his allocation of territory will depend on the profession of love each daughter makes for him. Goneril, the eldest, and Regan, the next eldest, make such extravagant professions of their love that Cordelia, the youngest, is so sickened by their hypocrisy that she merely states (I.i.91–2):

> I love your majesty
> According to my bond [indebtedness as a daughter], no more nor less.

And when Lear angrily describes her as 'So young and so untender' Cordelia replies 'So young, my lord, and true' (I.i.105–6). The word 'true' here carries weight as being completely sincere, in contrast to Regan's hypocritical 'my true heart' (I.i.69). Lear, however, immediately disowns Cordelia and divides her share of the territory between the two elder daughters and their husbands. They will have full powers of government, but Lear wishes to retain the title of king and, attended by a hundred knights, will reside with each of the two daughters on alternate months. One of Lear's courtiers, the Earl of Kent, unlike Lear, realises the sincerity of Cordelia's love and the hypocrisy of the other two daughters. He must speak out, he says, 'When power to flattery bows' (I.i.147), and he fearlessly condemns Lear (I.i.166): 'I'll tell thee thou dost evil.' For this plain speaking Kent is immediately banished. When Lear tells Cordelia's two suitors, the Duke of Burgundy and the King of France, that Cordelia will have no dowry in the form of territory, Burgundy backs out (ironically, later in the scene Lear addresses him as 'noble Burgundy', I.i.266), but France believes that true love should not be concerned with material considerations (I.i.238–40):

> Love's not love
> When it is mingled with regards that stand
> Aloof from the entire point.

He is happy to accept Cordelia as 'this unprized [not valued by Lear and Burgundy] precious maid' (I.i.259). At the end of this first scene Goneril and Regan admit in private that Lear showed 'poor judgment' (I.i.293–) in his treatment of Cordelia. They now agree to 'hit together' (I.i.300+) in curbing any authority that Lear may still try to wield.

The second scene introduces us to another family where disruption occurs. The Earl of Gloucester had already in the first scene (I.i.12–15) unashamedly acknowledged one of his two sons, Edmund, as being illegitimate (the result of adultery on Gloucester's part). The second scene begins with a soliloquy in which Edmund praises Nature ('Thou, Nature, art my goddess', I.ii.1) as a biological force especially associated with lust ('the lusty stealth of nature', I.ii.11), the force by which he himself was brought into the world. He is in fact proud of being a bastard, and there is dramatic irony in his description of his 'mind' as 'generous' (I.ii.8). This description is in fact belied by his expressed determination (I.ii.15–18) to have the land which, unfairly he thinks, will go to his 'legitimate' brother Edgar. (Actually the land would go to Edgar even if Edmund were legitimate since Edgar is older than Edmund, as we heard in I.i.15+, but this legal 'custom' is derided by Edmund at the beginning of his soliloquy, I.ii.2–6.) Edmund's soliloquy ends with a cynical appeal to the gods to support him (I.ii.22): 'Now, gods, stand up for bastards.' (Should Shakespeare's satirical presentation of Edmund be thought to imply an unfair attack on bastards in general, it should be remembered that the bastard Philip Faulconbridge in *King John* was the hero of that play.) Edmund proceeds to turn his father against Edgar by producing a forged letter which shows Edgar as suggesting to Edmund that their father should be put to death and his land be shared between them. Gloucester immediately denounces Edgar as a villain (I.ii.71+) and then cites astrology, with reference to recent eclipses of the sun and moon, as providing an explanation for evil in the human world (I.ii.96+):

> These late eclipses in the sun and moon portend no good to us... Love cools, friendship falls off, brothers divide. In cities mutinies, in countries discord, in palaces treason... This villain of mine [Edgar] comes under the prediction: there's son against father. The King falls from bias of nature: there's father against child.

(At one point in the first scene a similar assumption was made by Lear – in I.i.110–11 he spoke of 'the operation of the orbs/ From whom we do exist and cease to be'.) We may note that here Gloucester, unlike Edmund, refers to 'nature' as a source of benign instincts – Lear, in falling from the 'bias of nature', fails to show the instinctive love a father should have for his daughter. But Gloucester's remarks about the 'late eclipses' (and likewise Lear's remark about 'the orbs') must surely be regarded as a wrongful abdication of human moral responsibility (as shown in a more extreme form by Othello who, in *Othello* V.ii.112–14, when he receives from Emilia what he believes to be a report of Cassio's murder as instigated by Othello himself, pretends that such a murder was caused by the moon). We may take it that Edmund in his soliloquy after Gloucester has left is justified in mocking human attempts to blame the planets for human misdoings (I.ii.127–). Edmund's fault in this soliloquy lies in his complacent acceptance of himself as evil irrespective of the stars: 'I should have been that [what] I am had the maidenliest star in the firmament twinkled on my bastardising.' When Edgar appears, however, it suits Edmund's purpose to offer Gloucester's remarks about the recent eclipses as an explanation of the rage which, Edmund tells Edgar, has erupted in Gloucester against Edgar, and Edgar becomes convinced that he should stay away from his father. Edmund in his soliloquy at the end of the scene chuckles maliciously over the ease with which he was able to deceive Edgar (I.ii.170–2):

> a brother noble,
> Whose nature is so far from doing harms
> That he suspects none.

(Shakespeare thus repeats the point made in *Othello* I.iii.393–6 about an honest person being easily deceived as a result of being unsuspecting.)

After the first two scenes the forces of evil soon become dominant. Though Lear was guilty of evil in the first scene (as Kent pointed out), in the third scene he himself becomes the victim of evil, as committed by Goneril, with whom he spends his first month away from his palace. Goneril instructs her steward, Oswald, to behave provocatively towards Lear and his knights (I.iii.13–26), and she insists that Lear's hundred knights must be reduced because of alleged misconduct (I.iv.240–8). But Lear's response to this treatment is also evil in that he gives way to vindictive passion. In cursing Goneril he calls upon Nature to be destructive (I.iv.275–83):

> Hear, Nature, hear. Dear goddess, hear.
> Suspend thy purpose if thou didst intend
> To make this creature fruitful.
> Into her womb convey sterility... If she must teem,
> Create her child of spleen that it may live
> And be a thwart [perverse] disnatured torment to her.

Edmund (in I.ii.11) associated Nature with lust: Nature in Lear's mind is becoming associated with destruction. Goodness appears in the person of Kent who shows loyalty to Lear, despite Lear's banishment of him, by returning to serve Lear in disguise (he wishes to 'serve where thou [Kent himself] dost stand condemned', I.iv.5), but even Kent is infected by Lear's vindictive rage, as becomes apparent when he hurls an exceptionally long string of insults at Goneril's Oswald ('A knave, a rascal...a bawd...coward, pander, and the son and heir of a mongrel bitch', II.ii.10+). Lear turns from Goneril to Regan, trusting that she will be guided by the 'offices of nature' (II.iv.177, i.e. a child's natural sense of obligation to a parent – here we see Lear referring to 'nature' in its benign aspect), but he finds that, whereas Goneril had demanded that his hundred knights should be reduced to fifty, Regan refuses to let him have more than twenty-five knights, and he is duly provoked into leaving both daughters and going out into an oncoming storm. Meanwhile Edmund's evil plotting against Edgar is completely successful. He shows Gloucester a wound (actually self-inflicted) which he claims he received from Edgar when telling Edgar that he should respect his father, not be his father's murderer (II.i.40+ – the reference here of course is to Edgar as portrayed in Edmund's forged letter). Thereupon Gloucester sets about giving orders that Edgar is to be hunted down as a criminal. To evade capture Edgar disguises himself as 'Poor Tom', a mad beggar (a Bedlam beggar), almost naked, and begrimed with dirt, a representative of total human degradation (II.iii). Later, in the third Act, Edgar in his role of mad beggar speaks of his misery as being the result of his failure to defy the Devil ('the foul fiend', III.iv.96): his enumeration of his alleged sins (III.iv.82+) symbolically sums up the evil in debased human nature, and several of these sins ('lust', 'false of heart', 'bloody of hand', 'wolf in greediness') are exemplified by characters in the play.

    Much of the play is given over to the conflict between good and evil that takes place in Lear's own mind: here fleeting moments of true insight alternate with destructive rage and false perceptions of human life. Goneril's malevolent complaints about the conduct of his knights prompt Lear's first moment of insight – he realises his 'folly' in letting Cordelia's 'most small fault' draw away love from his heart (I.iv.266–72). But then he blinds himself to his own folly by uttering prolonged curses upon Goneril. Lear's personal jester (the 'Fool') – who 'pined' after Cordelia's departure (I.iv.71+) – directs numerous gibes against Lear's folly, and on one occasion Lear does say of his treatment of Cordelia 'I did her wrong' (I.v.25–), but most of the time the thrust of the Fool's remarks is ignored by Lear. When he is exposed to the storm in Act III Lear at first applauds the storm as a destructive force – he wants the thunder to crush the earth's whole surface and destroy all seeds of life (III.ii.6–9):

> And thou, all-shaking thunder,
> Strike flat the thick rotundity o' the world,
> Crack nature's moulds, all germens spill [destroy] at once
> That make ingrateful man.

(Because two of his daughters have treated him badly Lear regards the whole human race as 'ingrateful' – just as Timon, having suffered the ingratitude of certain members of the human race, calls upon Nature to let her 'womb' 'no more bring out ingrateful man', *Timon of Athens* IV.iii.186–7.) But Lear then contradicts himself by condemning the storm's attack on himself – he accuses the elements of conspiring with Goneril and Regan to attack 'a head/So old and white as this' (III.ii.21–4). Later, to his credit, he moves away from self-pity to pity for the dispossessed people of the world (III.iv.28–9) –

> Poor naked wretches, wheresoe'er you are,
> That bide [endure] the pelting of this pitiless storm–

and he pleads that a wealthy person should part with excessive wealth to alleviate poverty (III.iv.34–5):

> Expose thyself to feel what wretches feel,
> That thou mayst shake the superflux [superfluous wealth] to them.

But then, in an encounter with 'Poor Tom', Lear concludes that this poor creature is to be welcomed as presenting the undisguised truth about human beings – 'man is no more but such a poor, bare, forked animal as thou art' (III.iv.108–). This is perverted praise of human degradation, and contradicts what Lear said earlier to Regan (II.iv.265–6) when she questioned why he needed to be attended by even one of his knights:

> Allow not nature more than nature needs,
> Man's life is cheap as beast's.

By now Lear has been reduced to a state of madness (already, in III.ii.67, he himself had observed 'My wits begin to turn'), and as he wanders about the countryside after the storm he expresses a severely distorted view of life, now unrelieved by any moments of enlightenment. He praises lust for a reason we know to be completely wrong (IV.vi.114–15):

> Let copulation thrive, for Gloucester's bastard son
> Was kinder to his father than my daughters.

Then, again contradicting himself, he condemns lust, and he does so (rather as Hamlet, in condemning his mother as corrupt, condemned all women as corrupt – 'Frailty, thy name is woman', *Hamlet* I.ii.146) by making the wild generalisation that all women are lustful (IV.vi.124–5):

> Down from the waist they are centaurs [who were animal below the waist],
> Though women all above.

(This generalisation, which reflects Lear's hatred of Goneril and Regan, also, of course, shows blind prejudice by being applied entirely to women, without reference to men.) Lear makes another wild generalisation in denouncing everyone in authority as debased, so that human 'justice' is defeated by bribery (IV.vi.165–6):

> Plate sin with gold,
> And the strong lance of justice hurtless breaks.

Lear goes further by denouncing all human life on earth as folly (IV.vi.183–4):

> When we are born we cry that we are come
> To this great stage of fools.

And, with the husbands of Goneril and Regan in mind, he becomes consumed with a desire to commit murder (IV.vi.188):

> Then kill, kill, kill, kill, kill, kill!

Another character whose reactions we follow in some detail is Gloucester. Although he has been guilty of adultery and of grossly misjudging his son Edgar (as Lear misjudged Cordelia), there emerges in Gloucester a basic goodness. He is moved by 'pity' for Lear (III.iii.6–), and for this reason Regan and her husband, the Duke of Cornwall, have taken charge of Gloucester's house and forbidden him to help Lear. He nevertheless finds shelter for Lear (III.vi) and warns Kent of the need to convey Lear as quickly as possible to Dover (where a French army has landed) to escape from a plot (presumably by Cornwall and Regan) to have Lear put to death. Because of the help he has given to Lear Gloucester is subjected to an act of brutal cruelty – Cornwall, with encouragement from Regan, plucks out Gloucester's eyes (III.vii). The one good result of this barbaric act is that Gloucester, hearing that it was Edmund who informed against him (III.vii.87–8), becomes reconciled in his mind to Edgar: he asks the 'Kind gods' to forgive him for his treatment of Edgar (III.vii.90–1). In the next scene, however, the plight of 'Poor Tom' (whom he does not know to be Edgar but who does remind him of Edgar) causes Gloucester to regard the gods as tormentors (IV.i.37–8):

> As flies to wanton boys are we to the gods.
> They kill us for their sport.

And he describes 'Poor Tom' as the victim of 'the heavens' plagues' (IV.i.65) – but then he immediately swings round to the view that the 'Heavens' (IV.i.67) are concerned to promote among human beings a fairer distribution of wealth ('So distribution should undo excess/And each man have enough', IV.i.71–2 – these words parallel Lear's remarks about the need for 'wretches' to benefit from a wealthy man's 'superflux', III.iv.33–5). And when Edgar (as 'Poor Tom') cures Gloucester of the 'despair' (IV.vi.33) of wanting to commit suicide – Edgar tricks the blind Gloucester into believing he has fallen from a Dover cliff and has landed unharmed at the bottom – Gloucester comes to speak of the 'ever gentle gods', to whom he will leave the decision as to when he should die (IV.vi.219–21 – this is the view that Hamlet came to accept in *Hamlet* V.ii.210+). In contrast, therefore, to Lear's descent into moral chaos in the middle scenes of the play, there has been in Gloucester an increasingly firm hold on goodness.

In Act IV it becomes clear that the forces of goodness are asserting themselves. Goneril's husband, the Duke of Albany, a man completely different in character from Regan's evil husband Cornwall, comes out against Goneril and Regan, denouncing as atrocious their treatment of their father ('Tigers, not daughters, what have you performed?', IV.ii.40), and he hopes that heaven will intervene to overcome evil in the human world (IV.ii.46–50):

> If that the heavens do not their visible spirits
> Send quickly down to tame these vile offences
> It [i.e. destruction] will come.
> Humanity must perforce prey on itself,
> Like monsters of the deep.

(A similar hope was expressed by Titus in *Titus Andronicus* IV.iii.50–1:

> We will solicit heaven and move the gods
> To send down Justice for to wreak [avenge] our wrongs.)

In III.vii Cornwall, during his blinding of Gloucester, was attacked by one of his own servants who was appalled by this cruel act. Albany receives a report (IV.ii.70–8) that Cornwall has since died of the wound his servant inflicted upon him, and Albany sees Cornwall's death as showing that the heavens have already intervened (IV.ii.78–80):

> This shows you are above,
> You justicers, that these our nether crimes
> So speedily can venge.

The assertion of goodness is conspicuously represented by the return of Cordelia to Britain. Kent, after being given a description of Cordelia's grief on hearing of Lear's sufferings (IV.iii.25–32), finds it so difficult to account for the difference between Cordelia and her two sisters that he lapses into the error, similar to that of Gloucester earlier (I.ii.96+), of regarding the stars as responsible for human good and evil (IV.iii.33–5):

> The stars above us govern our conditions [dispositions];
> Else one self mate and make [the same two parents] could not beget
> Such different issues [children].

Cordelia herself proclaims 'love' to be the motive of her arrival in Britain in the company of French troops (IV.iv.27–8):

> No blown [bloated] ambition doth our arms incite,
> But love, dear love, and our aged father's right.

Cordelia's goodness is shown in her attitude to the natural world – in contrast with Edmund's association of Nature with lust (I.ii.11) and Lear's earlier desire for Nature to cause female sterility (I.iv.275–81), Cordelia gladly associates Nature, as represented by the plant world, with the healing properties of herbs, herbs that may help in the healing of Lear (IV.iv.16–18):

> All you unpublished [not generally known] virtues of the earth,
> ... be aidant and remediate
> In the good man's distress.

(Compare Friar Lawrence in *Romeo and Juliet* II.iii.15–16:

O mickle [great] is the powerful grace that lies
In plants, herbs, stones, and their true qualities.)

And an important remark is made about Cordelia by a 'Gentleman' (an upper-class servant) who speaks of Lear as having one daughter whose goodness redeems human nature from Original Sin (IV.vi.207–9):

Thou hast one daughter
Who redeems nature from the general curse
Which twain [Adam and Eve] have brought her to.

The presence of Cordelia restores Lear to sanity – as Lear, now in the safety of the French camp at Dover, comes out of a deep sleep, he at first imagines that he is physically dead and sees Cordelia in heaven as a 'spirit' (IV.vii.49), while he is punished by being in hell (IV.vii.45–7):

You do me wrong to take me out o' the grave.
Thou art a soul in bliss [heaven], but I am bound
Upon a wheel of fire...

(Compare Othello's vision, *Othello* V.ii.276–83, of meeting Desdemona on the Day of Judgement and being snatched away from Desdemona and heaven to be punished in hell for his treatment of her.) Lear's vision thus reveals a full awareness of Cordelia's true goodness and his own wrongdoing in disowning her.

Before the end of Act IV Edgar intercepts a letter from Goneril for delivery to Edmund which reveals a plot to murder Albany so that Edmund can take Albany's place in Goneril's 'bed' (IV.vi.260+) – after reading this letter Edgar exclaims (IV.vi.271) 'O indistinguished space of woman's will! [How boundless is woman's lust!]' and he describes both Goneril and Edmund as 'murderous lechers' (IV.vi.275). But the now widowed Regan is also interested in Edmund, and at the beginning of V.i we see that Goneril and Regan are jealous of each other. Meanwhile Edgar hands Goneril's letter over to Albany who is thereby informed of the plot against his life, and

Edgar (in disguise, though no longer as 'Poor Tom') presents himself as a challenger to Edmund in a duel. Edmund is struck down with what he knows to be a fatal wound, and Edgar, after revealing his true identity, says to Edmund with reference to their father (V.iii.170–3):

> The gods are just, and of our pleasant [pleasurable] vices [i.e. lust]
> Make instruments to plague us:
> The dark and vicious place where thee he got [begot]
> Cost him his eyes.

I assume that this is not to be taken as a true comment on Gloucester, since the loss of his sight was the direct result of his helping Lear and so can hardly be regarded as a just punishment. This speech seems rather to be Edgar's way of indicating that lust (Edmund's relationship with Goneril) has been the means by which Edmund has been brought to just punishment for the evil he has done. Edmund in his reply (V.iii.173–4) certainly takes Edgar's remarks as applying primarily to himself:

> Thou hast spoken right, 'tis true.
> The wheel is come full circle. I am here.

What we may take, then, to be the divine punishment of Edmund is quickly followed by further divine justice. Albany is informed that Goneril and Regan are both dead – Regan has died of poison put in her food by Goneril (presumably because Regan was a rival in the pursuit of Edmund) and Goneril has stabbed herself to death (presumably because of the exposure of the plot to murder Albany). Albany's response is (V.iii.231–2):

> This judgment of the heavens, that makes us tremble,
> Touches us not with pity.

In this last scene (V.iii), however, there are three deaths that most certainly do touch us with pity. Edgar reports that just before the fight with Edmund Gloucester had died, overwhelmed by conflicting emotions (V.iii.196–9) following

Edgar's revelation of his identity – Edgar says of Gloucester 'his flawed heart...Twixt two extremes of passion, joy and grief,/ Burst smilingly.' In V.ii, in the battle between the French and the British armies (with the British army led by Edmund), Lear and Cordelia were taken prisoner, and at the beginning of V.iii Lear feels that, despite being in prison, he and Cordelia, in the joy of one another's company, will seem to transcend life on earth, where even those of high rank are subject to changes in worldly fortune, as caused by intrigue at court – the two of them, says Lear (V.iii.16–19), will take on

> the mystery of things
> As if we were God's spies [angelic observers], and we'll wear out [outlast]
> In a walled prison packs [factions] and sects [cliques] of great ones
> That ebb and flow by the moon.

Edmund before he dies is suddenly overcome by a desire to do good ('Some good I mean to do,/Despite of mine own nature' he says, V.iii.243–4, thus no longer cynically complacent about being evil as he was in I.ii.127–), and so he reveals that he has given orders for Lear and Cordelia to be put to death, in the hope that action may now be taken to save them. But the action comes too late. Cordelia has already been put to death, and Lear's bereavement brings about his own death almost immediately – though just before he dies he is buoyed up by the belief that stirrings of life are visible in Cordelia's body (V.iii.310–11).

Despite these deaths the play ends with the earthly consolation that justice and order will be established in Britain. Albany announces (V.iii.302–4):

> All friends shall taste
> The wages of their virtue, and all foes
> The cup of their deservings.

And the responsibility of government is to be handed over to Kent and Edgar – they (though it appears that Kent will not live much longer) are to 'Rule in this realm and the gored state sustain' (V.iii.320).

It seems to me that the conflict between good and evil in this play cannot be fully understood unless it is seen in relation to the doctrine of Original Sin and seen also in more than worldly terms. Because of Original Sin (what in IV.vi.208 is called 'the general curse') suffering in human life is inevitable and some individuals suffer undeservedly in their life on earth – though this situation does not mean that in life on earth goodness can never prevail. What also has to be taken into account, over and above earthly fortunes, is the state of an individual's immortal soul. That Gloucester dies 'smilingly' (V.iii.199) may be taken as a sign that his soul is at peace. (Incidentally, this description of Gloucester's death, coming as it does shortly after Edgar's speech about the gods' punishment of lust, serves to dispel any impression that might have been given that Gloucester himself has been punished by the 'just' gods.) That Lear after his reunion with Cordelia feels he has become one of 'God's spies' (V.iii.17) may be a suggestion that his sins have been forgiven, so that he will not be 'bound upon a wheel of fire' (IV.vii.46–7) after all. And as for Cordelia, though she manifestly does not deserve to be killed, she represents the Christian martyr (very much applicable to her is what Lear says in V.iii.20–1: 'Upon such sacrifices...The gods themselves throw incense'), and we may take it that her soul will be as Lear saw it as being (IV.vii.46) – 'in bliss' (in heaven).

MACBETH (c. 1606)

Macbeth, like *King Lear*, is a vivid portrayal of the conflict between good and evil, but in *King Lear* the conflict is more general than it is in *Macbeth*, where the theme is the conflict between good and evil in connection with political power. A special feature of *Macbeth* is the presentation of evil as a force working through witches, creatures endowed with supernatural powers, and, just as evil human beings in Shakespeare characteristically employ deception to work their will on their victims, so too do the Witches – Macbeth, having been lured by them into evil, finds himself the victim of their deception.

At the beginning of the play Macbeth is a highly esteemed character who is contrasted with two evil characters – Macdonwald, a Scottish rebel leader ('The multiplying villainies of nature/Do swarm upon him', I.ii.11–12), and 'that most disloyal traitor/The Thane of Cawdor' (I.ii.53–4), who has been fighting on the side of the Norwegian enemy. Duncan, the Scottish king, praises Macbeth for his performance against the Scottish rebels ('brave Macbeth – well he deserves that name', I.ii.16), and, when told that Macbeth personally killed Macdonwald, Duncan exclaims 'O valiant cousin, worthy gentleman!' (I.ii.24). (This last praise comes after Duncan has heard that Macbeth ripped Macdonwald open from the stomach to the jaws – 'he unseamed him from the nave to the chaps', I.ii.22. It seems that this kind of violence carries Shakespeare's own approval when performed on a rebel.)

The Witches, in the brief first scene and at the beginning of the third scene, are associated with destruction – they are accompanied by thunder and lightning, and are especially concerned with raising storms when sailors are at sea. For them good is evil, evil good: 'Fair is foul, and foul is fair' (I.i.10). In the third scene they have come to encounter Macbeth and his fellow military commander, Banquo, as these two make their way across a heath after their victory over the Norwegians. The Witches hail Macbeth first as 'Thane of Glamis' (which he is), then as 'Thane of Cawdor', and finally as 'king hereafter' (I.iii.50). This last greeting startles Macbeth, so that Banquo asks (I.iii.51–2) 'Good sir, why do you start and seem to fear/ Things that do sound so fair?' (The wording here suggests that the Witches, for whom 'foul' is 'fair', I.i.10, also, in order to attract people to evil, make what is foul seem fair.) Banquo, in inviting the Witches to speak to him, makes it clear that he stands aloof from their influence (I.iii.60–1):

> Speak then to me, who neither beg nor fear
> Your favours nor your hate.

He is told that, though he will not be king, he will beget kings (I.iii.67). Almost as soon as the Witches have vanished two Scottish noblemen meet Macbeth to announce that the King has conferred on him the title of Thane of Cawdor which has been stripped from its previous bearer. Banquo immediately identifies the source of the Witches' prophetic knowledge – 'can the Devil speak true?' (I.iii.107) – and he goes on to describe them (I.iii.124–6) as 'The instruments of darkness' (i.e. of evil) who tell 'truths' to corrupt human souls ('to betray us/In deepest consequence'). But Macbeth is 'rapt' (I.iii.142), as he was (I.iii.57) after being hailed as 'king hereafter': he is now obsessed with the possibility of his becoming king, and he wonders whether this may entail 'murder' (I.iii.138) or whether it may happen without any action on his part ('Without my stir', I.iii.144). In the next scene (I.iv) Macbeth now contrasts unfavourably with Cawdor the traitor. We hear that Cawdor at least behaved honourably when he was executed: he showed 'deep repentance' (I.iv.7) and (I.iv.7–8)

> Nothing in his life
> Became him like the leaving it.

Macbeth, on the other hand, when later in the scene Duncan names his son Malcolm as his successor, talks in soliloquy of his 'black and deep desires' (I.iv.51) and of resorting to murder to attain these desires – 'yet let that be/Which the eye fears, when it is done, to see' (I.iv.52–3).

The coming of Duncan to Macbeth's castle as a guest (Lady Macbeth is informed of Duncan's intended visit in I.v) provides the opportunity for murdering Duncan, and in the scenes I.v to II.iii Macbeth and Lady Macbeth are contrasted in their reactions to evil. For most of this time Lady Macbeth is more inclined to evil than her husband. She fears that he is 'too full o' the milk of human kindness' (I.v.15–) to commit murder, and far from needing to be tempted by supernatural forces of evil (as Macbeth was by the Witches) she actually calls on these forces ('you spirits/That tend on mortal thoughts', i.e. are attentive to thoughts about murder, I.v.37–8; 'you murdering ministers',

I.v.45) to fill her 'top-full' with 'direst cruelty' (I.v.39–40). Macbeth, on the other hand, in his soliloquy at the beginning of I.vii is deterred by several considerations – that murder incurs punishment in this world as well as the next (I.vii.2–12), that he has obligations to Duncan as his kinsman, as a subject to him as king, and as his host (I.vii.12–16), that Duncan is a man of outstanding virtues (I.vii.16–20), and that his death would arouse widespread 'pity' and cause widespread grief (I.vii.21–5). When Lady Macbeth appears Macbeth says that they should 'proceed no further in this business' (I.vii.31) – but by the end of this scene Lady Macbeth has won him round. In II.ii we hear that Lady Macbeth's part in the murder was to ply with drink and drugs Duncan's two 'grooms' (attendants) – the nearest Lady Macbeth comes to showing any decent human feeling is her overcoming of an impulse to murder Duncan herself because the sleeping Duncan resembled her father (II.ii.12–13): she has otherwise been completely corrupted by the desire for power. When Macbeth rejoins Lady Macbeth after he has performed the actual murder he is horrified by what he has done. In his distraction he has carried away the daggers that were to be left in the bedchamber to make it appear that the grooms had killed Duncan in their state of drunkenness: Lady Macbeth denounces Macbeth as 'Infirm of purpose' (II.ii.52) and takes the daggers back. After the murder Macbeth feels that his guilt will never allow him to sleep (II.ii.35–43) and that he will never be able to wash the blood from his hands (II.ii.60–3):

> Will all great Neptune's ocean wash this blood
> Clean from my hand? No...

When Duncan's death is discovered, however, Macbeth plays the part of hypocrite with complete composure. Having been to the bedchamber officially to confirm Duncan's death for himself, he announces that he has killed the grooms out of 'fury' against them as Duncan's murderers (II.iii.105–6) and out of his 'violent love' for Duncan (II.iii.109) – his real motive, of course, being to ensure that the grooms cannot be interrogated. At this point Lady Macbeth collapses, and I think we are meant to take this apparent state of shock as a pretence, a continuation of her hypocritical profession of shock when Duncan's murder was discovered ('Woe, alas! What, in our house?', II.iii.85–6).

Immediately after the murder of Duncan his two sons, Malcolm and Donalbain, suspecting that they too will be murdered if they stay in Scotland, flee the country – Malcolm goes to England and Donalbain to Ireland. Macbeth, as Duncan's cousin, is accordingly crowned king. But one crime leads on to another. Macbeth, now that he is king, cannot bear the thought of the crown passing, as the Witches had foretold, to Banquo's offspring. If this happens, Macbeth feels, he has made over his soul to the Devil (by murdering Duncan) all to no purpose (III.i.63–9):

> If't be so,
> For Banquo's issue have I filed [defiled] my mind,
>   ... and mine eternal jewel [soul]
> Given to the common enemy of man,
> To make them kings, the seeds of Banquo kings.

And he tells Lady Macbeth that he would rather see the destruction of both earth and heaven (in this way Macbeth shows himself to be a spiritual ally of the Devil) than live in a state of unrest (III.ii.16–19):

> But let the frame of things disjoint [fall apart], both the worlds suffer [perish],
> Ere we will eat our meal in fear...

In immediate accord with her husband Lady Macbeth sees the solution as lying in the removal of Banquo and his son Fleance ('But in them nature's copy's not eterne', i.e. their lease on life is terminable, III.ii.38), and Macbeth proceeds to arrange for the double murder to be carried out. But this plan, when put into operation, fails to set Macbeth's mind at rest since, during a royal banquet (in III.iv), he is privately informed by one of the murderers that, though Banquo was killed, Fleance escaped, and this information is followed by the appearance of Banquo's ghost (which we may take to be a genuine ghost, not a devil, or the Devil, in the form of a ghost, as in *Hamlet*). Macbeth is terrified by the ghost, but since it is visible only to Macbeth himself Lady Macbeth calmly requests the guests to leave.

Uncertainty about the future sends Macbeth to the Witches to find out more from them. He greets them as beings concerned with destruction (IV.i.52–60) – with the raising of storms on land and at sea, with the toppling of castles and palaces, and with the destruction of the seeds of life ('nature's germens', IV.i.59 – compare Lear's raging desire that the storm in which he finds himself should 'Crack nature's moulds, all germens spill at once', *King Lear* III.ii.8). The Witches summon up three apparitions which in turn tell Macbeth that he should beware of Macduff, the Thane of Fife, that he can be harmed by no man born of woman, and that he can never be conquered until Birnam wood moves to Dunsinane hill. Macbeth finds reassurance in the last two pronouncements, but insists on knowing whether Banquo's offspring will ever reign in Scotland. In answer the Witches produce a 'show' of eight kings, with Banquo's ghost pointing to them as being descended from him.[72] This is indeed a straight answer, which draws from Macbeth a curse on the Witches and on those who trust in them (IV.i.138–9):

> Infected be the air whereon they ride,
> And damned all those that trust them.

Macbeth is thus condemning himself, but in desperation he proceeds even further along the path of evil. Learning that Macduff, whom he intended to kill in view of the first apparition's warning, has already fled to England, Macbeth decides out of sheer malice to order the murder of Macduff's wife and children. They are murdered in the scene immediately following (IV.ii).

In IV.iii the play moves to England where Macduff has joined Malcolm. Malcolm expresses his faith in the eventual triumph of goodness by saying (IV.iii.22) 'Angels are bright still, though the brightest fell' (referring to the Devil who as a rebellious angel fell from heaven).[73] But then Malcolm, wondering whether Macduff may have been sent by Macbeth to lead him into a trap, puts Macduff to the test by describing himself as being far too evil ever to be a king of Scotland. Shakespeare asserts the virtues desirable in a king by making Malcolm deny that he has them (IV.iii.91–4):

> But I have none: the king-becoming graces,
> As justice, verity, temperance, stableness [constancy],
> Bounty [generosity], perseverance, mercy, lowliness,
> Devotion, patience, courage, fortitude...

And after Malcolm has attributed to himself various vices, such as lust and avarice, Shakespeare introduces once again the theme of evil as a universally destructive force by making Malcolm say (IV.iii.97–100):

> Nay, had I power, I should
> Pour the sweet milk of concord into hell,
> Uproar [disrupt] the universal peace, confound [destroy]
> All unity on earth.

But Macduff's utter dejection convinces Malcolm of Macduff's sincere concern for the well-being of Scotland: he now acclaims Macduff as a man of 'integrity... truth and honour' (IV.iii.115–17), and he gives an assurance that he does not possess the vices he had attributed to himself (IV.iii.123–31). The murdered Duncan is described by Macduff as 'a most sainted king' (IV.iii.109), and in this scene the King of England (actually Edward the Confessor) is presented as another such king (he was briefly referred to earlier as 'the most pious Edward', III.vi.27). We hear that heaven has given him the gift of healing ('Such sanctity hath heaven given his hand', IV.iii.144), that 'he hath a heavenly gift of prophecy' (IV.iii.157 – we have here a counterpoise to the Witches' power of prophecy on the side of evil), and that in general (IV.iii.158–9)

> sundry blessings hang about his throne
> That speak him full of grace.

This king is providing Malcolm with support in the form of an English army, led by Siward, and the comment that there is no better soldier than Siward to be found in 'Christendom' (IV.iii.191–2) is the play's one direct reference to Christianity. The scene ends with the arrival of the tragic news of the murder of Macduff's wife and children. Malcolm says that a cure for Macduff's grief should be sought in a determination to inflict punishment on Macbeth – 'Let's make us medicines of our great revenge' (IV.iii.214). And Malcolm is confident that heaven is now working for the overthrow of Macbeth (IV.iii.237–9):

> Macbeth
> Is ripe for shaking, and the powers above
> Put on their instruments.

(Compare the references to heavenly intervention in *King Lear* IV.ii.46–50, 78–80.)

At the beginning of Act V Lady Macbeth is discovered to be in a state of dire mental distress. While sleepwalking she imagines that her hands are stained with Duncan's blood and, whereas after the murder of Duncan she had contemptuously dismissed Macbeth's guilt at the sight of Duncan's blood on his hands ('A little water clears us of this deed', II.ii.67), she now finds that guilt cannot in fact be so easily washed away – now, looking at her own hands, she says (V.i.41–2,49–50): 'What, will these hands ne'er be clean?... All the perfumes of Arabia will not sweeten this little hand.' As she recalls the occasions when she tried to allay Macbeth's fears she is now clearly trying to allay her own fears of the consequences of Macbeth's crimes: in particular there is the threat of punishment in hell ('Hell is murky', V.i.30+). Her death is reported soon afterwards (V.v.16), the result, it is thought, of suicide (V.viii.70–1). When Macbeth is told of her death he makes the well-known speech in which human life is dismissed as 'a tale/Told by an idiot' (V.v.26–7): this, of course, is not Shakespeare's own view (as it has sometimes been taken to be), but the view of a demoralised Macbeth. In this last Act Macbeth is 'sick at heart'

(V.iii.19) and commands the true allegiance of no one – he observes self-pityingly (V.iii.24–6):

> And that which should accompany old age,
> As honour, love, obedience, troops of friends,
> I must not look to have.

His downfall follows swiftly. In Birnam wood the combined English and Scottish forces, led by Siward and various Scottish nobles, camouflage their advance on Macbeth in Dunsinane by carrying before them branches from the wood. Macbeth sees (V.v.43–6) that he has been deceived by the Witches' third apparition, a 'fiend'

> That lies like truth. 'Fear not till Birnam wood
> Do come to Dunsinane' – and now a wood
> Comes toward Dunsinane.

And in the battle outside his castle Macbeth is confronted by Macduff, who, Macbeth learns, was not born of woman in so far as he was removed from the womb before time ('from his mother's womb/Untimely ripped', V.viii.15–16), so that Macbeth (told by the Witches' second apparition that he could not be harmed by any man born of woman) sees that he has again been deceived (V.viii.19–20):

> be these juggling fiends no more believed
> That palter with us in a double sense...

The play ends with Macduff displaying Macbeth's severed head and with Malcolm proclaiming that as Scotland's king he, 'by the grace of Grace' (V.viii.72), will set the country to rights.

ANTONY AND CLEOPATRA (c. 1607)

Just as *Troilus and Cressida* was about more than the love between Troilus and Cressida (it was much concerned with the need for integrity in military leaders), so *Antony and*

Cleopatra is concerned with more than the love between the two principal characters. The main theme of the play is the moral quality of rulers, seen especially in relation to love, but not exclusively to sexual love. *Antony and Cleopatra* is a sequel to *Julius Caesar* in that it presents the state of the Roman republic (territorially an empire) after the murder of Julius Caesar when power passed into the hands of the triumvirate of Antony, Octavius Caesar and Lepidus, and in *Antony and Cleopatra* Antony and Octavius Caesar are contrasted as political and military leaders. Antony, however, for all his failings, is presented more sympathetically than he was in *Julius Caesar*, where he was shown to be an irresponsible mob orator and was just as brutal as his fellow triumvirs in their joint condemnation of some seventy to a hundred senators to death (*Julius Caesar* IV.iii.171–6). *Antony and Cleopatra*, like *Julius Caesar*, derives its plot material from Plutarch's *Lives* (*Antony and Cleopatra* is based on Plutarch's Life of Antony), and Shakespeare follows Plutarch in showing that the chief cause of Antony's downfall was the fatal attraction exerted by Cleopatra.[74] But Shakespeare presents Octavius Caesar in a harsher light than Plutarch: in Shakespeare's play Octavius Caesar, in sharp contrast to Antony, is a hypocritical – and loveless – power politician.

The play opens in Cleopatra's palace in Alexandria, Egypt, where one of Antony's friends, Philo, talking to another friend, deplores the effect of Cleopatra on Antony as a general and a triumvir – Philo refers to Antony's 'dotage' (I.i.1) and to Antony as (I.i.12–13)

> The triple pillar of the world transformed
> Into a strumpet's fool.

And when Antony appears with Cleopatra he sweepingly dismisses his political responsibilities in favour of staying with Cleopatra (I.i.33–4):

> Let Rome in Tiber melt, and the wide arch
> Of the ranged empire fall! Here is my space.

But it soon becomes apparent that Antony's love for Cleopatra is hardly a source of true happiness, since his profession of love meets with the taunt from Cleopatra that, having been false to his wife Fulvia, he must also be false in what he says about his love for her (I.i.40–1):

> Excellent falsehood!
> Why did he marry Fulvia and not love her?

In the third scene Cleopatra indulges in the foolish whim of opposing Antony in mood – she says to her female attendant Charmian (I.iii.3–5):

> If you find him sad [in a serious mood],
> Say I am dancing; if in mirth, report
> That I am sudden sick.

And in this scene she continues the taunting in connection with Fulvia. Antony's infatuation is actually encouraged by another of his friends, Enobarbus, who calls Cleopatra 'a wonderful piece of work' (I.ii.147+), and in a later scene Enobarbus gives a glowing description of her sailing in a river boat on the occasion of Antony's first meeting her (II.ii.195–209). Cleopatra, says Enobarbus, was more beautiful than Venus as depicted in the imaginative works of painters – but Shakespeare, in making Enobarbus say that the winds were 'love-sick' with the perfumed sails of her boat (II.ii.197–8),[75] may be associating Cleopatra herself with the same kind of love-sickness that characterised Venus in the poem *Venus and Adonis* (lines 175 and 328). In this first Act of the play, however, Antony's political conscience is aroused by reports of trouble in the empire and in Italy itself. Serious inroads have been made in the eastern parts of the empire by a Parthian army led by Labienus (I.ii.96–100), and in Italy civil war has broken out (I.ii.177–9, I.iii.44–54) because of a widely supported bid for power made by Sextus Pompeius (a son of Pompey the Great, with whom Julius Caesar had been engaged in civil war, referred to at the opening of *Julius Caesar*). After hearing the report about

Labienus Antony applies to himself the word that Philo used of him in the first line of the play – he realises the need to free himself from 'dotage' (I.ii.113–14):

> These strong Egyptian fetters I must break,
> Or lose myself in dotage.

On receiving a further report that his wife has died Antony feels a pang of remorse – 'There's a great spirit gone!' (I.ii.119) – and, despite Enobarbus's cynical comment that Fulvia's death should make it easier for Antony to enjoy relations with Cleopatra ('your old smock brings forth a new petticoat', I.ii.165–), he prepares to return to Rome. Incidentally, as regards political responsibilities, Cleopatra as Queen of Egypt shows no concern at all with such responsibilities – as Antony remarks, she is the queen of 'idleness' (frivolity): 'your royalty/ Holds idleness your subject' (I.iii.91–2).

In the first scene to be set in Rome (I.iv) we hear Caesar (i.e. Octavius Caesar, who in this play is simply referred to as Caesar) telling his fellow triumvir Lepidus that he bears no malice towards Antony (I.iv.1–3):

> You may see, Lepidus, and henceforth know,
> It is not Caesar's natural vice to hate
> Our great competitor [partner].

He does however go on to deplore Antony's behaviour in Egypt as being a betrayal of 'judgment' (I.iv.33). In the early Roman scenes we hear a good deal about Pompey (i.e. Sextus Pompeius) as a leader. He is reputed to be able, in contrast to Caesar, to win people's love. A messenger tells Caesar (I.iv.36–8):

> Pompey is strong at sea,
> And it appears he is beloved of those
> That only have feared Caesar.

(Earlier Antony noted with some bitterness that the Roman people's 'love' was becoming increasingly linked to Pompey, I.ii.179–83.) But the messenger also reports that Pompey is supported by two pirates, Menecrates and Menas, whose men seize any ships they see (I.iv.48–55). In a later scene when Pompey meets both Caesar and Antony to discuss peace terms he describes the conspirators against Julius Caesar as 'courtiers [seekers] of beauteous freedom' (II.vi.17), a description that is hardly acceptable in view of Shakespeare's scathing satire in the earlier play at the point where the conspirators, having treacherously stabbed Caesar to death, claim to have done so in the name of 'Freedom' (*Julius Caesar* III.i.78). And Pompey has a dubious sense of 'honour' – when the three triumvirs are his guests on board his galley after he has accepted their peace terms, his pirate friend Menas suggests that the galley should be put out to sea and the three triumvirs murdered: Pompey rejects the suggestion as conflicting with his 'honour' (II.vii.75–6), but then adds that if this action had been taken without his previous knowledge 'I should have found it afterwards well done' (II.vii.78). We are also given a brief impression of Lepidus as a leader. He professes to admire the other two triumvirs, but there is no love lost between him and them – according to Pompey (II.i.14–16):

> Lepidus flatters both,
> Of both is flattered, but he neither [of them] loves
> Nor either [of them] cares for him.

And in a later scene Enobarbus (who has accompanied Antony to Rome) and Caesar's man Agrippa both mock Lepidus's insincere expression of devotion – 'O, how he loves Caesar!', 'Nay, but how dearly he adores Mark Antony' (III.ii.7–8).

In the Roman scenes it is of course Caesar who most commands our attention. When under threat from Pompey Caesar wants to be rejoined by Antony ('Pompey/Thrives in our idleness' Caesar tells Lepidus, I.iv.75–6). And when Antony does return to Rome Caesar is keen that friendship between them should be promoted by a marriage between his sister Octavia and Antony, now a widower after the death of Fulvia. Antony's acceptance of the offer is accompanied by a great display of brotherly love by the two leaders (II.ii.151–7), along with a declaration by Caesar of his great love for his sister. Says Antony:

> Further this act of grace, and from this hour
> The heart of brothers govern in our loves
> And sway our great designs.

And Caesar replies:

> A sister I bequeath you whom no brother
> Did ever love so dearly. Let her live
> To join our kingdoms and our hearts, and never
> Fly off our loves again.

The Roman Maecenas says of this marriage (II.ii.245–7):

> If beauty, wisdom, modesty can settle
> The heart of Antony, Octavia is
> A blessèd lottery [prize] to him.

But for Antony Octavia is clearly a political pawn, since at the end of the very next scene he says in soliloquy (II.iii.39–41):

> I will to Egypt,
> And, though I make this marriage for my peace,
> I' the East my pleasure lies.

As for Caesar, in so far as he is prepared to marry his sister off to the man whom (in I.iv) he had condemned as a debauchee, the implication is that he too is using Octavia as a political pawn. And doubts about the sincerity of his professed love for his sister are raised when he breaks into tears as she is about to leave with Antony for Egypt: in asides between Enobarbus and Agrippa (III.ii.51–9) the falsity of Caesar's tears is suggested by a comparison with the tears shed by Antony at the death of Brutus on the battlefield of Philippi, when, as Enobarbus recalls, 'What willingly he did confound [destroy] he wailed [bewailed]'. (Shakespeare did not actually show Antony doing this in *Julius Caesar*.) After Antony's departure from Rome

Caesar's true character is revealed beyond all doubt. In III.iv we hear that Caesar has violated the peace treaty with Pompey by going to war against him (presumably after Pompey has cleared the sea of pirates according to the terms of the treaty, II.vi.36–7). In the next scene (III.v) we hear that, having defeated Pompey, Caesar strips Lepidus of his power as a triumvir on the trumped-up charge of his having conspired with Pompey. And, now that Antony is no longer needed as an ally against Pompey, Caesar finds pretexts (III.vi) for going to war against Antony – one pretext being Antony's objection to the removal of Lepidus (III.vi.27–9). When Octavia arrives in Rome to plead for peace (III.vi), Caesar merely seizes upon Antony's betrayal of Octavia by his continued relations with Cleopatra as a further pretext for going to war. We see that Caesar, far from being a loving man, is a ruthless seeker of absolute power.

Earlier in the play Pompey had given it as his opinion that Antony's soldiership was twice that of Caesar and Lepidus together ('his soldiership/Is twice the other twain', II.i.34–5). But in the war with Caesar in the Third and Fourth Acts Antony's judgment is completely undermined by his blind attachment to Cleopatra. At Actium (on the west coast of Greece) Enobarbus and an unnamed soldier plead with Antony to fight against Caesar on land and not at sea where Caesar has superior ships, manned by experienced sailors, but Antony insists on a naval battle since his own navy will be joined by that of Cleopatra (III.vii). During the battle Cleopatra's fleet, with Cleopatra aboard her own flagship, suddenly withdraws, and Antony, 'like a doting mallard,/Leaving the fight in height, flies after her' (III.x.20–1). Enobarbus, who previously had been so much in favour of Antony's association with Cleopatra, is now appalled by its effect on Antony as a military leader – 'The itch of his affection [desire] should not then/Have nicked his captainship' (II.xiii.7–8). In fact Enobarbus is so ashamed of Antony that he decides to desert (III.xiii.200–1), but when Antony generously sends his personal 'treasure' after him (IV.vi.20–2) he is overcome by guilt (IV.vi.30–4) and later dies, saying 'O Antony,/Nobler than my revolt [desertion] is infamous' (IV.ix.18–19), so that we see that Antony, despite his folly, still inspires devotion. Caesar, after his victory off Actium, arrives in Egypt to confront Antony there, and in Alexandria Antony is now swayed by erratic changes of mood. Finding that Cleopatra is giving a friendly reception to Thyreus, sent by Caesar to negotiate Cleopatra's surrender, Antony furiously denounces Cleopatra and bitterly regrets that by turning his back on Octavia he has forgone 'the getting [begetting] of a lawful race,/And by a gem of women' (III.xiii.107–8), but then his mood changes to one of manic conviviality (III.xiii.182–4): 'Come,/Let's have one other gaudy night... fill our bowls once more.' After a brief advance against Caesar's troops outside Alexandria Antony is buoyed up by excessive optimism (IV.viii), but when he hears that his fleet has surrendered to Caesar Cleopatra again becomes the object of his rage ('This foul Egyptian hath betrayed me', IV.xii.10). After taking refuge from Antony Cleopatra foolishly tries to abate his rage by having him informed that she has taken her own life, with the result that Antony is immediately moved to join her in death. He survives his self-inflicted wound long enough to be taken to the living Cleopatra, and he dies expressing his love for her but also deceiving himself that he has fought heroically against his conqueror, Caesar – he describes himself as 'a Roman by a Roman/Valiantly vanquished' (IV.xv.57–8). Antony's death, however, is preceded by another example of the devotion he was able to inspire in his followers (as was previously shown by Enobarbus): when Antony decided to put an end to his life he called upon his faithful Eros to administer death by the sword, but Eros, rather than kill his 'dear master' (IV.xiv.89), killed himself. In this respect Antony contrasts favourably with Caesar, to whom no one, apart from his loving sister Octavia, is genuinely devoted.

As regards Caesar, during the Egyptian battle he gave instructions that Antony should be captured alive ('Our will is Antony be took alive', IV.vi.2), presumably in order that he might be publicly humiliated in some way. Any annoyance Caesar may have felt when told of Antony's death is concealed by a hypocritical display of grief for the loss of a comrade (V.i.40–8):

> But yet let me lament
> With tears...my brother...my mate in empire...

(When Caesar starts to weep over Antony's death Agrippa and Maecenas exchange what I can only assume to be satirical comments, V.i.28–35. In view of Caesar's determined efforts to secure Antony's downfall Agrippa talks of the strangeness of an urge 'to lament/Our most persisted deeds'. Both Maecenas and Agrippa seem to parody Caesar's apparent charitableness towards Antony's faults, as, for instance, when Agrippa says 'But you gods will give us/Some faults to make us men'. And Maecenas's remark 'When such a spacious mirror's set before him/He needs must see himself' seems to indicate Caesar's satisfaction in seeing himself as now occupying Antony's position of ruler of the spacious eastern part of the empire.) Caesar's public lament is cut short by the arrival of an Egyptian messenger from Cleopatra asking how Caesar intends to proceed with her, and Caesar assures the messenger that his intentions are 'honourable' since 'Caesar cannot live/To be ungentle' (V.i.58–60). Yet as soon as the Egyptian has gone Caesar instructs Proculeius to go to Cleopatra to ensure that she does not take her own life, so that she may be exhibited in his victory parade in Rome (V.i.65–6):

> for her life in Rome
> Would be eternal [bring eternal fame] in our triumph.

And when Proculeius has left there is more hypocrisy as Caesar tells his attendants that he had never wished to be drawn into a war with Antony (V.i.73–6):

> Go with me to my tent, where you shall see
> How hardly [unwillingly] I was drawn into this war,
> How calm and gentle I proceeded still
> In all my writings [letters to Antony].

Probably to point up Caesar as the loveless power-seeker,

Cleopatra in the last scene of the play (V.ii) is presented more sympathetically than in the earlier scenes, just as Antony, for all his folly, was presented more sympathetically in his last scenes. V.ii opens with Cleopatra saying:

> My desolation does begin to make
> A better life.

Despite being put under guard by Proculeius Cleopatra has contrived to have a countryman bring her some asps (small vipers) hidden under figs, and, though she is impelled to commit suicide as a means of escape from Caesar and though (like Antony himself) she indulges in self-deception about Antony's greatness ('His legs bestrid the ocean, his reared arm/Crested the world...', V.ii.82 ff.), she is inspired by the emotion of true love in wishing to join Antony in death and in wishing also to regard him as her husband ('Husband, I come', V.ii.285).[76] And, like Antony, she has devoted attendants. Iras, one of her female attendants, dies of shock as Cleopatra is about to submit to the fatal bites of the asps, and immediately after Cleopatra's death Charmian, her other female attendant, goes the way of her mistress by applying an asp to herself.

Caesar thus fails to take Cleopatra alive just as he failed to take Antony alive, and once again he shows no sign of his disappointment. The play ends with him putting on a show of generosity by announcing that a funeral will be held for both Antony and Cleopatra and that they will be buried beside each other. And he affects to be moved by 'pity' for the two lovers (V.ii.357–60):

> High events as these
> Strike [distress] those that make them, and their story is
> No less in pity than his glory which
> Brought them to be lamented.

The give-away word here is 'glory': in Caesar's view glory belongs to himself for having brought the lovers to their end. Earlier, just after he looked forward to Antony being taken alive, Caesar declared that 'The time of universal peace is near'

(IV.vi.5). The universal peace that prevails at the end of the play has been achieved by Caesar's removal of all those blocking his way to supreme power.

The essential tragedy of *Antony and Cleopatra* is that Antony, a man with a capacity for love, could not combine love with his responsibilities as a leader – as he might have been more successful in doing if he had been able to respond to the love of such a woman as Octavia.[77] The play thus stresses the need for love, but the right kind of love, in a ruler.

CORIOLANUS (c. 1607)

The plot material of *Coriolanus*, like that of *Julius Caesar* and *Antony and Cleopatra*, derives from Plutarch. The play is based on Plutarch's account of a Roman military leader in the early years of the Roman republic who, as a member of the patrician class, fell foul of the populace and became leader of the enemies of Rome, the Volscians, but was finally killed by a group of Volscians who conspired against him. For Plutarch Coriolanus was an outstandingly brave soldier whose downfall was due to his anger and churlishness. In Shakespeare's *Coriolanus* 'love' and 'hate' are key words, as they are in *Romeo and Juliet, The Merchant of Venice, Othello*, and *Timon of Athens*, and, though Plutarch too has something to say about hate in his account of Coriolanus, the main theme of *Coriolanus* is Shakespeare's own: the need for love rather than hate to be an activating force in the individual human being and in human society. (Shakespeare had already shown in *Antony and Cleopatra* the need for political leaders to be in tune with the true spirit of love.) Coriolanus is the central tragic character in that, though his personality has been warped by hate, he also has a capacity for love and pity, and just when these emotions become fully active he is struck down by the hate of the Volscians' own leader, Tullus Aufidius. In fact, though the play derives from Plutarch, in spirit it is closer to the Christian commandment 'That ye love one another' (*John* 13:34).

In the first scene rebellious Roman citizens, armed with various weapons, are complaining about the patricians (upper-class Romans) who in a time of famine are failing to arrange for a fair distribution of corn. These citizens regard their chief enemy amongst the patricians as being Caius Marcius (later to be known as Coriolanus – 'Caius Marcius is the chief enemy of the people', I.i.6–7), but there is one patrician, Menenius Agrippa, who, the citizens believe, 'hath always loved the people' (I.i.50). This belief proves to be unfounded when Menenius, after telling the citizens that 'most charitable care/ Have the patricians of you' (I.i.63–4), argues that the patricians need to be well supplied with food in order to care for the rest of society, just as the human belly consumes food to sustain the body as a whole (I.i.94–152), and he finishes up by calling these rebellious citizens 'rats' (I.i.160). At this point Marcius appears, immediately denouncing the citizens as 'curs' (I.i.166) and saying that he is proud to be hated by them – 'Who deserves greatness/Deserves your hate' (I.i.174–5). And in the second scene the Volscians, the enemy of the Romans (the Volscians inhabited an area to the south of Rome), receive a report from an informant in Rome which says that Marcius 'is of Rome worse hated than of you' (I.ii.13).

The third scene of the play gives us an insight into the kind of upbringing Marcius has had. His mother Volumnia has brought him up to be single-mindedly devoted to war. In her opening speech Volumnia tells Marcius's wife Virgilia that military 'honour' is more important than 'love' (this was the false view taken by Bertram in *All's Well That Ends Well*): Volumnia boasts of having sent Marcius to 'a cruel war' to make a man of him. When Virgilia, who clearly puts love before military honour, asks Volumnia how she would have felt if Marcius had been killed in battle, Volumnia replies that even if she lost numerous sons in war she would be glad to have them 'die nobly for their country' (I.iii.25–). Virginia is horrified by the thought of her husband suffering bloodshed in war ('O Jupiter, no blood!', I.iii.38), whereas Volumnia glories in such bloodshed ('The breasts of Hecuba... looked not lovelier/Than Hector's forehead when it spit forth blood', I.iii.40–2). And in a conversation between Volumnia and a visiting friend, Valeria, we hear about Marcius's young son. When Volumnia speaks of this son's keen interest in swords and drums (I.iii.55–6) Valeria immediately classifies him as 'the father's son' (I.iii.56+) and goes on to describe an occasion (I.iii.65–) when she saw him catch 'a gilded butterfly' which, after several times releasing it and catching it, he then 'mammocked' (tore to pieces). 'One on's [of his] father's moods' is Volumnia's comment (I.iii.66), and Valeria, whom we see to be of Volumnia's mind, praises the boy as 'a noble child' (I.iii.67).

In the scenes that follow in the first Act Marcius is involved in hostilities with the Volscians. His bravery and skill as a warrior are shown in his fighting his way out single-handedly after being shut within the gates of the Volscian capital Corioli: Roman soldiers are then able to enter and eventually capture this city. Before Corioli was captured, when the Roman soldiers had been forced to retreat, Marcius showed the same contempt for them ('Boils and plagues/Plaster you o'er', I.iv.31–2) as he showed for the citizens in Rome, yet he is capable of feeling intense love when he is reunited with the Roman commander-in-chief Cominius (I.vi.29–31):

> O, let me clip [embrace] ye
> In arms as sound as when I wooed, in heart
> As merry as when our nuptial day was done...

Tullus Aufidius, the Volscian military leader, is hated by Marcius – Marcius describes him as 'the man of my soul's hate' (I.v.10). (In the first scene of the play, however, Marcius did pay tribute to Aufidius as a leader and soldier – 'I sin in envying his noblity', I.i.228. Ironically this tribute is later shown in the play to be quite undeserved by Aufidius.) But Marcius does not hate all Volscians. When the fighting is over he remembers with gratitude the hospitality shown him by a Volscian in Corioli, and, having seen this man among the prisoners taken by the Romans, he asks that this prisoner should be released (I.ix.82–7). And, when Marcius returns to Rome (his mother, on hearing the news of Marcius's triumph, characteristically expressed delight that he was wounded – 'O, he is wounded: I thank the gods for't', II.i.112+), his first thoughts go to the weeping Volscian widows and mothers in Corioli – he says to his wife Virgilia (II.i.168–70):

> Ah, my dear,
> Such eyes the widows in Corioli wear,
> And mothers that lack sons.

Following his performance at Corioli Marcius is honoured with the name 'Coriolanus' (II.i.153–7), the name by which he is generally known for the rest of the play. There is a general wish that he should become consul, but custom requires that to become consul he must present himself to the people to ask for their votes or 'voices' (II.ii.137–42). Though this goes against his inclination, he complies with the custom and, being the hero of the hour, gains the people's consent (II.iii.129–33). But the tribunes Brutus and Sicinius (the tribunes are the people's elected leaders), fearing that as consul Coriolanus will try to curb their powers, have resolved to turn the people against him by stressing his 'hatred' of them (II.i.235–6). Immediately after the citizens have given their 'voices' to Coriolanus Brutus and Sicinius proceed to make the citizens change their minds (end of II.iii), and in III.i the two tribunes lead a riotous mob against Coriolanus who, however, is persuaded by Menenius, Cominius, and other patricians to withdraw. In the next scene it becomes apparent that Coriolanus derives his contempt for the common people from his mother – he recalls (III.ii.8–10) that she

> was wont
> To call them woollen vassals [coarsely clad underlings], things created
> To buy and sell with groats [coins of low value].

But now Volumnia, eager that Coriolanus shall become consul, wants him to ingratiate himself with the people (he should resort to 'policy', i.e. deception, III.ii.42,48, rather than express his true opinions), and to please his mother Coriolanus finally agrees to try to win the people over to him. As he prepares to face the people again Coriolanus is filled with a genuine desire to promote goodwill in the Roman state as a whole – he asks the gods to (III.iii.35–7):

> Plant love among us,
> Throng our large temples with the shows of peace,
> And not our streets with war.

(These words, in fact, sum up the play's central theme.) Though Coriolanus declares that he is willing to accept the will of the people and the authority of the tribunes (III.iii.43–7), this acceptance is ignored. Sicinius provokes Coriolanus by calling him 'a traitor to the people' (III.iii.66), and he plays into the hands of the tribunes by giving way to rage. When Sicinius incites the citizens to demand Coriolanus's banishment he responds by denouncing them as 'You common cry [pack] of curs, whose breath I hate' (III.iii.123) and says it is he who will banish them ('I banish you', III.iii.126) by turning his back on Rome (III.iii.136–8):

> Despising
> For you [because of you] the city, thus I turn my back.
> There is a world elsewhere.

Tenderness, however, is shown to his family and friends as he sets out on his departure from Rome (IV.i.48–50):

> Come, my sweet wife, my dearest mother, and
> My friends of noble touch [of proven worth]. When I am forth,
> Bid me farewell and smile.

Coriolanus decides to throw in his lot with the Volscians and arrives in Aufidius's home town of Antium, where again (as previously on returning to Rome from Corioli, II.i.168–70) he feels remorse for having made Volscian women widows (IV.iv.1–2): 'A goodly city is this Antium. City,/'Tis I that made thy widows.' He then reflects wryly (IV.iv.12–24) on how in earthly life love can turn into hate, hate into love: 'O world, thy slippery turns... My birthplace hate I, and my love's upon/

This enemy town.' Coriolanus presents himself to Aufidius, offering his services out of 'spite' (IV.v.82) against Rome. Surprisingly, in view of his previous avowals of his hatred of Coriolanus (I.x.24, III.i.14–15), Aufidius greets Coriolanus with a lyrical expression of love (IV.v.106–18 – this lyrical expression of love recalls the similar way in which Coriolanus expressed his love for Cominius in I.vi.29–32):

> Let me twine
> Mine arms about that body...here I clip
> The anvil of my sword, and do contest
> As hotly and as nobly with thy love
> As ever in ambitious strength I did
> Contend against thy valour...more dances my rapt heart
> Than when I first my wedded mistress [wife] saw
> Bestride my threshold.

We may be intended to take this as showing that Coriolanus is capable of inspiring love in a former enemy and that therefore what Coriolanus had been saying about hate turning into love applies also to Aufidius: if so, we are soon to find that Aufidius's new-found love turns back to hate. I think it more likely that we are meant to realise later that this profession of love is hypocrisy on Aufidius's part, arising from a quick perception that Coriolanus's services are to be welcomed as a means of securing the defeat of Rome. (There is at all events dramatic irony in the remarks made by Aufidius's servants that the alliance between Coriolanus and Aufidius in war against Rome shows that war is better than peace because peace 'makes men hate one another', IV.v.221ff. The play as a whole certainly does not subscribe to the view that war promotes love.) It is not long before Aufidius, having encouraged the Volscians to accept Coriolanus, is mortified to find himself outshone by Coriolanus – Aufidius's Lieutenant points out that Coriolanus is admired more than Aufidius by Aufidius's own men (IV.vii.3–6). At the beginning of the scene in which Aufidius avowed his hatred of Coriolanus early in the play (I.x.24) he said that because he could not defeat Coriolanus in honourable fight he was prepared to resort to dishonourable means to be rid of him (I.x.7–16), and now he is resolved to dispose of Coriolanus as soon as Rome has been conquered (IV.vii.56–7):

> When, Caius [Caius Marcius], Rome is thine,
> Thou art poorest of all – then shortly art thou mine.

As Coriolanus advances towards Rome at the head of the Volscian army, the Romans send individuals to plead with him to halt the advance. After the failure of Cominius on such a mission it is ironic that the tribunes Brutus and Sicinius appeal to Menenius to see what his 'love' for Coriolanus can do for Rome (V.i.39–41). Menenius too fails, despite Coriolanus's admission of his love for his friend ('Yet, for [because] I loved thee,/Take this [a letter] along', V.ii.85–6). Then Coriolanus's mother arrives at Coriolanus's tent, together with his wife and son. It is ironic indeed that Volumnia, who for so long had gloried in war, now finds herself pleading to her son to bring about 'peace' between Romans and Volscians (V.iii.138–40). She strikes a false note in trying to win Coriolanus's sympathy for her (V.iii.160–4):

> Thou hast never in thy life
> Showed thy dear mother any courtesy,
> When she, poor hen, fond of no second brood,
> Has clucked thee to the wars, and safely home
> Loaden with honour.

All Coriolanus's military accomplishments, according to one of the citizens in the first scene of the play, were performed 'to please his mother' (I.i.32 +), as later was his submission to the tribunes in order to become consul. And Volumnia's comparison of herself to a mother hen gives the impression that she was always protective, but far from ensuring that her son was brought 'safely home' she was quite happy that he should die for his country (I.iii.25–). But Coriolanus's love for his mother wins the day: he cannot help but relent. (Aufidius hypocritically says he was 'moved' by Volumnia's appeal, V.iii.194, but his aside, V.iii.200–2, reveals that he is glad to see here a means of discrediting Coriolanus in the eyes of the Volscians.) Coriolanus's spite against Rome has vanished, and he applauds the 'ladies' (Volumnia, Virgilia, and Valeria who is also present) for their part in bringing about 'peace' (V.iii.206–9).

When Coriolanus returns to Corioli from Rome to tell the Volscians that he brings peace terms honourable to both sides, Aufidius denounces him as a 'traitor' (V.vi.85) and Aufidius and his accomplices kill Coriolanus with their swords. Then in the last speech of the play Aufidius, no doubt because of the respect shown by certain Volscian lords for Coriolanus, professes sorrow (hypocritically, it must surely be assumed) for what he has done (V.vi.147–8):

> My rage is gone,
> And I am struck with sorrow.

Coriolanus's life is thus sacrificed in the cause of peace. For all his faults, mainly due to the warping effect of his upbringing, Coriolanus was responsive to the claims of love and peace.

PERICLES (c. 1608)

There has been some doubt about Shakespeare's authorship of *Pericles* because of its omission from the First Folio (the first collected edition of Shakespeare's plays, carrying the authority of having been compiled by, or at least under the supervision of, two actors in Shakespeare's own theatrical company), and, though the play was attributed to William Shakespeare when it was first published in mangled form in 1609, this attribution is not reliable.[78] However, it is generally accepted that much of the play, if not the whole of it, is by Shakespeare, and the overall theme of the play as we have it is by no means uncharacteristic of him. That theme is the overcoming by divine power of the effects of human evil and of adverse 'fortune', the two chief victims of human evil and adverse fortune being Pericles, Prince (i.e. King – see I.iii.2) of Tyre, and his daughter Marina.

Since a main source for the plot of the play was one of the stories in *Confessio Amantis*, a long work by the 14th-century

English poet John Gower, a substantial contribution to the play is made by 'Gower' as a narrator. (He appears at the beginning of each Act and on three other occasions, and for much of the time this Gower speaks in the form of verse adopted by the real Gower in *Confessio Amantis* – eight-syllable lines rhyming in pairs). At the beginning of the play Gower tells us that Antiochus the Great (who historically was a ruler of Syria, 223–187 BC) had a beautiful daughter with whom he committed incest, and suitors were warded off by being confronted with death if they failed to solve a riddle that was put to them. In the first scene Pericles, the young Prince of Tyre, offers himself as a suitor, but, on perceiving that the riddle refers to incest, he avoids giving a direct answer by saying that there are deeds of kings that are best not spoken about. Antiochus pretends that Pericles has misinterpreted the riddle and says that as a generous gesture he will allow Pericles to stay in Antioch for forty more days to ponder the answer to the riddle. Antiochus then instructs one of his lords to poison Pericles – but Pericles has already fled. On returning home (I.ii) Pericles is advised by his faithful minister Helicanus not to stay in Tyre for fear of an attempt being made on his life there, and Pericles decides to set off for Tarsus. It is not long before Antiochus's poisoner arrives in Tyre, and Helicanus sends word to Pericles in Tarsus, advising him to move on. Fortune strikes Pericles at sea since his ship is wrecked, but, as Gower tells us (Act II, Gower, lines 37–8), Fortune allows him to survive (he is the only survivor) by tossing him ashore:

> Fortune, tired with doing bad,
> Threw him ashore, to give him glad [gladness].

Pericles finds himself in the kingdom[79] of 'the good King Simonides' (II.i.43–4), and, having recovered his suit of armour from the sea, he competes in a jousting tournament held in honour of the birthday of the King's daughter Thaisa. Pericles is proclaimed the winner (he modestly attributes his victory to fortune rather than merit, II.iii.12), whereupon Thaisa falls in love with him and they marry.

The first indication of divine intervention in the play occurs in II.iv, where, according to a report received by Helicanus in Tyre, 'the most high gods' (II.iv.3) have punished Antiochus and his daughter for their incestuous relationship by striking them both dead with 'fire from heaven' (II.iv.9). As Helicanus observes (II.iv.13–15):

>   though
> This king were great, his greatness was no guard
> To bar heaven's shaft, but sin had his reward [i.e. was punished].

As for Pericles, since the people in Tyre have become impatient for his return, he embarks on a voyage home, accompanied by his wife Thaisa, now pregnant, and a nurse, Lychorida. But Fortune, having previously favoured Pericles by tossing him into Simonides's kingdom, turns against him ('Fortune's mood/Varies again' – III, Gower, lines 46–7). His ship is caught in a storm (III.i) and, though the ship is not wrecked, he is told by the nurse Lychorida that Thaisa has died in giving birth to a baby girl. The crew demand that Thaisa's body be cast overboard since, according to seamen's superstition, a ship must be cleared of the dead in order to be rid of a storm: arrangements are therefore made to put Thaisa's body to sea in a wooden chest. Meanwhile, since the newborn baby is too weak to travel further and Tarsus is near to hand, Pericles leaves the babe and the nurse with Cleon, the governor of Tarsus, who had been his host before (and to whom Pericles had presented a cargo of corn to relieve a famine in Tarsus – I.iv.88–96). Presumably because he is now a widower, Pericles asks Cleon and his wife to make themselves responsible for the bringing up of the baby daughter, whom Pericles has named Marina because she was born at sea (III.iii.12–13). Talking of the need to leave immediately for Tyre, Pericles says 'We cannot but obey/The powers above us' (III.iii.9–10), a remark that shows his respect for heavenly powers. As it happens, unbeknown to Pericles, heavenly powers have been acting through a physician in Ephesus, where Thaisa's coffin was washed ashore. Thaisa is restored to life by the physician

Cerimon who, according to a gentleman of Ephesus, is endowed with divine power (III.ii.101–3):

> The heavens
> Through you increase our wonder, and set up
> Your fame for ever.

After her restoration to life Thaisa, believing Pericles to be dead, accepts Cerimon's suggestion that she should become a priestess in the temple of the goddess Diana in Ephesus (III.iv).

Act IV is mainly concerned with the misfortunes of Pericles's daughter Marina. At the beginning of this Act Gower tells us that Marina (who by now is fourteen, as we hear later, V.iii.8) has been given by Cleon an education befitting a princess (in accordance with Pericles's request, III.iii.15–17), and this education has been so effective that she outshines Cleon's own daughter. The nurse Lychorida is now dead (says Gower) and Cleon's evil wife, Dionyza, is so angry that her daughter is outshone by Marina that she has arranged for Marina to be murdered. As she hands Marina over to the man who is to carry out the murder Dionyza displays all the hypocrisy of the Shakespearean villain – 'I love the king your father and yourself' she assures Marina (IV.i.34), and 'I must have care of you' (IV.i.51). But, just as Marina is about to be murdered on the seashore, pirates suddenly appear who seize her and take her off to Mytilene (IV.ii) where they sell her to a brothel keeper. In the brothel Marina preserves her virginity by converting clients to virtue, one of these clients being the governor of Mytilene, Lysimachus. (There is comic dramatic irony when the proprietor's wife, the bawd – procuress – of the establishment, hearing that Marina has 'spoken holy words to the Lord Lysimachus', exclaims 'O, abominable!', IV.vi.131–3.) Marina prays 'That the gods/Would safely deliver me from this place' (IV.vi.177–8), and almost immediately a partial answer to her prayer (it will be answered in full later) comes with her being allowed by the brothel keeper to go to 'an honest house' to teach singing, dancing and embroidery

(Gower, beginning of Act V), following her request at the end of IV.vi.

Earlier, at the beginning of IV.iv, we were told by Gower that Pericles made his way to Tarsus 'To see his daughter, all his life's delight...To fetch his daughter home', only to be informed that she was dead – the murderer employed by Dionyza had decided to say that he had carried out the murder (IV.i.100–1), and Dionyza had decided to say to Pericles merely that Marina had 'died at night' (IV.iii.16). Grief-stricken, Pericles departed from Tarsus, leaving it to 'Lady Fortune' to determine what would happen to him (IV.iv, Gower, lines 47–8). At the beginning of Act V we hear from Gower that Pericles's ship is anchored off Mytilene where he has been driven by winds, but what follows in V.i suggests that Pericles has been brought to Mytilene by the gods rather than by Fortune. In this scene, the most dramatically effective scene in the whole play, Lysimachus, the governor, introduces Marina to Pericles as a maid whose sweet singing voice ('sweet harmony', V.i.44) may help to rouse him out of his grief. Marina describes to Pericles how she has been the victim of 'wayward fortune' (V.i.88), and gradually Pericles comes to identify her as his lost daughter. With 'this great sea of joys rushing upon me' (V.i.191), Pericles asks Helicanus (who has accompanied Pericles on his journey) to fall on his knees to 'thank the holy gods' (V.i.197).

At the end of V.i the goddess Diana appears in a vision to Pericles, summoning him to go to her temple at Ephesus. Pericles does so, taking with him Marina and also the governor Lysimachus who, having been reformed by Marina in the brothel (IV.vi), is now going to marry her (V.ii, Gower, lines 10–11). In the last scene of the play Pericles is reunited with his wife Thaisa and is overwhelmed by the kindness of the gods (V.iii.41–2):

> No more, you gods! Your present kindness
> Makes my past miseries sports.

And, when Pericles asks Thaisa whom he should thank 'Besides the gods for this great miracle' (V.iii.59–60), she replies 'Lord

Cerimon...Through whom the gods have shown their power' (V.iii.61–2).

In the final speech of the play Gower sums up the main theme by saying that Pericles, his queen and his daughter, 'Although assailed with fortune fierce and keen', have been 'Led on by heaven and crowned with joy at last'. Gower also says that 'wicked Cleon and his wife' have been punished by 'the gods' by being burnt alive when the citizens of Tarsus, on coming to hear of the crime against Marina, set fire to Cleon's palace. (Here there seems to be a discrepancy. In V.i.170–1 Marina tells Pericles that 'cruel Cleon with his wicked wife/Did seek to murder me', but according to what Gower said at the beginning of Act IV, and according to what actually happened in IV.i, it was Dionyza alone who plotted the murder. And in IV.iii Cleon was horrified when Dionyza told him what she had done. Cleon's crime was thus confined to his keeping silent about the evil done by his wife.)

CYMBELINE (c. 1609)

Cymbeline has an historical setting derived from Holinshed, Cymbeline being a British king at the time of the Roman emperor Augustus. The plot is a complicated one, but the main theme of the play is clear enough: the overcoming of human evil by divine intervention (in this respect the theme is similar to that of *Pericles*), the evil in this play being evil in connection with love and politics.

At the beginning of the play evil is done to Cymbeline's daughter Imogen and her husband Posthumus Leonatus. As an orphan whose father achieved distinction in battle against the Romans, Posthumus has been brought up in Cymbeline's court where he was quick to acquire the learning imparted to him (I.i.43–6) and where he is 'most praised, most loved' (I.i.47). Yet, because Cymbeline, who had married again, wanted the Queen's own son to marry Imogen, Posthumus is banished and Imogen forced to stay in Cymbeline's court. Just before Posthumus leaves Cymbeline scornfully addresses him as

'Thou basest thing' (I.i.125) and Imogen as 'thou vile one!' (I.i.143). The Queen hypocritically pretends to be sympathetic to Imogen and Posthumus, but Imogen is not taken in by her ('Dissembling courtesy!', I.i.84), and after Posthumus has gone the Queen's evil nature becomes even more obvious when, because she knows that Pisanio, the servant Posthumus has left behind in the palace, is loyal to his master ('He's for his master/ And enemy to my son', I.v.28–9), she tries to kill him by making him a gift of what she says is life-preserving medicine but what is really poison.

In the first scene Imogen and Posthumus part with mutual vows of fidelity and exchange love tokens – Imogen gives Posthumus a diamond ring, and he gives her a bracelet. Posthumus goes to Rome to stay with Philario, who was a friend of his father, and here (in I.iv) he meets with evil in the person of Iachimo. Iachimo is cynical about the fidelity of women, and when Posthumus affirms his complete faith in Imogen Iachimo persuades him to enter into a wager whereby, if Iachimo, after visiting Imogen in Britain, can produce proof of having seduced her, Posthumus will part with the ring Imogen gave him, but if Iachimo fails to seduce Imogen he will pay Posthumus the sum of ten thousand ducats. On visiting Imogen Iachimo (believed by her to be Posthumus's friend) hides in a trunk that has been placed in her bedchamber, and when Imogen is asleep he removes the bracelet Posthumus gave her and takes note of a mole on her left breast (II.ii.37–8). Iachimo maliciously looks forward to provoking madness in her husband ('the madding of her lord', II.ii.37), just as Iago looked forward to provoking madness in Othello, to undermining 'his peace and quiet/Even to madness' (*Othello* II.i.304–5). Overwhelmed by the apparent proof of Iachimo's seduction of Imogen, Posthumus parts with the ring Imogen gave him and then becomes evil himself by giving way to destructive passion: 'O that I had her here to tear her limb-meal [limb from limb]' (II.iv.147 – compare Othello when convinced by Iago of Desdemona's infidelity: 'I'll tear her all to pieces', *Othello* III.iii.435). Like Hamlet ('Frailty, thy name is woman', *Hamlet* I.ii.146), Posthumus condemns *all* women (II.v.30–2):

They are not constant, but are changing still [incessantly]
One vice but of a minute old for one
Not half so old as that.

And he proceeds to arrange for the murder of Imogen – he writes to Imogen pretending he is in Milford Haven and luring her into meeting him there (in this play Milford Haven, a Welsh port, is used for travel between Rome and Britain) and he writes to his servant Pisanio instructing him to go to Milford Haven and murder Imogen (see III.ii and III.iv). Pisanio, however, is sure that Posthumus is mistaken about Imogen (III.ii.3–6). Accompanying her for most of the way to Milford Haven, he reveals Posthumus's instructions to him and says that he will merely send Posthumus some blood-stained item as apparent evidence that the murder has been carried out (III.iv.123–4). He then suggests that Imogen, dressed as a male, should try to gain employment with a Roman ambassador, Lucius, who is about to arrive in Milford Haven on his way back to Rome, so that she may be close enough to Posthumus in Rome to hear about his activities (III.iv.140–76).

Another evil character in the play is the Queen's son, Cloten. Because Imogen (in II.iii) firmly rejected his advances to her after Posthumus's banishment, Cloten is determined 'To be revenged upon her' (III.v.80). Following Imogen's disappearance from court, Cloten, sure that Pisanio has information about her whereabouts, threatens to kill Pisanio if Pisanio does not give him this information, and Pisanio shows him a letter in Posthumus's handwriting which indicates that Imogen has gone to Milford Haven (this must be Posthumus's letter to Imogen, perhaps passed on by her to Pisanio). In an aside (III.v.103–4) Pisanio seems confident that Cloten will be unable to catch up with Imogen (Pisanio presumably has in mind Imogen's intention to move on to Italy), but in soliloquy at the end of this scene he prays that heaven may protect her (III.v.160–1): 'Flow, flow,/You heavenly blessings, on her.' Cloten immediately decides (III.v.129+) that he will go to Milford Haven where he will kill Posthumus and where, dressed in a suit of Posthumus's clothes (which he sends Pisanio to fetch for him), he will rape Imogen – he wants to do this while wearing Posthumus's clothes as a cynical retort to the remark made by Imogen when she rejected him that Posthumus's 'meanest garment' was dearer to her than such a man as Cloten (II.iii.134–7). Nearing Milford Haven Cloten encounters three characters who first appeared in the play in III.iii – Belarius, victim of evil in the past because banished by Cymbeline on a false charge made by 'two villains' (III.iii.65–9), and two young men, Guiderius and Arviragus, who think they are Belarius's sons but who are actually the sons of Cymbeline, stolen when babes by Belarius in retaliation for the confiscation of his lands (III.iii.99–103). These three men live in a cave at the foot of Welsh mountains, and when Cloten arrives there he insults Guiderius by calling him a villain and a thief, a fight ensues, and Cloten is beheaded. Belarius, who had identified Cloten as soon as he arrived, becomes alarmed about what punishment may follow – but Arviragus is calmly prepared to leave this matter to the gods (IV.ii.146–7): 'Let ordinance [what is destined to happen]/Come as the gods foresay [determine] it.'

The killing of Cloten is the first example of evil being checked in the play, and the last Act shows the involvement of heavenly powers in the checking of human evil (such involvement having been hinted at in Posthumus's prayer that heavenly blessings would flow on Imogen, III.v.160–1, and in Arviragus's reference to the gods, as just quoted above). When war breaks out between Rome and Britain Posthumus arrives in Britain as soldier in the Roman army and, having received from Pisanio (as planned in III.iv.123–4) a blood-stained piece of cloth allegedly indicating the murder of Imogen, he is now bitterly repentant. He decides that in honour of Imogen's memory he will fight, dressed as a Briton, for her country against Rome (V.i.19–27), and on the battlefield he disarms Iachimo, who has become an officer in the Roman army, and assists in the rescue of Cymbeline from capture by the Romans (V.ii). But after the eventual British victory, to punish himself for the evil done to Imogen, Posthumus gives himself up as a defeated Roman soldier to the British (V.iii). When he is asleep in a British prison he has a vision in which his dead father asks the god Jupiter to help his son, and in response to this appeal Jupiter himself appears, saying to the father (V.iv.102–3):

> Be content.
> Your low-laid son our godhead will uplift.

In this vision Jupiter leaves a 'tablet' (a booklet for the writing of notes) for the father to lay on his son's body (V.iv.109), and when Posthumus awakes he finds the tablet, with a message in it prophesying that his miseries will end and all will be well in Britain (V.iv.135+).

In the long last scene (V.v), where nearly all the characters come together in Cymbeline's military camp, evil is completely overcome and the complications resulting from evil are resolved. The royal physician announces the death of the Queen and reports confessions made by her before her death: she confessed (V.v.37–56) that she had married Cymbeline, whom she detested, in order to become a queen and that she had intended to poison Imogen whom she also detested and Cymbeline himself in order to make her son king. On hearing how he has been deceived by the Queen Cymbeline now deeply regrets his misjudgment of Imogen ('O my daughter... it was folly in me', V.v.66–7 – there is an echo here of Lear's realisation of his 'folly' in misjudging Cordelia, *King Lear* I.iv.270–2). Lucius, the commander of the defeated Roman army (who formerly was the ambassador referred to by Pisanio in III.iv.140–2), is brought before Cymbeline, and along with Lucius comes Imogen, still in male disguise, who after a series of misfortunes became Lucius's personal attendant. (When Pisanio in III.iv suggested that Imogen should make her way to Rome in disguise he also passed on to her the poison given to him by the Queen, believing it to be a curative medicine as the Queen had told him. After parting with Pisanio Imogen, disguised as a young male, fell in with Belarius and the two young princes, who placed her in an open grave when she appeared to be dead after taking the curative medicine, as she thought it to be – IV.ii. Since this poison was not as deadly as the Queen had supposed, as indicated in asides in I.v.31–44 by the doctor supplying it, Imogen eventually recovered, and was then taken on by the Roman commander Lucius as his personal attendant – IV.ii.) Iachimo is among the Roman prisoners brought before Cymbeline, and, like Borachio in *Much Ado about Nothing* and Edmund in *King Lear*, Iachimo turns out to be a villain in whom evil finally gives way to good. When challenged by Imogen (still in disguise) as to how he comes to be wearing the ring which she knows to be the one she gave to Posthumus, Iachimo, with appropriate self-denunciation, makes a full confession of his treachery. Following Iachimo's confession Posthumus, who has also been brought in as a Roman prisoner, reveals his true identity and confesses to being guilty, as he thinks, of having caused Imogen to be murdered. Imogen then reveals that she is still alive, and she is reunited with her father and with Posthumus. Belarius, Guiderius and Arviragus are present, having been praised for the crucial part they played in bringing about the British victory (described in detail in V.iii). When, however, Guiderius admits to having killed Cloten Cymbeline says he must be put to death for doing so – at which point Belarius reveals that Guiderius and Arviragus are Cymbeline's sons. Cymbeline now sees that divine justice has been meted out to both the Queen and Cloten, on 'Whom heavens, in justice both on her and hers [her son],/Have laid most heavy hand' (V.v.462–3).

Apart from the Queen's political ambition for her son there is an important political element in the play which is put into clear perspective in the play's final speeches. This political element was first introduced in III.i where Lucius, at the time when he was a Roman ambassador, asks Cymbeline to make up the lapsed payments of tribute due to Rome. The Queen and Cloten both reject any obligation to pay tribute and speak in sturdily patriotic tones about Britain's ability to resist any foreign invader, thanks to her geographical location. Just as Gaunt in *Richard II* (II.i.61–3) had described England as

> bound in with the triumphant sea,
> Whose rocky shore beats back the envious siege
> Of watery Neptune,

so the Queen in *Cymbeline* describes Britain as an island (III.i.18–20)

> which stands
> As Neptune's park, ribbed and paled in
> With rocks unscaleable and roaring waters,

and Cloten speaks of 'our salt-water girdle' (III.i.75+). But, whereas Gaunt was meant to be admired as a true patriot, the patriotism of the Queen and Cloten is shown to be evil. In III.i Cymbeline accepts the view of the Queen and Cloten that Britain should refuse to pay tribute, and this refusal results in war between Rome and Britain. At the end of the play, however, Cymbeline tells Lucius that, despite the victory over the Roman army, Britain will in fact submit to the authority of Rome (V.v.458–61):

> Although the victor, we submit to Caesar
> And to the Roman empire, promising
> To pay our wonted tribute, from the which
> We were dissuaded by our wicked queen...

A Roman soothsayer who has come with Lucius to Britain sees this peace between Britain and Rome as having been promoted by 'the powers above' (V.v.464–5):

> The fingers of the powers above do tune
> The harmony of this peace.

In referring to 'the powers above' the Soothsayer has in mind the prophecy which Jupiter left with Posthumus and which at Posthumus's request the Soothsayer in this last scene has just been fully interpreting (V.v.441–56), noting that the prophecy ended with the promise of 'peace and plenty' for Britain. Earlier in the play (IV.ii.349–51) the Soothsayer had his own divine vision – after praying to the gods he saw an eagle, 'Jove's bird' (the eagle was associated by the Romans with Jupiter, or Jove), which arrived in western Britain from the 'south' and then vanished in sunbeams. At that time the Soothsayer had interpreted this vision as a prediction of 'success' for the Roman army in Britain (IV.ii.351–3), but now at the end of the play he realises that the vision pointed not to military victory but to Britain's peaceful union with Rome – this vision (V.v.471–4)

> foreshowed our princely eagle,
> The imperial Caesar, should again unite
> His favour with the radiant Cymbeline,
> Which shines here in the west.

And, following this exposition by the Soothsayer, Cymbeline says in the final speech of the play:

> Laud we the gods...
> And in the temple of great Jupiter
> Our peace we'll ratify...

This praise for international harmony surely marks a shift in Shakespeare's political viewpoint, away from Elizabethan patriotism as presented through Gaunt in *Richard II* and through *Henry V* (*Henry V*, it is true, ends in praise for peace between England and France – but peace on England's terms). We may also note that there is a complete contrast between the conception of the Roman emperor Augustus in *Cymbeline* and the presentation (as an on-stage character) of Octavius Caesar in *Antony and Cleopatra*. Historically they are the same person, but, whereas in *Antony and Cleopatra* Octavius Caesar is the ruthless power politician whose acquisition of complete power does not bode well for the empire, in *Cymbeline* Shakespeare follows Holinshed[80] in suggesting that Augustus presides over a peaceful international society.

THE WINTER'S TALE (c. 1610)

The main theme of *The Winter's Tale*, like that of *Pericles* and *Cymbeline*, is the triumph of good over evil in human life as aided by heavenly powers – though in *The Winter's Tale* we are not allowed to forget the deaths of some innocent people (two in particular). The title refers to the season symbolism of the play, winter being associated with evil in the first half of the play, and spring and summer with goodness in the second half.

In the first scene we hear that the King of Bohemia is a guest of the King of Sicilia and that the two kings have been close friends since childhood. Camillo, a lord at the Sicilian court, hopes that the affection between the two kings will long continue – 'The heavens continue their loves' (I.i.30). In the second scene Hermione, queen of Leontes, the Sicilian king, asks Polixenes, the Bohemian king, what the two of them were like as boys, and Polixenes says of their boyhood (I.ii.67–71):

> We were as twinned lambs that did frisk i' the sun
> And bleat the one at the other. What we changed [exchanged]
> Was innocence for innocence. We knew not
> The doctrine of ill-doing, nor dreamed
> That any did.

They seemed, says Polixenes, untainted by Original Sin – 'the imposition cleared/Hereditary ours' (I.ii.74–5). But then, with dramatic suddenness, we become aware that Original Sin, even if not apparent in childhood, may show itself in later life. After Hermione has prevailed upon Polixenes to stay longer as a guest when he had just refused Leontes's request that he should do this, Leontes praises Hermione's success – but an explosive aside (I.ii.108–19) reveals that Leontes is convinced that Hermione and Polixenes are involved in a sexual relationship. Leontes is possessed by jealousy (the word 'jealousy' is applied to him later in the scene, I.ii.451) as Othello was in connection with Desdemona, except that here there is no Iago to arouse such an emotion. Leontes proceeds to express doubt to his young son Mamillius as to whether Mamillius is in fact his son ('Mamillius,/Art thou my boy?', I.ii.119–20). When Leontes tells his courtier Camillo about his suspicions Camillo boldly condemns the utterance of such suspicions as 'sin' (I.ii.283 – rather as Kent in *King Lear* I.i.166 condemned Lear's treatment of Cordelia as 'evil'), and after being ordered by Leontes to poison Polixenes Camillo warns Polixenes of Leontes's intentions and escapes with Polixenes to Bohemia. In II.i a court lady speaks of Hermione as having spread 'Into a goodly bulk' (II.i.20), whereupon Leontes denounces Hermione as 'an adulteress' (II.i.78,88) and has her put in prison. (Leontes is motivated by 'vengeance', II.iii.22, whereas Hermione wishes her father were still alive to witness her plight 'with eyes/Of pity, not revenge', III.ii.120–1.) When Hermione gives birth to a daughter in prison, another lady of the court, Paulina, presents this daughter to Leontes as the child of his 'good queen' (II.iii.58), but Leontes orders Paulina's husband, Antigonus, to take this 'female bastard' to 'some remote and desert place' and leave the child there (II.iii.174–8).

After consigning Hermione to prison Leontes revealed to Antigonus and another of his lords (II.i.180–5) that to confirm what he took to be Hermione's guilt he had sent two of his courtiers to consult Apollo's oracle at Delphos. (Sicilia and Bohemia were really medieval Christian kingdoms, whereas the oracle at Delphi belonged to ancient Greek and Roman times, but Shakespeare here follows his plot source, Robert Greene's novel *Pandosto* – where Delphi was spelt 'Delphos'.) In *The Winter's Tale* Apollo is the chief representative of divine power as Jupiter was in *Cymbeline*, and, when the two courtiers return with Apollo's sealed answer and the seal is broken, the innocence of Hermione and Polixenes, and also of Camillo whom Leontes regarded as Polixenes's accomplice, is upheld. Leontes at first refuses to believe the oracle, whereupon there is an immediate announcement of the death of his son, Mamillius (described in I.i.34+ as a child that 'makes old hearts fresh'). Leontes now becomes a changed man, realising that (III.ii.143–4)

> the heavens themselves
> Do strike at my injustice.

He expresses deep remorse for his false suspicions and evil actions. But Hermione, who was being subjected to a legal prosecution when the oracle's answer arrived, collapses at the announcement of Mamillius's death, and a few moments later Paulina reports that Hermione too is dead.

In III.iii the scene shifts to Bohemia, which according to the play has a sea-coast (here again Shakespeare follows his plot source *Pandosto*). The ship carrying Antigonus and Hermione's newly born daughter touches upon a deserted part of the Bohemian coast, and Antigonus speaks of having had a dream (III.iii.17-37) in which Hermione appeared asking him to leave the babe in a remote place in Bohemia and give this babe the name Perdita, meaning one who is lost. Antigonus, who had left Sicilia before the oracle's verdict was known, assumes that Hermione was declared guilty by Apollo and that the dream indicated Apollo's will that the babe should be left in the land of its father, Polixenes (III.iii.42-6). Antigonus is of course wrong about Polixenes being the father, but the leaving of the babe in Bohemia, when seen in relation to the ultimate happy outcome, may in fact be taken as being divinely willed, as is suggested at the beginning of the scene when Antigonus, referring to 'The heavens', says 'Their sacred wills be done' (III.iii.5-7). The babe is soon discovered by a Bohemian shepherd who takes pity on it, but we hear from the shepherd's son (described in the stage directions as a 'Clown', which here merely denotes a country fellow) that the ship that was carrying Antigonus has been destroyed in a storm, with the loss of all those on board, and that Antigonus has been killed on land by a bear. (Antigonus's death was foretold by Hermione in his dream, III.iii.34-6.) The shepherd tells his son 'Thou mettest [you met] with things dying, I with things new born' (III.iii.105+), and these words point towards a rebirth of goodness in the last two Acts of the play.

Act IV opens with 'Time' as Chorus telling us that sixteen years have passed and that Perdita has 'grown in grace' (IV.i.24) while being brought up as a shepherd's daughter – the word 'grace' is important as conveying an impression not merely of physical beauty but of spiritual goodness. In the first half of the play it was winter time, as was indicated by Mamillius's remark, in connection with the telling of stories, that 'A sad tale's best for winter' (II.i.25), and the first half of the play had a sad tale to tell, dominated by evil. In Act IV, in symbolic contrast, it is summer time (IV.iv.80), with talk of a sheep-shearing feast at the shepherd's cottage (IV.iii.34+, IV.iv.3). Florizel, son of

King Polixenes, is in love with Perdita and, though it is summer time, the two young lovers themselves are associated with spring: Florizel describes Perdita, dressed for the sheep-shearing feast, as 'Flora/Peering in April's front' (the goddess of flowers appearing at the beginning of April – IV.iv.2–3), and Perdita says she wishes she could give Florizel 'some flowers o' the spring that might/Become your time of day' – flowers including daffodils, violets, primroses, oxlips and lilies (IV.iv.113–27). Spring and summer have a different significance for a rogue called Autolycus, who at the beginning of IV.iii sings of spring as a time when he can visit his 'doxy [mistress] over the dale' and steal sheets that are drying on hedges, summer being a time when he can 'lie tumbling in the hay' with women of easy virtue ('aunts'). But Florizel says of his love for Perdita (IV.iv.33–5):

> my desires
> Run not before mine honour, nor my lusts
> Burn hotter than my faith [faithfulness].

And as the young representatives of goodness in Act IV Perdita and Florizel belie the view of youth taken by the shepherd in III.iii.55+ when he first entered the play: 'I would there were no age between ten and three-and-twenty... for there is nothing in the between but getting wenches with child, wronging the ancientry [elderly folk], stealing, fighting.'

In the first part of the play, after hearing that Polixenes and Leontes were innocent of evil in their youth (there was an association with spring in the description of these two as 'twinned lambs', I.ii.67), we saw Leontes giving way to evil in later life, and now, in Act IV, we see a late eruption of evil in Polixenes himself. Polixenes decides to spy on his son's activities at the shepherd's cottage, and, in disguise, he is present when the shepherd expresses his willingness that Perdita should marry Florizel, who, as far as the shepherd knows, is a young rustic called Doricles. Polixenes, revealing his royal identity, is furious that his son, the heir to the throne, should be in love with 'a sheep-hook' (IV.iv.412): he threatens the shepherd with hanging, and says to Perdita 'I'll have thy beauty scratched with briers' (IV.iv.417). (In view of Polixenes's objection to a marriage between Florizel and a shepherdess, it is ironical that earlier in the scene, when he was talking to Perdita about flowers, he argued in favour of crossing wild plants with cultivated ones to 'make conceive a bark of baser kind/By bud of nobler race', IV.iv.94–5.) Florizel vows that he will abandon the throne rather than abandon Perdita (IV.iv.472–3), and he tells Camillo (who has been in Bohemia ever since he left Sicilia with Polixenes) that nothing will induce him to 'break my oath/ To this my fair beloved' (IV.iv.483–4). Camillo suggests that Florizel and Perdita should go to Sicilia where he is sure that Florizel, as Polixenes's son, will be welcomed by Leontes (IV.iv.535–42) – Camillo knows about Leontes's penitence since he was asked earlier by 'the penitent king' to return to Sicilia (IV.ii.9–). As Florizel and Perdita prepare to leave for Sicilia Camillo resolves to tell Polixenes of their escape, so that by accompanying Polixenes in pursuit of the young couple he may be able to see his native country once again (IV.iv.652–7).

In the last Act the play moves back to Sicilia and forward to a happy ending. Leontes, now 'saint-like' in his remorse (V.i.2), gives a reverential welcome to Florizel and Perdita (V.i.168–70):

> The blessed gods
> Purge all infection from our air whilst you
> Do climate here [during your stay in this country].

And when he receives word of Polixenes's arrival in Sicilia he promises to plead on Florizel's behalf (V.i.229–31). Then follows the revelation of Perdita's true identity. Near the end of IV.iv the shepherd and his son decided that they should show King Polixenes the various articles the shepherd had found along with the babe, but they were persuaded by Autolycus to contact Florizel who, Autolycus had by chance come to know, was about to board a ship. Autolycus contrived to have the shepherd and son and himself taken aboard the ship carrying Florizel and Perdita to Sicilia, and in V.ii gentlemen of the Sicilian court describe the great 'wonder' (V.ii.19–, 24) of the discovery, following the identification of the articles produced by the shepherd, that Perdita is Leontes's lost daughter. (Autolycus, though himself a rogue, was an unwitting instrument of the powers of goodness. He had hoped to gain personal 'advancement', IV.iv.817+, by bringing the shepherd and his son into contact with Florizel, but after the discovery of Perdita's true identity Autolycus can only envy the acclaim enjoyed by the two rustics – 'Here come those I have done good to against my will', V.ii.119+.) But amidst the atmosphere of goodwill and joyful discovery there are reminders in these first two scenes of Act V of the loss of innocent human lives. In V.i, when Paulina wishes that Mamillius were still alive so that he might have become a friend of Florizel who is of the same age as Mamillius would have been, Leontes winces (V.i.199–20): 'Prithee, no more. Cease. Thou know'st/He dies to me again when talked of.' And in V.ii one of the gentlemen of the Sicilian court refers to Antigonus's death and the deaths of all those aboard the ship that brought Antigonus to Bohemia (V.ii.57 ff.).

In the last scene (V.iii) comes another great revelation. Leontes and his Bohemian guests visit Paulina's house to see a life-like statue of Hermione, and this statue turns out to be Hermione herself, who did not in fact die after the shock of Mamilius's death in III.ii but has survived, to the knowledge only of Paulina, for the last sixteen years. (This dramatic return from assumed death thus parallels the return of Hero in *Much Ado about Nothing* and of Helena in *All's Well That Ends Well*.) Hermione embraces Leontes, and she asks the gods to bless her newly found daughter (V.iii.121–3):

> You gods, look down,
> And from your sacred vials pour your graces
> Upon my daughter's head.

The last part of Apollo's oracle had said 'the King shall live without an heir if that which is lost be not found' (III.ii.129+), and, since Paulina had taken these words as giving hope that Perdita was still alive, Hermione had 'preserved' herself to see whether Perdita would indeed be found (V.iii.125–8). (Hermione's motive in not letting even a repentant Leontes know that she herself was alive may have been to avoid the begetting of another child since that child, according to the oracle, would be doomed not to become an heir if Perdita were not found. In V.i.35–40 Paulina was insistent that it would be futile for Leontes, believing Hermione to be dead, to marry again in order to produce an heir because such an attempt would be flying in the face of the oracle.) The play ends with the widowed Paulina taking Camillo as her second husband, and with Leontes telling Hermione that, as directed by the heavens ('heavens directing', V.iii.150), Florizel is pledged to marry Perdita.

THE TEMPEST (c. 1611)

The general theme of *The Tempest*, like that of *Pericles*, *Cymbeline* and *The Winter's Tale*, is the triumphant assertion of good over evil. But *The Tempest* differs from those other plays in two notable respects. As in the other plays the triumph of good over evil is promoted by supernatural powers, but in *The Tempest* supernatural powers are wielded by a human being, Prospero, a magician who betrays human weaknesses that contrast with the pure goodness of Ariel, the supernatural spirit who is Prospero's faithful servant. And the play shows that, apart from what is achieved by supernatural means, an important part in the triumph of good over evil can be played by a movement towards good in an individual's moral development, as seen partly in Prospero himself but more remarkably in the savage creature Caliban. This moral development is a less sudden affair than the moral conversion of a villain at the end of a play – of Borachio at the end of *Much Ado about Nothing*, Edmund at the end of *King Lear*, and Iachimo at the end of *Cymbeline*.

The tempest that gives the play its title occurs in the short opening scene, and in the second scene we hear that the tempest has been raised by the magician Prospero who lives with his daughter Miranda on an island nearby. Prospero recalls that twelve years previously he became the victim of evil at the hands of his brother Antonio and of Alonso, the King of Naples.[81] At that time Prospero had been the Duke of Milan but had entrusted the governing of his dukedom to his brother while he himself gave his time to general learning and then to 'secret studies' (I.ii.77 – Prospero's studies as a magician represent a substantial advance on Cerimon's studies of medicine as a 'secret art' in *Pericles*, III.ii.32, which enabled him to bring Thaisa back to life). This brother made himself Duke of Milan by evicting Prospero from his dukedom with military assistance from the King of Naples, the price for this assistance being that Milan became a Neapolitan dependency. Prospero and Miranda, who was then less than three years old, were put to sea in a completely unseaworthy boat which, however, was brought to their island 'by Providence divine' (I.ii.159) – it is generally assumed that in setting the play on a remote island Shakespeare had in mind recent accounts given of the Bermuda islands by survivors of a shipwreck, but in the play the island is located, as becomes apparent from the conversation in II.i.64–105, somewhere between Italy and North Africa. The tempest was raised by Prospero because 'Fortune' (I.ii.178) had brought a ship carrying his enemies close to his island and he wanted to bring them ashore on the island.

In this second scene Miranda shows deep 'compassion' for the victims of the tempest (I.ii.5–13,27), but Prospero is able to assure her that they have all escaped unhurt. However, though Prospero has a tender regard for his daughter, there is a malevolent streak in his nature. He accuses his chief spirit, Ariel, who has carried out Prospero's instructions in every detail, of forgetting the debt he owes to Prospero for liberating him from a pine tree in which he had been imprisoned by the witch Sycorax: when Ariel insists that he has not forgotten this debt Prospero says, quite unjustifiably, 'Thou liest, malignant thing' (I.ii.257). When Prospero and Miranda arrived on the island there was only one creature with a human shape (I.ii.281–4) – Caliban, son of Sycorax (who had died, having originally been banished to the island because of her evil activities as a witch). Caliban became Prospero's slave, and, though he clearly deserved punishment for having attempted to rape Miranda

(I.ii.347–8), Prospero betrays a sadistic delight in threatening Caliban with torments (I.ii.368–71):

> If thou neglect'st or dost unwillingly
> What I command, I'll rack thee with old cramps,
> Fill all thy bones with aches, make thee roar
> That beasts shall tremble at thy din.

Ferdinand, the son of the King of Naples, has been separated by Ariel from the other castaways (I.ii.221), presumably on Prospero's instructions, and when, towards the end of this long second scene, Ferdinand encounters Miranda the two are instantly attracted to each other. This instant attraction is what Prospero had hoped for ('It goes on, I see,/As my soul prompts it', I.ii.419–20), out of a desire (presumably) to find a fit husband for Miranda. Yet here again Prospero's malevolent streak shows itself. In speaking to Miranda he describes Ferdinand as 'A goodly person' (I.ii.416) but, impelled by a perverse determination to prevent an easy courtship ('lest too light winning/Make the prize light', I.ii.451–2), he denounces Ferdinand as a 'spy' (I.ii.455) and a 'traitor' (I.ii.460,469) and says he will be severely punished (I.ii.461–4) – and in treating Ferdinand in this way Prospero ignores Miranda's protests ('O dear father,/Make not too rash a trial of him', I.ii.466–7).

In II.i the play moves to a part of the island where Alonso has come ashore along with his brother Sebastian, Prospero's usurping brother Antonio, and some Neapolitan courtiers. Alonso shows genuine affection for his son and daughter in that he mourns the loss of Ferdinand, whom he believes to be drowned, and the loss of his daughter who is now married to a distant African monarch (Alonso and his party had been sailing back to Italy after taking his daughter to Africa to marry the King of Tunis). One of the Neapolitan courtiers is the truly honourable Gonzalo, praised earlier by Prospero (I.ii.160–8) as a 'noble Neapolitan' who, when Prospero was put to sea after being evicted from Milan, had seen that in the boat were placed various 'necessaries' and also the books needed by Prospero to practise magic. Here on the island Gonzalo tries to relieve the sorrowful Alonso by diverting the attention of Sebastian who has been complaining that all their woes are due to Alonso's folly in marrying his daughter to an African. Gonzalo speculates about colonising this fertile island with 'innocent' people who might live in a community where there would be no need for learning, laws, private property, or work (II.i.137–62). After being ridiculed by Sebastian and Antonio Gonzalo tells Alonso that the purpose of his speculation was to give Sebastian and Antonio something to laugh at (II.i.164+). Shakespeare, however, seems to be making the point that it is indeed naive to believe that there can ever be a human society completely free of human sinfulness.[82] (In *2 Henry VI* IV.ii.60+ the rebel Jack Cade was satirised by Shakespeare for proclaiming that he would establish a society where all land would be held in common and where there would be no money and no lawyers.) The rest of II.i in *The Tempest* shows that Antonio and Sebastian take a cynical view of Gonzalo's utopia of innocents because of their own sinfulness. After Alonso and his courtiers have fallen asleep Antonio suggests to Sebastian that he could become the King of Naples if his brother Alonso were murdered here and now, and Sebastian needs little persuasion in accepting the suggestion, saying to Antonio 'As thou got'st Milan,/I'll come by Naples' (II.i.282–3). Antonio volunteers to carry out the murder of Alonso, but advises Sebastian to murder Gonzalo, the one Neapolitan courtier who would condemn the murder of Alonso. Sebastian gives hearty encouragement to Antonio to murder Alonso, but seems hesitant, presumably out of fear of being found out, of being involved in murder himself. Both acts of murder are forestalled, however, by Prospero's spirit Ariel, who causes Alonso and his courtiers to wake up.

On another part of the island two of Alonso's attendants have arrived on their own – Trinculo, identifiable as a jester because of his parti-coloured ('pied') costume (III.ii.60), and Stephano, referred to by Alonso at the end of the play as 'my drunken butler' (V.i.277). Stephano came ashore with a cask of wine ('butt of sack', II.ii.110+) thrown overboard from the ship, and Caliban, having been given some of this wine to drink, thinks that Stephano must be a god – 'That's a brave god and

[he] bears celestial liquor' (II.ii.109). Caliban wants Stephano to be his new master and persuades Stephano to agree to a plot to murder Prospero and become lord of the island in Prospero's place (III.ii.54–105). We then discover that Caliban is not totally depraved since he has an aesthetic sense as regards beautiful sounds – he tells Stephano and Trinculo in a poetic speech (III.ii.130–8):

> Be not afeard. The isle is full of noises,
> Sounds and sweet airs [tunes] that give delight and hurt not.
> Sometimes a thousand twangling instruments
> Will hum about mine ears...

In the middle of the play comes an affirmation of sheer goodness in a scene where Ferdinand and Miranda declare their love for each other. Ferdinand applauds Miranda as 'So perfect and so peerless' (III.i.47), and Miranda, prompted by 'plain and holy innocence' (III.i.82), asks Ferdinand to let her be his wife – though Gonzalo's description of a community consisting entirely of 'innocent' people was mere fantasy, Miranda is most certainly a shining example of the innocence that may be found in certain individuals. Ferdinand and Miranda join hands in a pledge to marry, and Prospero is filled with 'rejoicing' (III.i.93). In IV.i a 'pageant' (IV.i.155) is presented by spirits summoned by Prospero to mark the betrothal of Ferdinand and Miranda: in this pageant the spirits appear as goddesses (including Juno, wife of Jupiter) and nymphs to celebrate 'A contract of true love' (IV.i.84,133). At the beginning of the scene Prospero, who by now has released Ferdinand from the performance of punitive tasks, insists on the need for chastity to be observed until there can be a full ceremony of marriage (IV.i.15–19 – we hear at the end of the play, V.i.307–9, that the marriage ceremony will take place in Naples). Ferdinand's reply to Prospero shows that he is indeed aware of the need for chastity before marriage, and we are assured by goddesses in the pageant that before their marriage Ferdinand and Miranda will not be subjected to any 'wanton charm' by Venus or her son Cupid (IV.i.86–97). But the pageant is brought to an abrupt end as Prospero recalls Caliban's plot against him (of which he has been informed by Ariel), and in what is probably the best known speech in the play Prospero reminds us that, 'like this insubstantial pageant faded' (IV.i.155), all material things pass away – but Prospero tells Ferdinand to 'be cheerful' (IV.i.147) because (Prospero seems to be saying) we as human beings are not entirely material but have an affinity with the supernatural world, into which we pass at death (IV.i.156-8):

> We are such stuff
> As dreams are made on, and our little life
> Is rounded with a sleep.

(That dreams in this play are associated with the supernatural is suggested by Caliban in III.ii.133-8 where he talks of 'voices' on the island that cause him to have dreams in which 'The clouds methought would open and show riches/Ready to drop upon me'. And supernatural activity in the last scene in the play is likened to what happens 'in a dream', V.i.239 – by the boatswain of the ship that was struck by the tempest in the opening scene.)

Ariel deals effectively with Caliban and his fellow plotters. They are led by music into a stinking pool, and then, as they move towards Prospero's cell to murder him, they are confronted by a lime tree ('line', IV.i.193) on which Ariel has hung tawdry garments, garments which immediately distract the attention of Stephano and Trinculo from the plot. What is noticeable here is that Caliban is less foolish than Stephano and Trinculo. When Caliban first encountered them Trinculo scoffed at him for foolishly believing that the drunken Stephano was a god who had descended out of the moon – Trinculo called Caliban 'A most poor credulous monster', 'A most ridiculous monster, to make a wonder of a poor drunkard' (II.ii.137–, 155–6). Now, as Trinculo's interest is aroused by the clothing on the lime tree, Caliban cries out in anguish (IV.i.223) 'Let it alone, thou fool. It is but trash.' While Stephano and Trinculo, ignoring Caliban's appeal, are giving him a pile of clothes to carry away, Prospero and Ariel set spirits in the form of hunting dogs upon the three conspirators, and Prospero gives orders for them to be tormented by 'convulsions' and 'cramps' (IV.i.258–9).

As regards the original offenders against Prospero, Ariel in III.iii denounces Alonso, Antonio and Sebastian as 'three men of sin' (III.iii.53). (We learn from Ariel that Sebastian too was involved in the eviction of Prospero – 'you three/From Milan did supplant good Prospero', III.iii.69–70.) Ariel tells them that their sinful deed has not been forgotten: now that 'Destiny' ('Fortune' was the word used in I.ii.178) has brought them to this island (III.iii.53–6), 'The powers' (supernatural powers) have stirred up the seas against them (III.iii.73–5). Ariel goes on to tell them (III.iii.76–82) that their only escape from 'Lingering perdition' is through repentance and a reformed life ('heart's sorrow/And a clear life ensuing'). In the final scene of the play (V.i) the time comes for Prospero to pass judgment on these guilty men. At the end of the previous scene (IV.i) Prospero, after he had given orders for Caliban, Stephano and Trinculo to be subjected to physical torments, had reflected (IV.i.261–2):

> At this hour
> Lie at my mercy all mine enemies.

Prospero would seem, therefore, to be contemplating vindictive punishment for Alonso, Antonio and Sebastian. At the beginning of the final scene Ariel tells Prospero that Alonso and all the men with him have been reduced by a spell to such a state of misery as to evoke pity, and Prospero, moved by Ariel's expression of tender feeling, rejects his desire for vengeance against his enemies (V.i.25–30):

> Though with their high wrongs I am struck to the quick,
> Yet with my nobler reason 'gainst my fury
> Do I take part. The rarer action is
> In virtue than in vengeance. They being penitent,
> The sole drift of my purpose doth extend
> Not a frown further.

We see here that Ariel, the spirit who has been the servant of Prospero the magician, has brought about in Prospero the man a moral transformation. And in the soliloquy that follows (V.i.33–57) Prospero, recalling his egoism as a magician in wielding great powers of destruction (mainly by raising storms),[83] now vows to give up magic altogether ('this rough magic I here abjure').

When Prospero presents himself to the malefactors in the garb of the Duke of Milan Alonso is already penitent. In III.iii, after Ariel's denunciation of the 'three men of sin', Alonso was overcome with guilt concerning his 'trespass' against Prospero (III.iii.95–102): in fact, in Ariel's song about Alonso in I.ii.396–404 the drowned Alonso may represent Alonso's former evil self that has been transformed 'Into something rich and strange.' Now, in V.i, Alonso says he will give up the control he had acquired over Milan and he asks for his wrongs to be pardoned (V.i.118–19). He is overjoyed to find that his son Ferdinand is alive (V.i.179–80) and, gladly accepting Miranda as his future daughter-in-law, he asks her to forgive what he did to her father (V.i.196–8). Alonso is thus a character in whom there has clearly been a movement from evil to good. Prospero embraces Gonzalo as his 'noble friend' (V.i.120–1), and then, after telling Antonio and Sebastian in an aside (V.i.126–9) that he will 'tell no tales' about the plot to murder Alonso, he says publicly to Antonio that he will forgive him for his seizure of the dukedom on condition that the dukedom is given up (V.i.130–4). Miranda's innocence comes out with touching irony when she sees Alonso and his companions for the first time (V.i.182–3):

> How many goodly creatures are there here!
> How beauteous mankind is!

Evil in the human world is something Miranda will have to come to terms with. Meanwhile Gonzalo rejoices that the 'gods' have brought about a happy outcome to the past train of events (V.i.201–13).

Prospero offers pardon also to Caliban ('As you look/To have my pardon, trim it handsomely', i.e. justify it by good behaviour, V.i.292–3), but he fails to recognise that a

reformation has taken place in Caliban. In the second scene of
the play Prospero (if we accept the correction of what is almost
certainly an error in the Folio text) dismissed Caliban as a
savage incapable of taking 'any print of goodness' (I.ii.352 –
these words occur in a speech attributed in the Folio text to
Miranda, but many editors assign the speech to Prospero, to
whom it seems clearly to belong), and in IV.i Prospero describes
Caliban as 'a born devil on whose nature/Nurture can never
stick' (IV.i.188–9). In the final scene Prospero takes much the
same view of him (V.i.290–1): 'He is as disproportioned in his
manners/As in his shape.' Yet Caliban the born devil is moving
towards 'grace', and he now sees Stephano for what he is
(V.i.294–7):

> I'll be wise hereafter
> And seek for grace. What a thrice-double ass
> Was I to take this drunkard for a god
> And worship this dull fool.

Antonio and Sebastian show no signs of being penitent
(Sebastian says little in the final scene, and Antonio nothing at
all), but they are no doubt subdued by Prospero's knowledge of
their conspiracy against Alonso, and they can do nothing to
prevent Prospero's resumption of his dukedom. The ship that
had been secretly preserved by Ariel (I.ii.226–9) has been made
ready by him for use (V.i.222–6), and Prospero prepares to
return to Milan as a human being who no longer commands the
services of supernatural spirits – as he tells the audience in the
second line of the play's Epilogue, 'what strength I have's mine
own'.

HENRY VIII (c. 1613)

With *Henry VIII*, as with *Pericles*, there has been some
dispute about authorship. Unlike *Pericles*, however,
Henry VIII does carry the authority of being included in the
First Folio, and Shakespeare was generally assumed to be the
sole author until the appearance in 1850 of James Spedding's

essay 'Who Wrote Shakespeare's *Henry VIII*?'. Spedding argued that there are two different styles of language in *Henry VIII* and concluded that the play is partly by Shakespeare and partly by John Fletcher. Since Spedding's essay there has been some division of opinion as to whether Shakespeare was the sole author, but at least it is reasonable to assume that the general theme of the play is Shakespeare's. With Holinshed as its chief source (the most frequent source of Shakespeare's other English history plays), this play shows political intrigue, as practised by the power-seeking Cardinal Wolsey, and religious sectarianism (the clash between Lutheran Protestantism and allegiance to Rome) giving way to forgiveness and reconciliation and the happy anticipation of the reign of the future Queen Elizabeth. *Henry VIII* shares with the previous four plays (*Pericles, Cymbeline, The Winter's Tale* and *The Tempest*) the broad theme of the triumphant assertion of good over evil, but in *Henry VIII* this triumphant assertion occurs without any direct intervention by divine or supernatural powers.

In the first two Acts England is dominated by the evil Wolsey. In a conversation between the Duke of Buckingham and his friend the Duke of Norfolk we hear that Wolsey has advanced himself by organising an alliance between the King of England and the King of France, and then has been bribed by the Emperor (the Emperor Charles V) to break the alliance with France – as Buckingham says (I.i.191-3):

> thus the Cardinal
> Does buy and sell his [King Henry's] honour as he pleases,
> And for his own advantage.

Since Buckingham is Wolsey's enemy Wolsey has him arrested on a charge of high treason, and King Henry, in his first speech in the play (I.ii.1-4), shows that he has been convinced that he has narrowly escaped a plot against his life. The charge against Buckingham is based on the testimony of his former 'surveyor' (estate manager) who claims that Buckingham sought to make himself king (I.ii.132-5,146-71) – Buckingham is sure that the surveyor has been bribed by Wolsey (I.i.222-3), and Queen

Katherine[84] suspects malice on the surveyor's part following his dismissal from his job because of complaints by tenants (I.ii.171–5). Just after Buckingham has been declared guilty the second of two Gentlemen who are conversing in a Westminster street observes that the common people hate Wolsey but love Buckingham (II.i.49–53):

> All the commons
> Hate him [Wolsey] perniciously... this duke as much
> They love and dote on, call him bounteous Buckingham,
> The mirror of all courtesy.

As Buckingham is led off to execution he strikes the first note in the play of forgiveness (II.i.83–6):

> I forgive all.
> There cannot be those numberless offences
> 'Gainst me that I cannot take [make] peace with. No black envy [malice]
> Shall mark my grave.

Wolsey now turns his attention to Queen Katherine. Because the Emperor has refused Wolsey's request to be made Archbishop of Toledo (II.i.162–4) Wolsey in revenge seeks to humiliate Katherine who is the Emperor's aunt (II.ii.23 – see also I.i.176–7). He succeeds in arousing the King's conscience concerning his marriage to Katherine who was his brother's widow (II.ii.12–17), such a marriage being regarded at that time as incestuous (as was Claudius's marriage to Gertrude in *Hamlet*).[85] Wolsey advises a divorce from Katherine (II.ii.28), and he hopes to bring about a marriage between Henry and the sister of the King of France (II.ii.37–9, III.ii.85–6). In the presence of Cardinal Campeius, sent from Rome to consider the question of a divorce, Henry is pressed by Wolsey to give an assurance that it was not he, Wolsey, who had prompted the concern about the marriage (II.iv.143–55), and in a long speech Henry gives this assurance (II.iv.155–209) – Henry has clearly been deceived into believing that Wolsey had no part in arousing his conscience about his marriage. But his long speech shows how deeply disturbed he has been. In connection with an attempt to arrange a marriage between his daughter Mary and the Duke of Orleans Henry refers to doubt having been expressed by the French ambassador as to whether Mary, because of her father's marriage to his brother's widow, could be regarded as 'legitimate' (II.iv.170–81), and Henry talks also of his anxiety about Katherine's inability to give birth to a surviving male heir (II.iv.186–99). The play thus indicates that, though the issue of divorce had been promoted by Wolsey for his own malicious purposes, there are good reasons for a divorce. And in this scene Henry's treatment of Katherine is presented as honourable in that, though a divorce may be necessary, he expresses high respect for her as a person – he praises her 'rare qualities' (II.iv.137–40) and describes her as 'The queen of earthly queens' (II.iv.141). But the movement towards divorce does not proceed as Wolsey had intended. For his second queen Henry has in mind, not the French king's sister, but Anne Bullen (known in our history books as Anne Boleyn) whom Wolsey scorns as 'A spleeny Lutheran' (III.ii.99). When Henry learns that Wolsey has now asked the Pope to delay granting Henry a divorce (III.ii.30–6) Wolsey's influence over Henry is at an end: Henry turns to the English churchman Cranmer who sanctions his divorce and arranges for his marriage to Anne to be proclaimed (III.ii. 63–8 – Henry has gone ahead with the marriage to Anne, III.ii.41–2, before its proclamation).

Wolsey is soon completely disgraced. His amassing of wealth for the purposes of bribery comes to the knowledge of the King (III.ii.210–13), and he is charged with various abuses of his powers (III.ii.310–30). But surprisingly the general spirit of goodness that now begins to prevail in the play shows itself even in Wolsey. He undergoes a genuine moral conversion. In the well-known soliloquy in which he bids 'a long farewell to all my greatness' (III.ii.351) he rejects worldly vanity (III.ii.365–6): 'Vain pomp and glory of this world, I hate ye./I feel my heart new opened.' And in his advice to Cromwell, who having served Wolsey is now about to enter the King's service, Wolsey embraces the Christian doctrine of loving one's enemies

(III.ii.443): 'Love thyself last. Cherish those hearts that hate thee.' This prevailing spirit of goodness in the play shows itself especially in forgiveness. The Earl of Surrey, son-in-law of the ill-fated Duke of Buckingham, condemns Wolsey's ruthless 'ambition' (III.i.i.254), and he is bitter about having been sent by Wolsey to Ireland to be out of the way when Buckingham was executed (III.ii.259–64), but when Wolsey is disgraced Surrey is forgiving, as was his father-in-law before him (II.i.83) – 'I do forgive him' says Surrey of Wolsey (III.ii.336). And when Wolsey's death occurs soon afterwards Katherine, who previously had condemned Wolsey for his 'arrogancy, spleen and pride' (II.iv.110), says (IV.ii.31): 'So may he rest [in peace], his faults lie gently on him'. Wolsey's death is shortly followed by Katherine's own death, and Katherine, who said she would always pray for Henry even if no longer his queen (III.i.180–1), dies blessing him (IV.ii.163–4). (Before she dies Katherine in her sleep has a vision in which celestial beings promise her 'eternal happiness', IV.ii.90.)

Henry is now confronted by an outbreak of sectarianism led by Gardiner, Bishop of Winchester, formerly Henry's secretary as advanced by Wolsey (II.ii.113–17). Cranmer, who has been made Archbishop of Canterbury, is denounced by Gardiner as an 'arch heretic', i.e. a Lutheran (V.i.45 – Cranmer had already been denounced as an arch heretic by Wolsey earlier on, III.ii.102), and Cromwell (who has become the King's new secretary) and Anne Bullen are also denounced by Gardiner, presumably as Lutherans since they are associated by him with Cranmer (V.i.29–32). But Henry firmly supports Cranmer as a man of 'truth' and 'integrity' (V.i.114), and he brings about a reconciliation between Gardiner and Cranmer – Gardiner, called upon by Henry to 'Embrace and love' Cranmer, responds by doing this 'With a true heart/And brother-love' (V.iii.170–2).[86]

The play ends joyfully with the christening of the daughter born to Henry and Anne (the need for a male heir seems at this point to have been forgotten) – this daughter, the future Queen Elizabeth, will become, Cranmer predicts, 'A pattern to all princes' (V.v.22).[86] (Two brief prophecies of this kind were made earlier in the play. The Lord Chamberlain thought it possible that from Anne Bullen 'may proceed a gem/To lighten all this isle', II.iii.78–9, and the Duke of Suffolk was persuaded that from Anne 'Will fall some blessing to this land', III.ii.50–1.) And Cranmer further predicts that this Elizabeth will bequeath to her successor 'Peace, plenty, love, truth, terror' (V.v.47 – 'terror' here means terror to all foes), her successor being King James I of England, the reigning monarch when *Henry VIII* was first performed.

Henry VIII, it will be noted, says nothing about what happened in Henry VIII's reign after his marriage to Anne Boleyn and the birth of their daughter. Politically the play is concerned to give an idealised portrayal of Henry as the forerunner of the great Queen Elizabeth. But the play's celebration of the spirit of goodness makes it more than a political play.

A Note on THE TWO NOBLE KINSMEN

The Two Noble Kinsmen, a play probably composed in 1613,[87] was published in 1634 as being by John Fletcher and William Shakespeare. But, whereas it seems reasonable to assume that the main themes of *Pericles* and *Henry VIII* are Shakespeare's even though these plays may not have been composed entirely by him, I can see no reason for making this kind of assumption about *The Two Noble Kinsmen*.

As regards the plot (which derives from *The Knight's Tale* by Chaucer), two cousins, Palamon and Arcite, fight for Thebes against Athens but are taken prisoner, and in Athens they both fall in love with Emilia, sister-in-law of Theseus, the Duke of Athens (this is the Duke who appeared in *A Midsummer Night's Dream*). The crux of the plot occurs in the last Act where, as arranged by Theseus, the winner of Emilia is to be decided by an armed combat. Before the combat Arcite prays to the god Mars, Palamon to the goddess Venus, and Emilia herself to Diana, goddess of chastity – Emilia, who has a high regard for both contenders, prays that the winner may be the one 'that best loves me' (V.i.158). The winner of the combat is Arcite, but just after the combat he is thrown by his horse and he dies leaving Emilia, with his blessing, to Palamon. The main theme is announced by Theseus at the end of the play: justice has been done by the gods. Observing that Mars gave Arcite victory in the combat and Venus gave Palamon the love of Emilia, Theseus remarks (V.iv.107–8):

> So the deities
> Have showed due justice.

Theseus then adds that justice has also been done in that Palamon was the first to see Emilia and fall in love with her ('you first saw her and/Even then proclaimed your fancy', V.iv.116–17). Thus the gods, says Theseus, have taken from him the responsibility of administering justice himself (V.iv.119–20):

> The gods my justice
> Take from my hand.

It is incredible that such a conception of divine justice could have come from Shakespeare. In Shakespeare justice is administered by the divine powers against truly evil people. In *King Lear* (V.iii.231) the 'judgment of the heavens' is directed against Goneril and Regan. In *Pericles* (II.iv.1–15) 'the most high gods' mete out 'justice' to the incestuous Antiochus and his daughter. And in *Cymbeline* (V.v.461–3) 'justice' is done by the heavens on Cymbeline's 'wicked queen'. But in *The Two Noble Kinsmen* Palamon and Arcite are, as indicated in the title, both 'noble', and both honourably accept the conditions laid down by Theseus – that the winner of the combat shall be the winner of Emilia but that the loser shall be beheaded, along with 'all his friends' (III.vi.289–301). As for Arcite's offence in not respecting Palamon's prior claim to Emilia, this prior claim was surely a slender one – Arcite saw Emilia and fell in love with her only minutes after Palamon did (see II.i.176 ff.) and before Emilia knew anything about the feelings of either of the men. (The situation in this play may be contrasted with that in the Shakespeare play with a somewhat similar title – *The Two*

Gentlemen of Verona – where Proteus is indeed treacherous in trying to steal the girl who is already in love with his friend Valentine.) As regards the gods, though divine power over events in human life is represented by Jupiter in *Cymbeline* and by Apollo in *The Winter's Tale*, in Shakespeare Mars and Venus never represent more than aspects of human nature – soldiership and sexual attraction. And in Shakespeare the gods act as a collective force in their enforcement of justice, whereas in *The Two Noble Kinsmen* justice is a balancing act performed by two individual gods. (Incidentally we are told nothing about the contribution made to justice by Diana, the goddess whom Emilia asked to grant her the man who loved her 'best'. Diana would have had a difficult decision to make since the play suggests that Palamon and Arcite loved Emilia with equal ardour – see III.vi.252–71.) In comparison, therefore, with divine justice as conceived by Shakespeare, divine justice in *The Two Noble Kinsmen* is a frivolous and muddled affair.

Brief Notes on the Chronology of Shakespeare's Works

Since it is impossible to be precise about the order in which Shakespeare's works were written, here are brief notes which may help to show how I have arrived at my choice of dates. For information about possible dates of composition I have consulted various editions of Shakespeare, but especially the Arden editions – much of this information is summarised in two useful reference books: *A Shakespeare Companion* (1952, revised 1964) by F. E. Halliday, and *A Shakespeare Encyclopaedia* (1966), edited by Oscar J. Campbell and E. G. Quinn (this was published in New York under the title *A Reader's Encyclopedia of Shakespeare*). Where (as is often the case) the date of composition has been placed by scholars within a period of two or three years, I have tended to choose a date that would make for a fairly even spacing of the works, on the grounds that it is less likely (though certainly not impossible) that Shakespeare would have written, say, three or four plays in one particular year and only one or none in the next. I list the works below in the order I have already chosen, and the accompanying date in brackets is the date (often very tentative) already shown at the head of each section in this book. I then briefly present facts or arguments that have influenced my choice of date, and to the facts or arguments taken from textual scholars I occasionally add observations of my own.

In these notes the abbreviation 'pub.' indicates the first date of publication, and 'reg.' indicates the date of registration (entry of the title of the work in the Stationers' Register prior to publication). The date of a play's publication was unlikely to have been very close to its date of composition since arrangements were not usually made to publish a play until after it had been in performance for some time. Evidence as to whether a work was in existence before 1598 is provided by Francis Meres's book *Palladis Tamia: Wit's Treasury* (reg. 7 September 1598) which gives a full (but not quite complete) list of the works of Shakespeare known by that date: in what follows 'Meres' denotes that the work was mentioned in *Palladis Tamia*. Many of the plays were not published at all until their inclusion in the 1623 First Folio collected edition of Shakespeare's plays: the date 1623 in these notes indicates publication in the First Folio. It should of course be recognised that plays in existence for some time before publication (including, especially, those never published before their inclusion in the First Folio) might well have undergone revision after they were first composed, but there can hardly have been much alteration as regards their themes.

1 Henry VI (c. 1590), *2 Henry VI* (c. 1590), *3 Henry VI* (c. 1591), *Richard III* (c. 1591)

I follow the dating suggested by the Arden editions of these plays (the dates of these Arden editions themselves being as follows: *2 Henry VI*, 1957; *1 Henry VI*, 1962; *3 Henry VI*, 1963; *Richard III*, 1981). The 'Date' sections in the Arden editions of *1 Henry VI* and *2 Henry VI* mention the influence on both these plays of Spenser's *The Fairie Queene* (Bks. I–III pub. Jan. 1590[88]). *3 Henry VI* was clearly in existence in 1592 since the dramatist (and general author) Robert Greene, in a pamphlet written just before his death on 3 Sept. 1592, denounced Shakespeare as an upstart by referring to a line in *3 Henry VI* (I.iv.137). The Date sections in the Arden editions of all four plays speak of evidence of verbal borrowing from *Richard III* in the anonymous play *The Troublesome Reign of King John* (pub. 1591).

Titus Andronicus (c. 1591)
Pub. 1594. There is an apparent reference to *Titus Andronicus* in an anonymous play *A Knack to Know a Knave* which is known to have been performed on 10 June 1592, and verbal borrowings from *Titus Andronicus* in *The Troublesome Reign of King John* (1591) are detected in the 'Date and Authorship' section in the 1953 Arden edition.

The Comedy of Errors (c. 1592)
First known performance 28 Dec. 1594. The description of 'Time' as a thief (IV.ii.59–60) may anticipate the numerous references to Time in the Sonnets – Sonnet 77 speaks of 'Time's thievish progress'.

The Taming of the Shrew (c. 1592)
A play called *The Taming of a Shrew* was reg. 2 May 1594 and pub. 1594 ('As it was sundry times acted'). *The Taming of the Shrew* would have been composed some time before *The Taming of a Shrew* if those editors are right who assume *A Shrew* to be a 'bad' Quarto (an unauthorised version) of *The Shrew*. In the Induction (ii.47–51) of *The Taming of the Shrew* a reference to Cytherea (i.e. Venus) and Adonis may point forward to the poem *Venus and Adonis* (1593).

Sonnets (c. 1592–3), *Venus and Adonis* (1593), *A Lover's Complaint* (c. 1593), *The Rape of Lucrece* (1594)
Venus and Adonis was reg. 18 April 1593 and pub. 1593, and in the accompanying dedication of this poem to the Earl of Southampton Shakespeare talks of a 'vow' to write another poem that would be 'some graver labour' – this clearly became *The Rape of Lucrece*, reg. 9 May 1594 and pub. 1594. *The Rape of Lucrece*, therefore, cannot have been composed long before its publication, and it seems likely that the same was so with *Venus and Adonis*. The opposite seems to be true of the Sonnets and *A Lover's Complaint*. These were not published until 1609, but the Sonnets (mentioned by Meres) are very close in theme to *Venus and Adonis* and *The Rape of Lucrece*, and *A Lover's Complaint* is written in the same stanza form (rhyme royal) as *The Rape of Lucrece* and also as Samuel Daniel's *The Complaint of Rosamond* (pub. 1592) – *A Lover's Complaint* may have been prompted by Daniel's poem. (Daniel's *Delia* sonnets, pub. Feb. 1592, may have supplied the rhyme scheme for Shakespeare's Sonnets – *a b a b c d c d e f e f g g* – though this rhyme scheme had also been employed by Edmund Spenser in three of the four poems in sonnet form in *Complaints*, 1591.)

The Two Gentlemen of Verona (c. 1593)
(In my commentaries in this book I have dealt with *The Two Gentlemen of Verona* immediately after the poem *Venus and Adonis*.) Meres. In theme this play is the closest of all Shakespeare's plays to the Sonnets.

Love's Labour's Lost (c. 1594)
Pub. 1598. Meres. The inclusion in this play of love poems in sonnet form suggests that the play is close to the Sonnets period, and the Date section of the 1951 Arden edition specifies verbal parallels between the play and the Sonnets.

King John (c. 1594)
Meres. I place this play at a point between the Sonnets and *Richard II* since it carries over into politics the concern of the Sonnets with 'constancy' and 'truth' and the Bastard's spirited patriotism is akin to that of Gaunt in *Richard II*.

Romeo and Juliet (c. 1595)
Pub. 1597 ('As it hath been often... plaid publiquely').

Richard II (c. 1595)
Reg. 29 Aug. 1597 and pub. 1597. Performed in Sir Edward Hoby's house on 9 Dec. 1595. (Sir Edward Hoby was the son of Sir Thomas Hoby, whose English translation of Cortegiano's *Il Libro del Cortegiano – The Book of the Courtier* – is frequently cited in the General Notes at the end of the present book.)

A Midsummer Night's Dream (c. 1596)
Pub. 1600. Meres. In the 'Date and Occasion' section in the 1979 Arden edition the editor favours the hypothesis that the play was written with a view to being performed on the day of the marriage of Elizabeth Carey and the son of Lord Berkeley – 19 Feb. 1596.

The Merchant of Venice (c. 1596)
Reg. 22 July 1598. Meres. 'Andrew', the name of Antonio's ship in I.i.27, is probably a reference to a Spanish ship of that name

that was captured by the English fleet at Cadiz, news of this capture having reached the English Court on 30 July 1596 – see the Date section in the 1955 Arden edition.

1 Henry IV (c. 1596), *The Merry Wives of Windsor* (c. 1597)
2 Henry IV (c. 1598)
1 Henry IV reg. 25 Feb. 1598 and pub. 1598. *The Merry Wives of Windsor* reg. 18 Jan. 1602 and pub. 1602. *2 Henry IV* reg. 23 Aug. 1600 and pub. 1600. Meres refers to '*Henry the 4*', which may or may not include *2 Henry IV*. It is highly probable that *The Merry Wives of Windsor* (see section 5 in the Introduction of the 1971 Arden edition) was written in connection with the ceremony of the election of knights to the Order of the Garter in April 1597 and the installation of these knights in Windsor in May – there are references to the Order of the Garter in V.v.59–70 of the play. Since, according to tradition, *The Merry Wives* was written to meet Queen Elizabeth's request for a play about Falstaff in love, Shakespeare, having responded to this request, would then have been free to proceed with the writing of *2 Henry IV*, which he may not have completed until 1598 (see section 6 in the Introduction of the Arden edition of *The Merry Wives*).

Much Ado about Nothing (c. 1598)
Reg. 4 Aug. 1600 and pub. 1600 ('As it hath been sundrie times publikely acted'). The play could have been completed in late 1598, just too late to be mentioned by Meres, whose *Palladis Tamia* was reg. 7 Sept. 1598.

Henry V (1599)
Pub. 1600. A firm dating is given by a reference in the play (Chorus at the beginning of Act V, lines 29–34) to the Earl of Essex as having gone to Ireland to suppress rebellion. Essex left for Ireland on 27 March 1599 and returned on 28 Sept. – the Chorus in the play speaks of Essex as not having yet returned.

Julius Caesar (c. 1599)
First known performance probably 21 Sept. 1599.

As You Like It (c. 1600)
Reg. 4 Aug. 1600 (but not pub. until 1623).

Hamlet (c. 1600)
Reg. 26 July 1602. Pub. 1603 (a 'bad' Quarto). The scholar Gabriel Harvey referred in a written note (on a page in an edition of Chaucer) to the play *Hamlet* and also to the Earl of Essex as a living person: since Essex was executed on 25 Feb. 1601, it would seem that Hamlet had already been performed early in 1601, if not in 1600.

The Phoenix and Turtle (1601)
The book which included the poem attributed to Shakespeare was pub. 1601.

Twelfth Night (c. 1601)
First known performance 2 Feb. 1602. (In its Date section the 1975 Arden edition rejects the argument, put forward by Leslie Hotson in 1954, that this play was first performed on Twelfth Night – 6 Jan. – 1601.)

Troilus and Cressida (c. 1602)
Reg. 7 Feb. 1603 (but not pub. until 1609).

All's Well That Ends Well (c. 1603)
No external evidence of date (not pub. until. 1623), but the play touches on the honour-in-love-and-in-war theme of *Troilus and Cressida*, and it is linked to *Measure for Measure* by a particular kind of incident common to both plots – in both plays a lustful male character (Bertram in *All's Well*, Angelo in *Measure for Measure*) is tricked into having sexual relations with the woman to whom he is married or to whom he is betrothed. In *All's Well* this incident derives from the source story, but in *Measure for Measure* this incident has been added to the source story, as the result perhaps of *All's Well* having been written before *Measure for Measure* – this is the suggestion made in a footnote in the Date section in the 1959 Arden edition.

Othello (c. 1603)
First known performance 1 Nov. 1604, but a letter from Alfred Hart in *The Times Literary Supplement* of 10 Oct. 1935 quoted examples of words and phrases from *Othello* that had been incorporated in the 'bad' Quarto of *Hamlet*, pub. 1603. This 'bad' Quarto was apparently compiled by actors who had recently been performing in *Othello* – see the 1957 Cambridge edition of *Othello*, Introduction, pp. xiv–xv.

Measure for Measure (c. 1604)
First known performance 26 Dec. 1604.

Timon of Athens (c. 1605)
No external evidence of date (not pub. until 1623), but Timon's speech in IV.i decries order in words that recall Ulysses's 'degree' speech in *Troilus and Cressida* (I.iii.83–124), and Timon's savage praise of sexual promiscuity (IV.i.3,6–8,12–13) seems to anticipate this aspect of the mad Lear's misanthropy (*King Lear* IV.vi.114–23).

King Lear (c. 1605)
First known performance 26 Dec. 1606 (this performance is mentioned in the registration entry, 26 Nov. 1607), but according to E. K. Chambers's *William Shakespeare: A Study of Facts and Problems* (1930), vol. 1, p. 468, a conversation between Lear and Kent was imitated in a play called *The Fleir* by Edward Sharpham, reg. 13 May 1606, so that *King Lear* was probably in existence well before May 1606.

Macbeth (c. 1606)
First known performance 7 Aug. 1606, according to evidence advanced in H. N. Paul's *The Royal Play of Macbeth* (1950) – this book is cited in Appendix E of the 1951 Arden edition. Probably written after March or even May 1606, since the Porter's talk at the beginning of II.iii about an 'equivocator' almost certainly refers to the Jesuit priest Henry Garnet who, charged with being involved in the Gunpowder Plot, was tried on 28 March 1606 and hanged on 3 May: Garnet defended his

use of equivocation, or lying for an allegedly justifiable purpose – see the Date section in the 1951 Arden edition.

Antony and Cleopatra (c. 1607)
Reg. 20 May 1608 (but not pub. until 1623).

Coriolanus (c. 1607)
Not pub. until 1623. The play is unlikely to have been composed before 1605 since Menenius's allegorical story of a rebellion by bodily 'members' against the belly (I.i.94–152) partly draws on William Camden's *Remains of a Greater Work Concerning Britain*, pub. 1605 – see the Date section in the 1975 Arden edition of the play. *Coriolanus* seems to belong to the same period as *Antony and Cleopatra* in that both plays are based on Plutarch, but it seems to precede *Pericles*, the first of Shakespeare's last plays, notable for their serene faith in the power of goodness to triumph over evil.

Pericles (c. 1608)
Reg. 20 May 1608 and pub. 1609 ('As it hath been divers and sundry times acted').

Cymbeline (c. 1609)
First known performance seen by the astrologer Dr Simon Forman in 1611, probably in April.

The Winter's Tale (c. 1610)
First known performance seen by Dr Forman on 15 May 1611.

The Tempest (c. 1611)
First known performance 1 Nov. 1611.

Henry VIII (c. 1613)
First known performance 29 June 1613 (when the first Globe theatre was burnt down).

General Notes

1. (page 1) For Kott Shakespeare's history plays show that 'politics is only an art aiming at capturing and securing power'. *Hamlet* should enable us 'to get at our modern experience, anxiety and sensibility'. And *A Midsummer Night's Dream* reveals 'the dark sphere of sex' – when Titania (as a result of fairy magic) falls in love with Bottom, who has had an ass's head put on him by Puck, she is indulging a secret longing for 'animal love' and so is freed from her 'inhibitions'.

2. (page 1) Theories of literature, prominent in the 1970s and 1980s, which would reject the approach I advocate here, and which have been applied to the study of Shakespeare, have been examined and refuted by Brian Vickers in his *Appropriating Shakespeare: Contemporary Critical Quarrels* (1993).

3. (page 2) At least in my interpretation of each play I am concerned with meaning as arising out of the play as a whole, in contrast to what Brian Vickers has to say about the interpretations of Shakespeare in recent times by Deconstructionists, New Historicists, Freudians, Feminists, Marxists and others: 'Each group appropriates that part of the work that echoes its own interests, and discards the rest.' (*Appropriating Shakespeare*, Epilogue.)

4. (page 5) Apart from Shakespeare himself (1564–1616), examples of prominent Renaissance Christian authors are, in Italy, Marsilio Ficino (1433–99), Pico della Mirandola (1463–94) and Baldassare Castiglione (1478–1529), and in England Sir Thomas Elyot (c.1490–1546, author of *The Book Named the Governor*, 1531) and the poets Edmund Spenser (c.1552–99) and John Milton (1608–74).

5. (page 6) St Augustine, writing early in the 5th century AD, said that the wicked spirits whom the Greeks took to be gods encouraged Greek dramatists to write immoral plays so that human minds might be lured into damnation to keep these

spirits company – *De Civitate Dei* (*The City of God*), Bk. II, Ch. 10, p. 49 of the English translation in the Everyman series.

6 (page 8) 'God sees those future events which happen of free will as present events...man's freedom of will remains inviolate...God has foreknowledge and rests a spectator from on high of all things.' Boethius's *De Consolatione Philosophiae* (*The Consolation of Philosophy*), written about 525 AD, was a highly influential book, especially on the subject of Fortune, throughout the Middle Ages and on into Shakespeare's own time, when Queen Elizabeth herself made an English translation of the book from the Latin. (The words quoted are from Bk. V of the *Consolation*, pp. 167–8 of the 1969 Penguin Classics translation by V. E. Watts.) Prior to Boethius the same point was made by St Augustine in *The City of God*, Bk. V, Ch. IX (p. 152 of the translation in Everyman): 'Nor let us fear that we do not perform all our actions by our own will, because He [God], whose foreknowledge cannot err, knew before that we should do thus or thus.'

7 (page 9) It has been argued, and is still being argued (as in Anthony Holden's *William Shakespeare: His Life and Work*, 1999), that Shakespeare in his teens was a Catholic, to be identified with one William Shakeshafte who was employed in the household of a Lancashire Catholic family, the Hoghtons. (Such an identity, concludes Park Honan in his scholarly *Shakespeare: A Life*, 1998, 'so far has not been capable of proof or disproof' – see the Note on pp. 430–1 of Honan's book.) But in view of the attacks on the Papacy in the plays I have cited Shakespeare during the time he was a playwright can hardly have been a committed Catholic.

8 (page 11) In Ch. 3 of *Shakespeare's History Plays* Tillyard notes that William Baldwin in his prose Introduction to *A Mirror for Magistrates*, a series of poems about the fall of famous people from power (1559, with further poems in subsequent editions), says that the 'office' (function, responsibility) of a magistrate 'is God's office, yea his chief

office. For as justice is the chief virtue, so is the ministration thereof the chiefest office.' According to Tillyard, *A Mirror for Magistrates* 'must be added to Hall's Chronicle and the Homilies as one of the important formative influences of Shakespeare's youth.'

9 (page 15) Shakespeare's view of love seems to have been strongly influenced by what is said by the courtier Bembo near the end of the book that was a classic statement of Renaissance ideals – Castiglione's *Il Libro del Cortegiano* (1528), which as *The Book of the Courtier* appeared in English translation by Sir Thomas Hoby in 1561 (the book takes the form of a discussion between courtiers about the qualities of an ideal courtier). According to Bembo, in Hoby's translation, 'sensuall love...is a very rebel against reason' (p. 306 of the Everyman edition of Hoby's translation), but in the ascent to true love there is a period when 'the soule is alwaies in affliction and travell [travail] and (in a manner) waxeth woode [mad] until the beloved beautie commeth before her [the soul] once againe' (Everyman ed., p. 317): love in its highest form, however, enables the soul to experience 'heavenly harmony' (Everyman ed., p. 321). Though there is no direct evidence that Shakespeare was acquainted with *The Courtier*, it seems highly probable that he was, and I shall refer to it in further Notes. That Shakespeare was influenced by *The Courtier* was first argued by George Wyndham in his Introduction (in the section entitled 'The Idea of Beauty') to *The Poems of Shakespeare* (1898), but here Wyndham considers the influence of *The Courtier* only in relation to Shakespeare's Sonnets.

10 (page 16) Shakespeare here must be condemning his younger self, since his wife Anne Hathaway gave birth to a child barely six months after the granting of the marriage licence (at the end of November 1582, when Shakespeare was eighteen).

11 (page 18) It is just possible that here Shakespeare was influenced by Aristotle's famous doctrine of the 'mean', as stated in Book II of *Ethics* – Aristotle states, for example,

that courage is a desirable 'mean' between cowardice and rashness. (An English translation of Aristotle's *Ethics* by J. A. K. Thomson, 1953, was published in Penguin Classics, 1955.) Shakespeare does in fact refer to Aristotle's *Ethics* twice – in *The Taming of the Shrew* (I.i.32) and in *Troilus and Cressida* (II.ii.166–7) – but it must be admitted that the numerous examples given by Aristotle of the 'mean' differ from the examples to be found in Shakespeare of the need for a balance between opposites, except that Aristotle does at one point deprecate an excess of 'pity' (see p. 65 of the Penguin Classics edition).

12. (page 19) This kind of balance is described in Bk. IV of Castiglione's *The Book of the Courtier* (in Hoby's translation) as 'temperance' – 'that which in affections [i.e. passions, such as anger or hatred] is corrupt and strong against honestie, she [temperance] bringeth to obey unto reason': in this way the mind is brought into a state of 'harmony'. (Everyman edition, p. 272.)

13. (page 19) In connection with 'temperance' *The Courtier* (Bk. IV) dwells on the need for 'reason' to control 'greedie desire' (Hoby's translation, Everyman ed., pp. 269–71), though desire here is not limited to sexual desire.

14. (page 20) Compare *The Courtier* (Bk. II): 'Whatsoever therefore causeth laughter, the same maketh the mind jocunde and giveth pleasure, nor suffereth a man in that instant to mind the troublesome griefes that our life is full off.' (Hoby's translation, Everyman ed., p. 138.)

15. (page 21) This type of character derives from Christopher Marlowe's play *The Jew of Malta* (c.1589), which opens with 'Machiavel' (i.e. the Italian political philosopher Machiavelli) introducing the Jew Barabas as a disciple of his. In Act II of the play Barabas enjoys reciting a list of his villainies, a list which begins:

> As for myself, I walk abroad o' nights
> And kill sick people groaning under walls...
> Among his past activities he mentions that as a usurer
>   with extorting, cozening [cheating], forfeiting

[defaulting],
And tricks belonging unto brokery,
I filled the gaols with bankrupts in a year.

The name 'Machiavel' occurs twice in Shakespeare – in *1 Henry VI* (V.iv.74) and *3 Henry VI* (III.ii.193). The qualities attributed to the Machiavel type of character are a travesty of the real Machiavelli. It is true that in his *Il Principe* (*The Prince*, 1513) he recommended that a ruler should not feel bound by pledges and that he should practise deception, but at least Machiavelli's concern was with promoting the interests of a particular state, not those of a particular individual.

16 (page 23) Since the full title and the date of Hall's chronicle were given earlier (page 10), it may be helpful to the reader to state here that Holinshed's *The Chronicles of England, Scotland, and Ireland* first appeared in 1577, and a second edition, with additional material, appeared in 1587. The work as a whole included material from various authors, but Holinshed himself wrote the history of England.

17 (page 24) Historical note. In the 12th century Henry II (1154–89), as the result of what he inherited from his mother and acquired through his own marriage, ruled over an extensive amount of territory in France, but most of this was lost in the reign of King John (1199–1216). The loss of territory reported in the opening scene of *1 Henry VI* refers to territory that had been gained through conquest by Henry V (1413–22). It should perhaps be mentioned that there is a good deal of historical inaccuracy in *1 Henry VI*. For instance, when Henry VI became king (1422) he was not quite nine months old, and by the time Joan of Arc was taken prisoner (in V.iii of the play) in May 1430 Henry would have been only eight years old, yet before that in the play he is seriously involved in affairs of state.

18 (page 25) Throughout the play Shakespeare follows the chronicles of Hall and Holinshed in giving a completely slanderous view of Joan. At the end of the play – in V.iv – Shakespeare, following Holinshed, shows the so-called Maid

as being pregnant.

19 (page 26) The play insists on referring to Charles as the Dauphin (i.e. heir to the French throne), even though he had already been crowned King (as reported in the play, I.i.92).

20 (page 32) 'Lancaster' refers to Henry VI as being descended from Edward III's fourth son, John of Gaunt, Duke of Lancaster. (The Duke of York in the *Henry VI* plays was given that title by King Henry because, although through his mother he was descended from the third son of Edward III, through his father he was descended from Edward III's fifth son, Edmund of Langley, Duke of York.)

21 (page 34) This tidal image was probably suggested by Hall's chronicle, and Shakespeare may also have followed Hall in pointing to the tragedy of father and son fighting against each other: 'The one parte some time flowyng, and sometime ebbyng... This conflict was in manner unnaturall, for in it the sonne fought against the father...' See the 1964 Arden edition of the play: the footnote on II.v.6, and the excerpts from Hall in Appendix I, p. 155.

22 (page 34) This is not the unnamed brother who is reported killed in II.iii. Confusingly, in the first two scenes of the play Montague is referred to as the brother of the Duke of York (I.i.14,116, I.ii.4,36,55,60). This attribution is wrong historically since Montague was York's uncle – see the footnote on I.i.14 in the 1964 Arden edition of the play.

23 (page 35) This reference to Machiavelli is of course anachronistic (as is the reference to him in *1 Henry VI* V.iv.74) since Machiavelli (1469–1527) was born only two years before Henry VI's death (1471).

24 (page 37) In the Quarto editions of the play Vaughan is denounced by Richard (in I.iii) as one of Queen Elizabeth's 'allies', along with Rivers and Grey, but some modern editions, including the Collins *Complete Works* (I.iii.333), follow the Folio edition of the play which substituted the name of Dorset (elder brother of Grey) for that of Vaughan.

25 (page 42) Though the argument in favour of a Yorkist claimant to the throne is set forth in II.v of *1 Henry VI* and in

II.ii of *2 Henry VI*, Shakespeare gives no explanation of how Richmond (who ascended the throne as Henry VII) came to be the Lancastrian claimant – Richmond was in fact able to trace a line of descent from Edward III's son, John of Gaunt, Duke of Lancaster (from whom Henry VI was descended).

26 (page 43) See the 'Source' section of the Introduction in the 1953 Arden edition of the play. In the 'Sources' section of the Introduction in the 1995 Arden edition, however, it is argued that the plot of *Titus Andronicus* was Shakespeare's own invention.

27 (page 44) The play is historically wrong in assuming that the common people had a say in the choice of a Roman emperor.

28 (page 46) Though Shakespeare may well have had in mind the similar incident in Seneca's *Thyestes*, he quite clearly was aware (as Seneca himself might have been) of another such incident in Ovid's *Metamorphoses*, Bk.VI, where Procne, wife of Tereus, having learnt that Tereus has raped her sister Philomela (and cut out her tongue), kills the son of Tereus and herself and, after serving a meal to Tereus, tells him he has been eating his own son's flesh. Ovid's story is directly referred to by Titus in Shakespeare's play (V.ii.195–6), with the suggestion that it is Ovid's story that gives Titus the idea for his act of revenge.

29 (page 47) I refer here to the last four lines of this final speech, lines which are omitted in some modern editions, including the Collins *Complete Works*, since these lines were not included in the very first edition of the play (the 1st Quarto, 1594). These lines were, however, included in the next three editions (the 2nd and 3rd Quartos and the First Folio).

30 (page 50) Mention has been made in previous Notes (9, 12, 13, 14) of the possible influence on Shakespeare of Hoby's translation (1561) of Castiglione's *The Book of the Courtier* (1528 in Italian). The conception of love expressed by Antipholus of Syracuse may well derive from the discourse on love by the courtier Bembo in the last part (Bk. IV) of *The Courtier*. Bembo speaks of the human soul as languishing in its 'earthly prison' where it is subject to 'errours' – which are

attributed here to the blinding of the soul by 'the senses' and 'sensuall love'. Love in its highest form enables human souls to 'forsake this earthly basenesse and flee up unto heaven'. Bembo prays that the Lord may 'like a trustie guide in this blinde mase [maze] shew us the right way'. (Hoby's translation, Everyman ed., pp. 305–6, 320–1.)

31 (page 56) In the Church of England marriage service the pledge made by the wife to the husband is in answer to the question 'Wilt thou obey him, and serve him, love, honour, and keep him in sickness and in health...?'

32 (page 57) In the Church of England marriage service the husband has to promise 'to love and to cherish' his wife.

33 (page 57) It is often assumed that Shakespeare's Sonnets are directly autobiographical but, as James Winny points out in his *The Master–Mistress: A Study of Shakespeare's Sonnets* (1968), there was no suggestion that the Sonnets were autobiographical until 1790 when Edmond Malone in his edition of Shakespeare's works expressed the view that the Sonnets might partly derive from Shakespeare's own life. (During the course of the 19th century opinion on the matter was divided: in a footnote on the Sonnets Edward Dowden in his *Shakspere: A Critical Study of His Mind and Art*, 1875, cites examples of various shades of opinion, ranging from the view that the Sonnets portray what is entirely imaginary to the view that they are entirely autobiographical.) Among those who reject the view that Shakespeare's Sonnets are directly autobiographical are, besides James Winny, Sidney Lee in his *A Life of William Shakespeare* (1898) and L. C. Knights in his essay 'Shakespeare's Sonnets' (1934), included in *Explorations* (1946).

34 (page 60) What Sonnet 69 has to say about the need for physical beauty to be accompanied by beauty of the mind may show the influence of Castiglione's *The Courtier*. In Bk IV (in Hoby's translation) the courtier Bembo speaks of the importance of 'the beautie of the soule' and regrets the lack of 'stedfastnesse' (which may be taken as meaning the same as Shakespeare's 'constancy' and 'truth') to be found in some

beautiful women and some beautiful men. A little later Bembo says that a man should love a woman for 'the beautie of minde' no less than for the beauty of the body. (Everyman ed., pp. 310–11, 314.)

35 (page 60) As regards love between male friends, in Bk. II. of *The Courtier* Bembo says '...it hath happened to mee more than once to be deceived of him whom I loved best, and of whom I hoped I was beloved above any other person', but Federico ('Sir Fredericke' in Hoby's translation) is confident that among those actually present where this discussion is taking place (at the court of the Duke of Urbino) there are male friends 'whose love is indissoluble and without any guile at all, and [is] to endure untill death'. (Hoby's translation, Everyman ed., pp. 119–20.)

36 (page 60) Compare Bembo in *The Courtier* (Bk. IV): 'most commonly it happeneth that yong men be wrapped in this sensuall love, which is a very rebel against reason.' (Hoby's translation, Everyman ed., p. 306.)

37 (page 60) Compare Bembo in *The Courtier* (Bk. IV) who talks of 'the blinde judgement' of sensual love. (Hoby's translation, Everyman ed., p. 313.)

38 (page 61) These two lines as originally published were:
   Poor soul, the centre of my sinful earth,
   My sinful earth these rebel powers that thee array
The repetition of 'my sinful earth' appears to be a printer's error. 'Fooled by...' is one of the emendations suggested by editors.

39 (page 61) The word 'rebel' was used in connection with lust by Bembo in *The Courtier*, as quoted in Notes 9 and 36 ('sensuall love, which is a very rebel against reason'). 'Poor soul, centre of my sinful earth' may relate to Bembo's remarks about 'the lustinesse of the flesh' causing the soul to be 'drowned in the earthly prison' (Hoby's translation, Everyman ed., pp. 305–6). The actual phrase 'sinful earth' seems to derive from Edmund Spenser's poem *The Ruines of Time* (published 1591) where 'sinful earth' occurs twice (in lines 44 and 290 of that poem). Other echoes of Spenser's

poem can be found in Shakespeare's Sonnets.

40 (page 62) In Notes 9, 36 and 39 I have quoted Bembo in *The Courtier* as saying that sensual love is 'a very rebel against reason'. In view of Venus's eagerness to identify human 'desire' with that of horses, it is worth mentioning here that Bembo goes on to distinguish true love between man and woman from 'what beastes without reason doe'. (Hoby's translation, Everyman ed., p. 306.)

41 (page 64) As suggested in Note 9, Shakespeare, in connection with love's irrationality, may have had in mind the remarks of Bembo in *The Courtier* who says of the young lover: 'the soule is alwaies in affliction and travell [travail] and (in a manner) waxeth woode [becomes mad], until the beloved beautie commeth before her [the young man's soul] once againe.' (Hoby's translation, Everyman ed., p. 317.) Though Bembo is here speaking of a young male lover, Shakespeare sees young lovers of both sexes as being liable to irrational behaviour. A more significant difference is that Shakespeare does not follow Bembo in attributing this irrational behaviour to one particular cause – the physical absence of the loved one. In *The Two Gentlemen of Verona* Shakespeare shows Silvia behaving irrationally in the actual presence of Valentine.

42 (page 67) This interpretation is one of the suggested interpretations listed in the footnote on V.iv.82–3 in the 1969 Arden edition of the play.

43 (page 71) Shakespeare's use of the word 'knighthood' here and in line 197 probably derives from Chaucer – in Chaucer's account of the story Lucresse appeals to Tarquinius to behave as a true knight should (*The Legend of Good Women*, line 1821).

44 (page 73) Compare Bembo in Castiglione's *The Courtier* (Bk. IV): 'I say, therefore, that since the nature of man in youthfull age is so much enclined to sense, it may be graunted the courtier, while hee is yong, to love sensually' – after which an ascent should be made to a higher kind of love. (Hoby's translation, Everyman ed., p. 312 ff.)

45 (page 73) As a matter of historical fact Navarre had ceased in 1589 to be an independent kingdom, separate from the kingdom of France.

46 (page 73) Compare *The Courtier* (Bk. III): 'no court, how great soever it be, can have any sightlinesse or brightnesse in it, or mirth, without women.' (Hoby's translation, Everyman ed., p. 188.)

47 (page 75) *The Courtier* (Bk. III) dwells on the importance of the eyes as 'a guide in love' (Hoby's translation, Everyman ed., p. 247). And when Berowne talks about 'The nimble spirits in the arteries' (IV.iii.302) in connection with love, he comes close to what is said in *The Courtier* about 'those lively spirits that issue out at the eyes', spirits that 'are engendred nigh the hart [heart]' (Everyman ed., p. 247).

48 (page 75) In *The Courtier* (Bk. IV) Bembo speaks of love in its highest form as 'heavenly harmony' (Hoby's translation, Everyman ed., p. 321).

49 (page 77) In Shakespeare's play John is seen as a usurper even though Holinshed states that Richard I, having previously declared Arthur to be his heir, in his final will assigned the crown to his brother John. This will is briefly referred to in Shakespeare's play (II.i.191-4), only to be contemptuously dismissed as 'A woman's will', meaning that Richard in making it was dominated by his mother, Elinor. (See the footnotes on II.i.192 and 194 in the 1954 Arden edition of the play. The Arden editor comments: 'Shakespeare belittles the will in order to make John seem a usurper.')

50 (page 89) We are not told in the play what Richard's motive was for wanting Gloucester to be put to death. Gloucester was in fact the leader of a group of nobles who had opposed Richard's authority: as Holinshed put it, Gloucester 'was ever repining against the king in all things, whatsoever he wished to have forward.'

51 (page 90) It has been pointed out that Shakespeare seems to have forgotten that England itself, without Wales and Scotland, is not an island!

52 (page 93) See *Matthew* 27:22-4.

53 (page 93) Compare Holinshed: 'in this dejecting of the one [Richard], and advancing of the other [Bolingbroke], the providence of God is to be respected, and his secret will to be wondered at.'

54 (page 97) Katharine M. Briggs in her *The Anatomy of Puck: An Examination of Fairy Beliefs among Shakespeare's Contemporaries and Successors* (1959), Ch. XI, notes that, although fairies were often regarded as devils, there was also a widely held view in Shakespeare's time that they 'were not devils but an intermediate creation between humanity and pure spirits': they lived longer than human beings but were still mortal, with 'an eternal destiny still unfixed, so that they were capable of salvation'.

55 (page 99) Theseus goes on to mock the male lover for imagining his beloved to be more beautiful than she is – 'the lover ... Sees Helen's [Helen of Troy's] beauty in a brow of Egypt [of a gipsy woman]' (V.i.10–11). But Bembo in *The Courtier* (Bk. IV) commends such imagination – he says of the male lover: 'through the vertue of imagination hee shall fashion with himselfe that beautie much more faire than it is in deede.' (Hoby's translation, Everyman ed., p. 317.)

56 (page 99) There can be little doubt that we are not meant to accept these allegations. They derive from Plutarch's *Lives* (translated into English by Sir Thomas North), whereas Theseus in *A Midsummer Night's Dream* is based primarily on Theseus as he is presented in Chaucer's *The Knight's Tale*: Chaucer's Theseus, though he has become ruler of Athens by conquest, is a man of 'noble' character. But even Plutarch in his Life of Theseus (the first of the *Lives*) casts doubt on the reliability of at least some of the stories told about Theseus. See Harold F. Brook's Introduction (p. lxxix) to his 1979 Arden edition of *A Midsummer Night's Dream*.

57 (page 105) In connection with these lines editors refer to the description given near the end of Plato's *The Republic* (c. 380 BC) of the universe as seen after physical death by human souls that have aspired to goodness: music accompanies the movements of planets and stars. Shakespeare may well have

had in mind the following passage from *The Courtier* (Bk. I): 'it hath beene the opinion of most wise Philosophers that the worlde is made of musike, and the heavens in their moving make a melodie, and our soule is framed after the verie same sorte and therefore lifteth up it selfe, and (as it were) reviveth the vertues and force of it selfe with Musicke.' (Hoby's translation, Everyman ed., p. 75.)

58 (page 105) In *The Courtier* (Bk. I) it is said of music in relation to the individual human being: 'who so savoureth it not, a man may assuredly thinke him not to be well in his wits.' (Hoby's translation, Everyman ed., p. 76.)

59 (page 126) The play omits the details. In fact Henry's claim was based on his descent from Edward III's mother, Isabella, daughter of the French King Philip IV: each of Isabella's three brothers had been king, all having died without a male heir, and after the death of the third brother the French crown had passed to Philip IV's nephew. It has been pointed out that, if succession through a female had been accepted as valid, then descendants of the daughter of Isabella's brother Louis (King Louis X), older than Isabella herself, would have had a prior claim over Isabella's descendants.

60 (page 131) In his view of Caesar Shakespeare may have been influenced by his beloved Ovid. In Bk. I of *Metamorphoses* Ovid says of the gods when they hear that a mortal has plotted against Jupiter: 'Their dismay was such as was felt by the human race when a wicked band of fanatics tried to extinguish the Roman name by shedding Caesar's blood.' (Penguin Classics translation by Mary M. Innes, p. 37.) The crime of Caesar's murder is described in some detail in the final Book (Bk. XV) of *Metamorphoses*.

61 (page 136) We have here but one example of how Shakespeare has altered Plutarch in order to create sympathy for Caesar – in Plutarch's account Caesar made many attempts to read the written note given him by Artemidorus but was prevented from doing so by the persistent attentions of the crowd. Other examples of sympathetic touches added by Shakespeare are Caesar's consideration for Calphurnia's

wishes when she begs him not to go to the Senate House, and his greeting of the conspirators as friends: these details are not to be found in Plutarch.

62 (page 147) The 3rd and 4th Quarto editions of *Hamlet* have 'a devil' in the earlier part of this line and 'the devil' in the later part of the line, but the 1st Quarto edition and the First Folio edition have 'the Devil' in both parts of the line. (I have obtained this information from the Textual Notes on *Hamlet* in the American Riverside edition, 1974 and 1997, of Shakespeare's complete works.)

63 (page 147) In a detailed commentary on Belleforest's *Histoires Tragiques*, a direct source of Shakespeare's *Hamlet* if Shakespeare was able to read Belleforest in French, Harold Jenkins in his 1982 Arden edition of *Hamlet* points out (Arden Introduction, p. 95) that 'Belleforest speculates whether Amleth [Shakespeare's Hamlet], instructed by the "malign spirit" which "abuses men", has become susceptible through his "melancholy" to diabolic revelations'. (In a footnote Jenkins quotes the relevant passage from Belleforest's work in the original French.) Further reference to Hamlet's remarks about the Devil is made in two of Jenkins's Longer Notes (p. 483 of his Arden edition). Here Jenkins quotes from authors in Shakespeare's time who speak of the Devil's practice of appearing before a victim as the ghost of a person known to the victim, and as regards the Devil taking advantage of Hamlet's 'melancholy' Jenkins quotes Thomas Nashe as saying in his *The Terrors of the Night* (1594): 'The Devil, when with any other sickness or malady the faculties of our reason are enfeebled and distempered, will be most busy to disturb and torment us.'

64 (page 147) The reference to Purgatory here can hardly be intended by Shakespeare to be taken as an accepted belief since Shakespeare was writing at a time when there was religious censorship of plays and when the established Church of England condemned Purgatory as a 'Romish [Roman Catholic] doctrine...repugnant to the Word of

God' (no. XXII of the 'Articles of Religion'). Shakespeare had referred to Purgatory before, when in *Romeo and Juliet* (III.iii.18) he makes Romeo say that anywhere away from the city where Juliet lives is for him 'purgatory, torture, hell itself', but here (in a play that, after all, is set in a Roman Catholic country) the reference to Purgatory is very brief and could be taken as little more than a metaphor for a place of suffering. (The same applies to a later reference to Purgatory in *Othello* IV.iii.75.) As regards the claim of the Ghost in *Hamlet* to have come from Purgatory, it has been pointed out by Eleanor Prosser in her book *Hamlet and Revenge* (1967, 2nd ed. 1971) that, even according to Roman Catholic belief, no soul in Purgatory would show vindictiveness as the Ghost in *Hamlet* does. (See pp. 136–7 of the 2nd ed. of Eleanor Prosser's book.) It would seem therefore that the Ghost's claim to have come from Purgatory points to his being an impostor.

65 (page 154) In *The Courtier* (Bk. IV) Bembo says of the souls of a man and woman in love: 'And one alone [i.e. a single soul]...ruleth (in a manner) two bodies.' (Hoby's translation, Everyman ed., p. 315.)

66 (page 163) Chaucer's long narrative poem *Troilus and Criseyde* (c. 1385), Shakespeare's main source for the Troilus and Cressida story, refers to Troilus's young Trojan companions as knights ('knyghtes', *Troilus and Criseyde*, Bk. I, line 184), and of Hector it is said 'In al this world ther nys [is not] a bettre knyght/Than he' (Bk. II, lines 177–8).

67 (page 173) Though skins of varying hue are to be found among Moors, Othello is regarded by Shakespeare as black-skinned. Aaron, the Moor in *Titus Andronicus*, seems also to be black – certainly the child that Tamora (a Goth, not a Moor) has by him is referred to as 'a blackamoor child' in a stage direction and is described as 'black' by its nurse (*Titus Andronicus* IV.ii.50 + ,66).

68 (page 174) Ben Jonson, in his *Discoveries* (published posthumously, 1640), said of Shakespeare himself: 'He was (indeed) honest, and of an open and free nature.'

69 (page 178) It is interesting to note that Othello too is presented as a Christian, even though we might have expected that as a Moor he would have been a Muslim. When he sees Cassio brawling with a Venetian, following the destruction of the Turkish fleet by a storm (reported in II.ii), he deplores such fighting amongst those on the Venetian side, and he aligns himself with Venetian Christians against Turkish Muslims (II.iii.162–4):

> Are we turned Turks, and to ourselves do that
> Which heaven hath forbid the Ottomites?
> For Christian shame, put by this barbarous brawl.

70 (page 184) The phrase 'measure for measure' appeared previously in Shakespeare's *3 Henry VI* (II.vi.55), where it is used by the Earl of Warwick who as a Yorkist orders that the publicly displayed head of the Duke of York should be replaced by the head of the Lancastrian Clifford who had stabbed York to death. The phrase as used by Warwick denotes mere revenge, but as used by the Duke in *Measure for Measure* it suggests just retribution.

71 (page 188) 'Love your enemies, do good to them which hate you' (*Luke* 6:27). See also *Matthew* 5: 43–4.

72 (page 208) Holinshed (Shakespeare's source for the plot of the play) says merely that the Scottish Stewart family of kings was descended from Banquo, but Shakespeare indicates more specifically that there had been eight Stewart kings up to the time when *Macbeth* was first performed – the eighth being James VI of Scotland who in 1603 had also become James I of England (and the patron of Shakespeare's own company of actors, who became known as the King's Men).

73 (page 208) Compare this line from *Macbeth* with lines 83–4 of Edmund Spenser's poem *An Hymn of Heavenly Love* (1596):

> The brightest Angel, even the Child of Light,
> Drew millions more against their God to fight.

(Satan is described as the 'brightest' angel because of Christ's remark 'I beheld Satan as lightning fall from heaven', *Luke* 10:18, and the Christian Church's identification of Satan with the morning star in *Isaiah* 14:12 – 'How art thou fallen from heaven, O Lucifer, son of the morning!')

74 (page 212) Plutarch says of Antony (in North's translation): 'the last and extremist mischief of all other (to wit, the love of Cleopatra) lighted on him... and if any spark of goodness or hope of rising were left him Cleopatra quenched it straight...'

75 (page 213) Enobarbus's description of Cleopatra in her river boat is closely based on the description in North's Plutarch, but the point about the winds being love-sick is Shakespeare's own.

76 (page 220) Historically Antony did in fact marry Cleopatra and divorce Octavia (Antony's marriage to Cleopatra is briefly mentioned by Plutarch), but there is nothing about this marriage or this divorce in Shakespeare's play (where Cleopatra, just before Antony dies, refers to 'Your wife Octavia', IV.xv.27).

77 (page 221) In Bk. III of *The Courtier* (p. 205 of the Everyman edition of Hoby's translation) Octavia is cited as an example of a woman deserving of high praise (as also is Portia, Brutus's wife in *Julius Caesar*).

78 (page 228) *Pericles* was included in the second issue (1664) of the Third Folio, along with six other plays not included in the previous Folios. These other plays, like *Pericles*, had been published in Shakespeare's lifetime and had been attributed either to William Shakespeare or to 'W.S.' (one of them was not actually attributed to Shakespeare until three years after his death). Yet there is little acceptance of any of these six plays as being by Shakespeare.

79 (page 229) This kingdom is referred to later in the play (III, Gower, line 34) as being Pentapolis, which actually was on the north coast of Africa – but in the play it is assumed to be in Greece (II.i.64)

80 (page 240) According to Holinshed an ambassador from Augustus thanked Cymbeline for having 'kept his allegiance toward the Romane empire: exhorting him to keepe his subiects in peace with their neighbors, sith [since] the whole world, through meanes of the same Augustus, was now in

quiet, without all warres or troublesome tumults.'

81 (page 247) In this scene Prospero does not mention the King of Naples's personal name, but I give it here and shall be referring to him as Alonso even though in the dialogue of the play we are not given this name till quite late on – in III.iii.75.

82 (page 250) Editors point out that Gonzalo's utopia is based on a passage in an essay on 'Cannibals' (1580) by the French essayist Montaigne (John Florio's English translation of Montaigne's *Essays* appeared in 1603). Montaigne reports with enthusiasm what he has been told about the virtues of certain South American Indians who (in Florio's translation) have 'no kinde of traffike [trade], no knowledge of Letters, no intelligence of numbers, no name of magistrate, nor of politike superioritie; no use of service, of riches or of povertie; no contracts, no successions, no partitions, no occupation but idle...no manuring of lands, no use of wine, corne, or mettle.' Shakespeare can hardly have been impressed by the claims made on behalf of such a society.

83 (page 254) It is known that Shakespeare, in the description of Prospero's destructive powers, drew on a passage in Ovid's *Metamorphoses*, Bk. VII, where Medea recites her powers as a sorceress. To indicate Prospero's egoism as a magician Shakespeare adds a point of his own: Prospero's self-satisfaction in observing that the supernatural power of elves was 'weak' ('Weak masters though ye be', V.i.41) except when employed to serve his own much greater power.

84 (page 257) This name is spelt Katharine in many editions of Shakespeare – it is spelt Catherine in our history books – but in the First Folio, the edition in which the play was first published, the spelling was Katherine.

85 (page 257) Historical note. Catherine (to adopt the spelling in our history books) was married to Prince Arthur, the eldest son of Henry VII, in 1502, but Arthur died soon after the marriage. Catherine was then betrothed to the future Henry VIII after the granting of a dispensation by the Pope enabling Henry to marry his brother's widow. The young Henry was only eleven at the time of the betrothal: he did not actually

General Notes

marry Catherine until just after his ascent to the throne in 1509. He divorced her in 1533.

86 (page 259) V.iii in the Collins *Complete Works* is part of V.ii in other editions, and V.v (the last scene) in the Collins edition is V.iv in other editions.

87 (page 260) See pages xxv–vi of the Introduction in the Signet edition of this play. In my scene and line references to the play the numbering is that of the Signet edition. *The Two Noble Kinsmen* is not included in the Collins *Complete Works*.

88 (page 264) It should perhaps be mentioned that according to the calendar ('Old Style') in use in Shakespeare's time the year did not end in December but continued until the following March, with the new year beginning on 25 March. Following the usual practice of modern historians with dates of this period, all dates in these notes referring to January–March are accompanied by the year numbered according to the 'New Style' calendar (adopted in England in 1752).

Index

As regards Shakespeare's themes, a summary of these will be found in the survey of Shakespeare's view of life (pages 5–24), and the central theme of each of his works is noted in the first or second paragraph of each detailed commentary. The themes listed in this index represent a broad selection, but the list is by no means exhaustive.

As regards Shakespeare's works, since the list of Contents makes it clear where each work is dealt with in detail, page numbers in this index indicate where works are referred to other than in the sections where they are dealt with in detail.

Act to Restrain Abuses of Players, 5, 6
Aristotle *Ethics* 273–4 (Note 11)
Augustine, Saint *The City of God* 271–2 (Notes 5, 6)

Belleforest, François de *Histoires Tragiques* 284 (Note 63)
Bible *Genesis* 8 *Isaiah* 286 (Note 73) *Matthew* 180, 281 (Note 52), 286 (Note 71) *Mark* 180 *Luke* 180, 286 (Notes 71, 73) *John* 221 *Epistle to the Romans* 8, 9 *Epistle to the Ephesians* 17
Boethius *The Consolation of Philosophy* 272 (Note 6)
Bogdanov, Michael (director) 1
Briggs, Katharine M. *The Anatomy of Puck* 282 (Note 54)

Campbell, Oscar J., and Quinn, E. G. *A Shakespeare Encyclopaedia* 263
Castiglione, Baldassare 271 (Note 4) *Il Libro del Cortegiano*, translated by Hoby – see Hoby, Sir Thomas
Chambers, E. K. *William Shakespeare: A Study of Facts and Problems* 269
Chaucer, Geoffrey *The Legend of Good Women* 71, 280 (Note 43) *The Knight's Tale* 260, 282 (Note 56) *Troilus and Criseyde* 285 (Note 66)
Church of England Homilies 10 Marriage

Index

Service 16, 56, 278 (Notes 31, 32) Condemnation of Purgatory 284 (Note 64)

Daniel, Samuel *The Complaint of Rosamond* 68, 265 *Delia* sonnets 265
Dowden, Edward *Shakspere: A Critical Study of His Mind and Art* 278 (Note 33)

Elyot, Sir Thomas *The Book Named the Governor* 271 (Note 4)

Ficino, Marsilio 271 (Note 4)

Gower, John *Confessio Amantis* 228–9
Greene, Robert 264 *Pandosto* 242, 243

Hall, Edward (chronicler) *The Union of the Two Noble and Illustre Families of Lancaster and York* 10, 275 (Notes 16, 18), 276 (Note 21)
Halliday, F. E. *A Shakespeare Companion* 263
Hart, Alfred Dating of *Othello* 269
Hoby, Sir Edward (son of Sir Thomas Hoby) 266
Hoby, Sir Thomas *The Book of the Courtier* (English translation of Castiglione's *Il Libro del Cortegiano*) 266, 273 (Note 9), 274 (Notes 12, 13, 14), 277–9 (Notes 30, 34, 35, 36, 37, 39), 280 (Notes 40, 41, 44), 281 (Notes 46, 47, 48), 282–3 (Notes 55, 57, 58), 285 (Note 65), 287 (Note 77)
Holden, Anthony *William Shakespeare: His Life and Work* 272 (Note 7)
Holinshed, Raphael *Chronicles* 10, 126, 190, 233, 256, 275 (Notes 16, 18), 281–2 (Notes 49, 50, 53, 286 (Note 72), 287 (Note 80)
Homer *Iliad* 162
Honan, Park *Shakespeare: A Life* 272 (Note 7)

Jenkins, Harold (editor of the 1982 Arden edition of *Hamlet*) 284 (Note 63)
Jonson, Ben *Discoveries* 285 (Note 68)

Knights, L. C. *Explorations* 278 (Note 33)
Kott, Jan *Shakespeare Our Contemporary* 1, 271 (Note 1)
Kyd, Thomas *The Spanish Tragedy* 43, 46

Lee, Sidney *A Life of William Shakespeare* 278 (Note 33)
Livy (Roman historian) 71
Lodge, Thomas *Rosalynde* 139, 141

Machiavelli, Niccolo 35, 274 (Note 15), 276 (Note 23)
The Prince 275 (Note 15)
Marlowe, Christopher *The Jew of Malta* 23, 274 (Note 15)
Meres, Francis *Palladis Tamia* 263–4, 265, 266, 267
Milton, John 271 (Note 4)
A Mirror for Magistrates 272–3 (Note 8)
Montaigne, Michel de Essay on 'Cannibals' 288 (Note 82)

Nashe, Thomas *The Terrors of the Night* 284 (Note 63)
North, Sir Thomas – see Plutarch

Ovid *Metamorphoses* 6, 61, 99, 277 (Note 28), 283 (Note 60), 288 (Note 83)
Fasti 71

Paul, H. N. *The Royal Play of Macbeth* 269
Pico della Mirandola 271 (Note 4)
Plato *The Republic* 282 (Note 57)
Plautus *Menaechmi* 48, 49
Amphitruo 48
Plutarch *Lives*, as translated by Sir Thomas North 131, 212, 221, 270, 282 (Note 56), 283–4 (Note 61), 287 (Notes 74, 75, 76)

Prosser, Eleanor *Hamlet and Revenge* 285 (Note 64)

Seneca *Thyestes* 43, 277 (Note 28)
Shakespeare's themes:
  Compassion or pity 17, 18–19, 21, 33, 34, 35, 79, 98, 104, 140, 182, 190, 195, 197, 206, 220, 242, 248, 253, 274 (Note 11)
  Divine intervention 5, 6, 42, 46, 51, 87, 93, 125, 127, 129, 146, 152, 153, 169, 183, 198–9, 201, 210, 230, 232–3, 233, 236, 237, 238, 239, 242, 247, 248, 254, 261, 281–2 (Note 53)
  Forgiveness 17, 67, 85, 153, 178–9, 189, 254, 256, 257, 259
  Fortune 6–7, 19, 22, 49, 72, 79, 85, 86, 87, 150, 228, 229, 230, 232, 233, 248, 253
  Hate (as opposed to love) 21, 82, 83, 87, 100, 101,

104, 121, 140, 172, 173, 176, 185, 187, 189, 221, 222, 223, 224, 225, 226

Honour 13–14, 30, 90, 94, 108, 111, 116, 125, 126–7, 129, 130, 132, 138, 162, 164, 167, 170, 180, 209, 211, 215, 222

Hypocrisy 13, 30, 35, 38–9, 44–5, 70, 79, 101, 118, 129, 136, 147, 148, 188, 190, 206, 207, 212, 219, 226, 227, 228, 231, 234

Integrity (or 'truth') 13–14, 27, 34, 77, 80, 81, 131, 136, 148, 162, 163, 164, 165, 166, 167, 180, 184, 187, 209, 211, 259

Justice 11, 44, 46, 47, 72, 87, 88, 89, 119–20, 180, 182, 184, 187, 189, 196, 198–9, 202, 209, 238, 261–2, 272–3 (Note 8)

Love, various aspects:
1) True love between man and woman 53, 63, 66, 82, 85, 95, 96, 97, 100, 102, 106, 112, 113–14, 130, 143, 155, 156, 157, 158, 159, 161, 165, 167, 170, 190, 191, 220, 251
2) Irrationality in the early stages of true love 15, 20, 64–5, 85, 96, 99, 141–2, 273 (Note 9), 280 (Note 41)
3) Constancy in love 59, 64, 65, 66, 68, 95, 102, 154, 162, 165, 278 (Note 34)
4) Chastity 15–16, 69, 70, 86, 150–1, 154–5, 168, 251
5) Love between members of a family 14, 49–50, 151, 152, 158, 190, 192, 195, 199, 218, 227, 232
6) Love between males 14, 57, 60, 61, 159, 223, 226, 279 (Note 35)
7) Love of one's fellow human beings 10, 25, 130, 185, 221, 225, 259
8) Other forms of love, including friendship 14, 67, 100, 137, 139, 140, 141, 188, 214, 225–6, 227, 233, 241, 257, 258–9

Lust 15, 60, 61, 62, 63, 69, 70, 71, 72, 112, 115, 144, 191, 194, 196, 200, 201, 279 (Note 39)

Mirth 20–1, 109, 152, 274 (Note 14)

Moral conversion 13, 22, 40, 114, 124, 137–8, 145, 172, 184, 202, 238, 242, 247, 253, 254, 255, 258

Music 11, 77, 104–5, 133, 175, 282–3 (Notes 57, 58)

Order and disorder 10, 11,

24, 27, 31–2, 43, 47, 82, 107, 111, 115, 116, 119, 120, 126, 136, 172, 187, 202–3
Original Sin 8, 181, 200, 203, 241
Patriotism 11–12, 126, 238–9
Revenge as malicious retaliation 17–18, 33, 42, 43, 44, 45, 46, 103, 104, 145, 147, 151, 161, 166, 176, 178–9, 235, 242, 253, 257, 285 (Note 64), 286 (Note 70)
Revenge as rightful punishment 18, 72, 89, 138, 147, 210, 286 (Note 70)
Shakespeare's works:
All's Well That Ends Well 16, 183, 222, 246, 268
Antony and Cleopatra 7, 21, 221, 240, 270, 286 (Notes 74, 75, 76, 77)
As You Like It 14, 17, 155, 185, 268
The Comedy of Errors 15, 51, 57, 87, 95, 96, 265, 277–8 (Note 30)
Coriolanus 10, 13, 21, 270
Cymbeline 6, 12, 22, 23, 240, 242, 247, 256, 261, 270, 287 (Note 80)
Hamlet 7, 19, 178, 187, 196, 198, 208, 234, 257, 268, 269, 271 (Note 1), 284–5 (Notes 62, 63, 64)
1 Henry IV 8, 20, 23, 112, 115, 116, 117, 118, 125, 127, 131, 132, 267
2 Henry IV 20, 107, 111, 112, 125, 127, 128, 129, 180, 187, 267
Henry V 6, 10, 12, 13, 14, 22, 23, 119, 133, 162, 240, 267, 283 (Note 59)
1 Henry VI 5, 6, 7, 9, 10, 22, 23, 27, 28, 29, 31, 32, 33, 38, 131, 264, 275 (Notes 15, 17, 18), 276 (Notes 19, 23, 25)
2 Henry VI 10, 13, 18, 21, 32, 33, 34, 41, 95, 131, 250, 264, 276 (Note 25)
3 Henry VI 7, 18, 19, 21, 25, 29, 36, 37, 40, 41, 42, 43, 72, 77, 82, 131, 264, 275 (Note 15), 276 (Notes 20, 21, 22, 23), 286 (Note 70)
Henry VI plays as a whole 7, 9, 24, 36, 43, 77, 88, 94, 131, 276 (Note 20)
Henry VIII 9, 13, 270, 288–9 (Notes 84, 85)
Julius Caesar 22, 73, 146, 172, 212, 213, 215, 216, 267, 283–4 (Notes 60, 61)
King John 9, 12, 14, 17, 87, 88, 162, 180, 192, 266, 281 (Note 49)
King Lear 14, 17, 22, 203,

Index

208, 210, 237, 238, 241, 247, 261, 269
A Lover's Complaint 70, 265
Love's Labour's Lost 15, 96, 266, 280–1 (Notes 44, 45, 46, 47, 48)
Macbeth 5, 7, 8, 11, 13, 14, 17, 18, 23, 269–70, 286 (Notes 72, 73)
Measure for Measure 8, 9, 268, 269, 286 (Note 70)
The Merchant of Venice 8, 16, 18, 20, 23, 109, 120, 133, 140, 172, 181, 189, 221, 266–7, 282–3 (Notes 57, 58)
The Merry Wives of Windsor 17, 117, 130, 267
A Midsummer Night's Dream 5, 6, 14, 15, 17, 20, 64, 142, 154, 260, 266, 271 (Note 1), 282 (Notes 54, 55, 56)
Much Ado about Nothing 9, 22, 23, 137, 172, 181, 238, 246, 247, 267
Othello 17, 19–20, 22, 23, 185, 187, 192, 193, 200, 221, 234, 269, 285 (Notes 64, 67, 68), 285–6 (Note 69)
Pericles 7, 9, 233, 240, 247, 255, 260, 261, 270, 287 (Notes 78, 79)
The Phoenix and Turtle 16, 268
The Rape of Lucrece 6, 15, 18, 68, 86, 132, 265, 280 (Note 43)
Richard II 8, 11, 12, 13, 18, 23, 107, 108, 119, 125, 146, 147, 151, 180, 238, 240, 266, 281–2 (Notes 50, 51, 52, 53)
Richard III 5, 7, 8, 13, 17, 23, 24, 35, 43, 79, 87, 122, 146, 264, 276–7 (Notes 24, 25)
Romeo and Juliet 6, 7, 9, 15, 16, 21, 64, 95, 100, 120, 123, 140, 154, 165, 172, 199, 221, 266, 285 (Note 64)
Sonnets 14, 15, 19, 61, 63, 64, 65, 69, 70, 71, 72, 73, 77, 79, 96, 154, 159, 265, 266, 273 (Note 9), 278 (Notes 33, 34), 279 (Notes 35, 36, 37, 38, 39)
The Taming of the Shrew 1, 16, 71, 85, 103, 114, 130, 265, 274 (Note 11), 278 (Notes 31, 32)
The Tempest 6, 15–16, 17–18, 256, 270, 288 (Notes 81, 82, 83)
Timon of Athens 195, 221, 269
Titus Andronicus 13, 18, 19, 21, 48, 71, 72, 122, 180, 198, 264, 277 (Notes 26, 27, 28, 29), 285 (Note 67)

Troilus and Cressida 7, 11, 167, 169, 180, 211, 268, 274 (Note 11), 285 (Note 66)
Twelfth Night 9, 14, 155, 268
The Two Gentlemen of Verona 15, 17, 71, 77, 79, 85, 95, 142, 162, 261–2, 266, 280 (Notes 41, 42)
Venus and Adonis 6, 15, 70, 71, 96, 213, 265, 280 (Note 40)
The Winter's Tale 6, 9, 16, 22, 247, 256, 262, 270

Spedding, James 'Who Wrote Shakespeare's *Henry VIII?'* 255–6

Spenser, Edmund 271 (Note 4) *The Fairie Queene* 264 *Complaints* 265 *The Ruines of Time* 279 (Note 39) *An Hymn of Heavenly Love* 286 (Note 73)

Tillyard, E. M. W. *The Elizabethan World Picture* 5 *Shakespeare's History Plays* 10, 24, 272–3 (Note 8)

Vickers, Brian *Appropriating Shakespeare: Contemporary Critical Quarrels* 271 (Notes 2, 3)

Winny, James *The Master-Mistress: A Study of Shakespeare's Sonnets* 278 (Note 33)

Wyndham, George *The Poems of Shakespeare* 273 (Note 9)